Middle School Curriculum, Instruction, and Assessment

A Volume in
The Handbook of Research In Middle Level Education

The Handbook of Research In Middle Level Education Series

Vincent A. Anfara, Jr. Series Editor

The Handbook of Research in Middle Level Education (2001)
   Vincent A. Anfara, Jr.

Middle School Curriculum, Instruction, and Assessment (2002)
   Vincent A. Anfara, Jr. and Sandra L. Stacki

Middle School Curriculum, Instruction, and Assessment

Edited by
Vincent A. Anfara, Jr.
University of Tennessee

and
Sandra L. Stacki
Hofstra University

NMSA

National Middle School Association
Westerville, Ohio

INFORMATION AGE
PUBLISHING

80 Mason Street • Greenwich, Connecticut 06830 • www.infoagepub.com

Library of Congress Cataloging-in-Publication Data

Middle school curriculum, instruction, and assessment.
    p. cm. – (Handbook of research in middle level education ; v.
2)
Includes bibliographical references and index.
  ISBN 1-931576-76-9 (pbk.) – ISBN 1-931576-77-7 (hard)
  1. Middle school teaching–United States. 2. Middle schools–United
States. 3. Educational change–United States. I. Series.
  LB1623.5 .M54 2002
  373.1102–dc21
                                                                    2002010589

Copyright © 2002 Information Age Publishing Inc.

All rights reserved. No part of this publication may be reproduced,
stored in a retrieval system, or transmitted, in any form or by any means,
electronic, mechanical, photocopying, microfilming, recording or otherwise,
without written permission from the publisher.

ISBN: 1-931576-76-9 (paper); 1-931576-77-7 (cloth)

Printed in the United States of America

CONTENTS

PREFACE

Middle schools have been attacked for a less-than-rigorous curriculum resulting in poor student performance on high-stakes tests like the Third International Mathematics and Science Study (TIMSS). Even researchers who have been intimately involved with the middle-school movement have noted, "We have not seen the widespread dramatic improvement in academic outcomes we had hoped for" (Lipsitz, Mizell, Jackson, & Austin, 1997, p. 535). Many practitioners and scholars had faith in the reforms that were delineated in *Turning Points* (Carnegie Council on Adolescent Development, 1989) and *This We Believe* (National Middle School Association, 1982). We assumed that if schools implemented the recommended structural changes (i.e., advisory programs, teaming of teachers, flexible block scheduling), students' academic, behavioral, and socioemotional development would improve.

While exemplary middle schools have implemented many middle school reforms with a high degree of fidelity, the reform as recommended by *Turning Points* and *This We Believe* did not receive widescale implementation. Many middle schools adopted parts of the total reform package. Many more simply changed the name above the schoolhouse door from junior high to middle school. As Cuban (1992) noted, structural changes that have been at the core of most middle-grades reform recommendations may do little to change the fundamental experiences of students. Getting to the heart of the problem, Cuban goes on to say that these structural changes are "too distal to improve students' learning and attitudes" (p. 229). In short, there is "too little linkage between the implementation of these structural changes and actual changes in the practices and experiences of teachers and learners" (Felner et al., 1997, p. 532).

As early as 1993, Mergendollar argued that changes in instructional and curricular practices in schools advanced more slowly than structural

Middle School Curriculum, Instruction, and Assessment, pages vii–viii
Copyright © 2002 by Information Age Publishing
All rights of reproduction in any form reserved.

changes. In similar fashion, the National Governors' Association (1989) concluded that "Few reform reports have touched on the heart of the educational process, what is taught and how it is taught" (p. 1). The Council of Chief State School Officers (1989) added that structural changes are being treated as ends in themselves rather than as means to improved learning for students. Fundamentally, these structural changes are decoupled from the very outcomes they were created to improve.

Cognizant of the need to link the middle school movement to high student achievement and to focus on what is taught and how it is taught, Volume 2 of *The Handbook of Research in Middle Level Education* is dedicated to looking at issues of middle level curriculum, instruction, and assessment. I am confident that the chapters in this volume will engage readers. At this juncture in the history of middle school reform, middle-level practitioners and scholars need to focus on the core technology of schools—teaching and learning. I hope that our understanding of these processes will be advanced, that our assumptions will be challenged, and that the relational nature of teaching and learning will be highlighted.

—V. A. Anfara, Jr.

REFERENCES

Carnegie Council on Adolescent Development. (1989). *Turning points: Preparing American youth for the 21st century.* New York: Carnegie Corporation of New York.

Council of Chief State School Officers. (1989). Success for all in a new century. *Education Week, 8*(39), 1, 20.

Cuban, L. (1992). What happens to reforms that last? The case of the junior high school. *American Educational Research Journal, 29*(2), 227–251.

Felner, R., Jackson, A. W., Kasak, D., Mulhall, P., Brand, S., & Flowers, N. (1997). The impact of school reform for the middle years: Longitudinal study of a network engaged in *Turning Points*-based comprehensive school transformation. *Phi Delta Kappan, 78*(7), 528–532, 541–550.

Lipsitz, J., Mizell, M. H., Jackson, A. W., & Austin, L. M. (1997). Speaking with one voice: A manifesto for middle-grades reform. *Phi Delta Kappan, 78*(7), 533–540.

Mergendollar, J. R. (1993). Introduction: The role of research on the reform of middle grades education. *Elementary School Journal, 93*, 443–446.

National Governors' Association. (1989). *Results in education 1989.* Washington, DC: Author.

National Middle School Association. (1982). *This we believe.* Columbus, OH: Author.

INTRODUCTION: MIDDLE-LEVEL CURRICULUM, INSTRUCTION, AND ASSESSMENT

Evolution or An Innovation at Risk?

Steven Jay Gross
Temple University

ABSTRACT

Curriculum, instruction, and assessment (referred to here as CIA) in middle-level education can be seen as a dynamic, interrelated system. At present the middle level CIA may be characterized as an evolving, complex innovation that faces dramatic turbulence in the form of the accountability, standards, and high-stakes testing movements. Thus we must consider the question, are we looking at an evolving middle level concept or an innovation at risk? This introduction seeks to respond to the question by establishing a CIA framework, describing the evolution of the middle level CIA through the previous century, and depicting the development of the countermovement that seeks to replace it.

Middle School Curriculum, Instruction, and Assessment, pages ix–xxviii
Copyright © 2002 by Information Age Publishing
All rights of reproduction in any form reserved.

OVERVIEW

This is a complex story, one requiring systemic thought. I have four purposes in approaching the task of describing curriculum, instruction, and assessment, referred to as CIA, in middle level education as a system. First, I would like the reader to avoid getting lost in the detail of specific approaches by showing the big picture. Second, it will help the reader to appreciate the complex elements that surround the question of CIA in middle level education. Third, it will help in understanding the contradictions between conflicting sides in the emerging struggle for the middle level CIA. Finally, I believe this will help those who have a strong affiliation to exercise a degree of choice and strategic behavior.

To provide a careful overview, I organized this introduction in the following way: I start by describing the dynamics of the curriculum–instruction–assessment triangle and how this can be used as a powerful lens to appreciate the interrelationship of key elements in a single educational movement as well as depict differences between rival movements. Next, I briefly examine the CIA in the middle level movement, including its philosophical origins, core beliefs, and the manifestation of these in practice. Having established the CIA lens and applied it to the middle-level movement, I consider the challenges to that movement, which include limits in its implementation as well as the rise of conflicting movements for middle-level students based on quite different philosophical beliefs that form a counter CIA triangle. I will conclude with an illustration showing the conflict between these two ways of organizing curriculum, instruction, and assessment at the middle level.

USING THE CIA LENS

While serious discussions centering on curriculum, instruction, or assessment are often separate areas of study, I find it most useful to connect them for the purpose of this introduction. Simply, curriculum may be considered to be the learning agenda, instruction involves the ways that agenda is shared, and assessment raises the question of the extent to which the agenda affected the learners. Once this connection among the three elements is established, the question then becomes, how might they work together? Many writers (English, 1988; Taba, 1962) have described the relationship among curriculum, instruction, and assessment (referred to below as CIA). In further work, the question of alignment among CIA has become an important issue (English & Larson, 1996; Jacobs, 1998). In a recent study of 10 innovative schools and districts in North America (Gross, 1998), I found a dynamic relationship among CIA. If a school, for instance, worked to establish a literature-based reading program for elementary and middle level students, it soon will need to rethink older teaching methods since those were tied to the structure of the basal readers. Likewise, when it comes time to assess student learning, teachers and administrators will need to move beyond the traditional tests and consider new ways to help students demonstrate their learning.

Seeing the connection and understanding the dynamic relationship among the three CIA elements is crucial. First, these are arguably at the heart of our work with students. What is more important than establishing an agenda, communicating it, and learning the extent to which it has had an impact on learners? Second, these central forces influence one another regardless of which is activated first. A change in assessment will likely lead to changes in curriculum and instruction. Similarly, a change in instruction or curriculum will almost certainly translate into altered instruction and assessment. This is both good news and a challenge for planners, practitioners, and scholars who study changes in schools. On one hand, there is a certain freedom to begin where there is an opening. On the other hand, changes at any point need to be carefully thought through, since they will very probably mean changes in the whole CIA pattern.

Changes in any long-lived movement such as middle level education are complex and rich in detail. Understanding the flow of change and trying to establish patterns can be challenging; therefore, seeing developments in the context of an organizing framework is useful. For this introduction, I use the CIA dynamic relationship as a lens through which to describe the course of the middle level over time. Morgan (1997) advises us that any metaphor obscures just as it illuminates and I acknowledge that connecting the three elements so closely will mean not describing some qualities of each that might deserve serious reflection. However, in this orienting chapter, I believe that establishing an evolving interrelationship among the elements will be most useful to the reader.

In the next section, I examine the CIA triangle in the middle-grades context, including foundational concepts, supporting structures, and evolution over time. In the third section, I raise the question of turbulence as the middle level CIA faces questions surrounding implementation and confronts the standards movement, the accountability movement, and high-stakes testing, all of which present possible challenges and combine to form a rival CIA. This raises the issue that the middle-level CIA could be an innovation currently at risk. I conclude with an illustration of the conflict between the two views on organizing curriculum, instruction, and assessment for middle level learners.

EARLY CONCEPTS THAT UNDERGIRD THE CIA OF TODAY'S MIDDLE LEVEL MOVEMENT

As Kliebard (1986) has established, the American curriculum at all levels has been a scene of contending forces and ideologies. He starts his depiction in 1892 with the convening of the National Education Association's Committee of Ten. Its work, under the direction of Harvard President Charles W. Eliot, established a humanist-oriented curriculum for secondary education that was intended to expose all students to a content-enriched learning agenda. While their focus was beyond middle-level education, the impact of the report above and below secondary school was intentional.

Yet, other voices were vying for a place in curriculum discussions at the turn of the last century and several of these became the philosophic antecedents to what has become the middle level education movement of our time: These include the Child Study advocates, the American Herbartians, and the Social Meliorists. Taken together, these movements became part of the building blocks of the Progressive Education movement. I contend that the middle-level movement of today is an outgrowth of Progressive Education.

The Child Study Movement: G. Stanley Hall and His Heirs, the Developmentalists

Instead of exposing all students to a standard curriculum, G. Stanley Hall, famed early 20th-century psychologist, insisted upon a flexible program based upon differences in learners at various stages. Hall's work led to an enriched interaction between educators and the students with whom they worked. It also led to the rationale for a specific kind of education for students at different ages.[1] Beyond his own writings, Hall was a pioneer in the developmentalist approach to understanding children and their educational needs. Of particular importance in this light are the works of Piaget, Erikson, and Vygotsky. While many other psychologists have been highly significant in shaping our ideas on children and young people's development, I include these three because they have held a central place in the training programs of preservice educators for decades and are often key characters in early educational psychology courses.

Piaget's (1952) famous observations of his own children led to the concept of specific stages of development, each with its own needs, potentials, and limits. Students were not to be lumped into one category but were best understood by their developmental stage. Interestingly enough for middle level educators, students between the ages of 10 and 13 stand at the dividing line separating concrete from formal operations. One other aspect of

Piaget's work deserves mention here because of its impact. Piaget held that change in learners came from two forces: assimilation and accommodation. Children can assimilate small differences in their environment into their current models of reality. Larger changes require a restructuring of their models of reality and lead to accommodation. Middle level educators can make the case that young adolescents face a significant accommodation that requires a specific organizational response with serious implications for curriculum, instruction, and assessment.

Erikson's (1963) theory of development has also been highly influential in understanding the series of adjustments we make throughout the life cycle. Outlining eight psychosocial crises, Erikson taught that human beings are continually faced with opposing choices. Of particular importance to middle level educators are the two stages facing students in the middle years. Joseph and Kirby (2000) describe Erikson's developmental theory as it applies to middle-school students:

> The stages that are important for middle grades are stages 4 and 5, which are: [sic] industry versus inferiority (ages 6–12) and identity versus identity confusion (ages 12 and up). During these stages, the young adolescent asks the question: Am I important? Am I successful? Who am I? Am I in control? (Seghers, 1995). Middle school scholars (Erikson, 1963; Milgram, 1992; Thornburg, 1983) believe that it is imperative at these stages that the young adolescent's needs to accomplish something, gain independence from adults, make choices, and build positive relationships with others are fulfilled.[2] (p. 166)

Soviet psychologist Lev Vygotsky's (1978) concepts of zone of proximal development (ZPD) and scaffolding also became important foundations for middle level educators. For Vygotsky, ZPD was the space between where a student currently was in his or her growth and where he or she could be with the help of a teacher. Understanding how much a single student could move meant carefully observing children and becoming sensitive to their needs and current levels of understanding. Equally, this meant carefully helping the student by constructing what Vygotsky called *scaffolds*. Scaffolds are intentionally designed bridges to help the learners cross from their current abilities. Thus, Vygotsky's work serves to amplify the underlying message of Piaget and Erikson; learners are unique, going through stages of development, and require the attentiveness of a well-educated professional who can craft specific educational experiences that meet their current needs. We may look upon the middle level CIA and its supporting structures as a specific kind of scaffold designed to help young adolescents bridge the space between childhood and young adult life.

These three psychologists, all highly influential, have taken the child-study thinking of Hall and placed it into the mainstream of our thinking about schools. Each has made a case for specific attention to young adolescents, and their impact upon the design of the middle level movement is clear and considerable.

The American Herbartians

Far less well known today than Hall and those who followed in his tradition are the American Herbartians. This group was inspired by the work of early 19th-century German philosopher Johann Friedrich Herbart (1776–1841), who advocated for the integration of learning. According to Herbart, "the business of instruction is to form the person on many sides, and accordingly to avoid a distracting or dissipating effect. And instruction has successfully avoided this in the case of one who with ease surveys his well-arranged knowledge in all of its unifying relations and beholds it together as his very own" (cited in Graves, 1912, p. 180). The Herbartian's concepts of concentration and correlation are directly related to some of today's middle level movement's core instructional concepts because they form the basis of what we now refer to as interdisciplinary studies and thematic units. In both cases, the idea is to unify the content through themes and to help the young learners understand the overarching unity of the disciplines in their world.

The Social Meliorists

L. Frank Ward became leader of the third foundational movement, which forms the base of the middle level movement of our time, the social meliorists. Like many social reformers of the late 19th century, Ward became convinced that education itself was a way out of the social and economic inequality of his time. This stand put him at odds with many others, including those who were influenced by the work of British sociologist Herbert Spencer and his popular belief in Social Darwinism.[3] Ward's view was just the opposite; our inherent awareness of social ills was hardly an excuse for inaction, but rather proof that a problem existed and that society itself was responsible to improve conditions. Since schools were one powerful tool in the hands of society, they should be a major stage upon which to engage in social healing. As Kliebard (1986) describes Ward's position, "The key to progress and the great undertaking that lay before us was the proper distribution of cultural capital through a vitalized system of education" (p 27). We will find the same agenda as a central element in the middle level movement. Today's middle level proponents aim to protect children from the ill effects of teenage pregnancy and tobacco, alcohol, and drug addiction through their special program of middle level education. They have also brought a concern for the issues of race, class, gender, and sexual orientation to bear in their work.

Dewey, Progressive Education, and the Amalgamation of Earlier Movements

The Child Study Movement, the American Herbartians, and the Social Meliorists contributed to the ideas of John Dewey and to the American Progressive educational movement to which he gave birth. At the heart of Dewey's approach to education were four guiding principles described in his *Democracy and Education* (1916). These ideas included a respect for learner's feelings and interests, investigation and problem solving as cornerstones of learning, and an insistence that learning be connected to direct social experience. Progressives' concern over social conditions was directly related to the social meliorist tradition. Building upon Hall's strong interest in the specifics of children and their development, the Progressives gave today's middle level educators a strong vision of such instructional approaches as hands-on learning. William H. Kilpatrick, a colleague of Dewey at Teachers College, was heavily influenced by the latter's philosophy and added a powerful component to the evolving CIA mixture in the form of the Project Method (Kilpatrick, 1926). Over the decades, Kilpatrick influenced many thousands of classroom teachers and school administrators with this concept.[4] The Progressive Educators' platform can therefore be seen as a reflection of earlier ideas and a forecast of the middle level's focus on learners and their social, emotional, and physical state, as well as their need to find meaning through active learning.

THE EMERGENCE OF TODAY'S MIDDLE LEVEL CIA

Despite the efforts of the Progressives and developmental psychologists, contending forces in the United States kept many of these ideas from being practiced on a large scale for decades at the middle level. Middle-years education remained a smaller imitation of the high school CIA, and the term "junior high school" was often highly accurate. Learners roughly between the ages of 11 and 15 were relegated to a watered-down version of senior high school with its departmentalized curriculum, lecture format, and regimented assessment program.

While the junior high school model was prevalent in U.S. public schools during the 1940s, 1950s, and 1960s, it did not go unchallenged. As Faunce and Clute (1961) point out:

The traditional procedure neither provides for nor permits any relationship except that of an individual pupil with his teacher. Talking to others or sharing materials is sternly prohibited as a form of cheating, or an example of willful avoidance of duty. Such social behavior is regarded as an interference with the real tasks of learning, such as hearing assignment s by the teacher, preparing that assignment without help, and proving one's mastery of the assignment by recitation and writing tests. It will be noted that such expectations polarize relationships in a class, limiting them to teachers and individual pupil. (p. 162)

Like the work of educators much earlier in the 20th century, this kind of critique began to influence thinking and foreshadowed a robust middle level movement starting in the 1970s and culminating in the late 1980s.

By the end of the 1980s and into the 1990s a powerful middle level philosophy, built upon many of the ideas described above, began to take shape. Two hallmarks of this nascent movement were the concepts found in crucial documents such as the original *Turning Points* and the supporting positions taken by sympathetic scholars.

Turning Points (Carnegie Task Force on Education of Young Adolescents, 1989) was written by the Carnegie Council on Adolescent Development and has become familiar to those in the middle level movement. This work, and the allied *Fateful Choices* (Hechinger, 1992), build the case for a completely redesigned middle level education, based on the needs, challenges, and interests of students. The authors of *Turning Points* advocated a core of common knowledge including five elements: thinking critically, developing healthy lifestyles, becoming active citizens, integrating subject matter across disciplines, and learning and testing successfully (p. 42).

In terms of curriculum, instruction, and assessment, this document staked out a clear path. The key is not isolated content, but "the disciplining of young adolescents' minds, that is, their capacity for active, engaged thinking" (Carnegie Task Force, 1989, p. 43). To accomplish this, there needs to be, "a disposition toward inquiry, discovery, and reasoning across subjects" (p. 43). Themes and clusters of subjects are pivotal since they help students see connections. "The student learns to reason even while absorbing basic information about the subject matter" (p. 43). According to the authors, breadth must be exchanged for a carefully selected depth for this approach to work.

Regarding assessment, the authors of *Turning Points* criticized the practice of overtesting since they believed it negatively influenced curriculum and instruction. Tests need to "more closely resemble learning tasks" (p. 48). State and national use of portfolios was also recommended in addition to standardized tests, as a link connecting statewide assessment to school-level work. Instructional processes that fit included cooperative learning, de-tracking or heterogeneous grouping, and flexible block scheduling.

Moving in the same direction, the National Middle School Association published a statement of guiding principles in 1995 titled *This We Believe*. This document set forth the conditions that NMSA attached to successful middle level education and has been used by that organization to advocate significant changes in practice. Supporting programs that they believed helped learners to grasp their world and themselves, the document called for problem-solving studies and engaging, hands-on learning as well as the inclusion of authentic assessment. Traditional approaches, on the other hand, such as a departmentalized curriculum with isolated instruction and testing, were criticized. Equally unacceptable was the domination of content over process in a textbook- and workbook-driven classroom.

Supporting the call of *Turning Points* and *This We Believe*, sympathetic scholars have added their own voices. Much of their work has informed the kinds of instruction they felt to be required to meet the needs of middle level learners. Others have brought issues of values and ethical orientations into the formation of the middle level movement.

A crucial question raised by some scholars is the relationship between subject-matter content and engaging method. Chris Stevenson (1993) makes the point that the question should not be one of *what* middle-grades students should learn but *how* they learn. He states, "I contend that there is not a single framework, no universal design that will be valid and appropriate for the diverse school contexts that exist...I propose further that the question itself is misleading. The real issue is, 'How should the middle level be?'" Stevenson continues, " I have seen that our preoccupation with 'what' typically diverts us from the essence of authentic learning: engagement. By engagement I refer to a personal intellectual investment in learning that enhances a youngster's scholarly competence and confidence" (p. 76). Clearly, Stevenson's emphasis on active learning is aligned with *Turning Points*.

Others feel that using a core curriculum and fashioning a school that meets the needs of middle-level learners are not so much in opposition. Beane (1993a) suggests this harmony: "One conclusion seems quite apparent. The purposes of the middle school, the needs of emerging adolescence and core curriculums are entirely compatible" (p. 18). This raises the obvious question of what the term "core" means. For Beane, Alberty's (1953) vision is useful. This includes eight elements and is organized in "Pre-planned units which focus on youth needs and social problems. Within the unit, organization is characterized by a number of elements" (Beane, 1993a, p. 18). These units include use of resources. They do not need to contain specific, predetermined fields of study or basic skill in this vision. They do need to relate to students' needs and interests, however.

Beane (1993b) answers the need to give middle level students a broad, integrated education while not ignoring the development of skills with the thematic unit. "The main component would consist of thematic units whose organization centers are drawn from the intersecting concerns of early adolescents and issues in the larger world" (p. 46). Beane further illustrates the content of these units:

> In each case we can also imagine early adolescents reading, tabulating data from surveys, researching information, thinking about consequences of decisions, formatting hypotheses, listening to the ideas of others, constructing models, artistically displaying ideas, writing reports, and examining ethical issues, in other words, developing and applying a wide array of skills. And we can easily see how such a curriculum creates a sense of unity and coherence among the concepts and skills the school seeks to promote. (p. 46)

Leading middle level thinkers such as Stevenson and Beane have made important judgments about the relative role that specific content needs to play versus a more generalized approach to learning. Their emphasis rests upon holistic, hands-on thematic learning, allowing for skill development with much less in the way of highly defined academic goals.

Finally, an expanded view of ethics exists in the middle-level movement. The ethic of care (Gilligan, 1982) is an important element in the evolving shape of the middle level CIA, according to Brown (2000). Certainly, the fact that middle-level education has seen itself as child-centered is one indication of ethical orientation. In addition to the ethic of care, the ethic of critique (Shapiro & Stefkovich, 2001) is also evident. One aspect of the ethic of critique is raised by West-Olatunji (2000) when she raises the question of culturally appropriate pedagogy. When "addressing the African-American student experience," West-Olatunji argues that pedagogy should "advocate critical thinking around the socio-political context of the learner" (p. 145).

Organizational theorists like Sergiovanni (1996) believe that schools need to bridge the communal values of the home and the more competitive values of the larger society. In the context of middle level education, this is especially relevant. If there is a continuum starting with the all accepting home and ending with the judgmental wider society, planners for middle level education have clearly made a statement that their enterprise needs to be positioned near the center. This position well depicts an environment where the curriculum is exploratory and integrated since these qualities allow for reaching beyond the narrower confines of childhood without the consequences of choices made in the adult world. Cooperative learning and authentic assessment also fit this center position on the continuum because these are strategies that require learner responsibility while at the same time allow for individualized contributions. The middle level CIA is thus sheltered but open to explorations; a net exists underneath learners at this stage.

BRINGING THE PIECES OF
THE MIDDLE LEVEL CIA TOGETHER

What comes out of this analysis is a strong theoretical movement with a clear agenda and implications for CIA. This CIA has its origins in the work of child-study advocates (Hall), developmental psychologists (Piaget, Erikson, Vygotsky), social meliorists (Ward), Herbartists, Progressive Educators (Dewey, Kilpatrick), ethicists (Gilligan, Starrat), and organizational theorists (Sergiovanni). Carnegie (1989) and National Middle School Association (1995) among others have given the movement organizational support and a focus that brings specific recommendations for curriculum, instruction, and assessment. Recent scholars have spent careers bringing detail to the vision. Figure 1 shows the ingredients that form the middle level CIA. Figure 2 illustrates the key components of this CIA combination. However, the question remains: Has this movement become fully realized and is its place secure in the vast majority of middle schools?

CHALLENGES

In contrast to this compelling middle-level vision are equally powerful challenges that form a dramatic counterpoint. Major challenges to the middle level movement described above fall into two categories: First, some scholars raise an open question regarding the degree to which the movement's vision has been brought to life in school settings. Simply put, how many schools do a thorough job of implementing the ideals of the theorists? Second, there is a growing challenge to the middle level movement by a vigorous combination of countermovements. These rival movements take the form of accountability, nationally designed academic standards, and high-stakes testing for all students and form their own, powerful CIA.

The Challenge of Implementation

The question of implementation of the middle level vision has been on the minds of many scholars. Erb (2000) considers the *Turning Points* recommendations as something of a black box problem asking us to consider what happens inside of the box. He believes that time and focus on these recommendations shows results. "There is now evidence that middle schools demonstrating high levels of implementation of the eight *Turning Points* recommendations show positive results across the core curriculum. This means understanding the importance of supporting structures such as interdisciplinary teams and taking these very seriously" (p. 5).

Early Concepts:	Leading To:	More Recently:	Lead to the Middle Level CIA
SocialMeliorism: The belief that schools must help correct social ills	The Progressive Education Movement: Led by John Dewey and his followers.	Expanded concepts of ethics, such as the Ethic of Caring and the Ethic of Critique have expanded the mission of middle level educators	Curriculum (Agenda): Core Curriculum, Connection of subject matter. Topics that relate to student needs and interests.
The Child Study Movement (followed by the develomentalists) The belief that students are all different and that we can understand those difference through investigation. We then can adjust education to better meet the needs of individual students at different times in their lives.	The Progressives blended the ideas of the Child Study Movement, the Social Meliorists and the American Herbartians and added the concept that education needed to be connected to the life of the society in order to sustain democracy.	In addition, applying a growing sensitivity to racial, gender, ethnic and sexual orientation, middle level planners have also increased the range of their concerns.	Instruction (Communicating the Agenda): Cooperative learning, Team teaching, hands-on learning. Interdisciplinary approaches. Thematic units.
The American Herbartians: The central ideas of concentration and correlation raise the need to teach in broad themes that unify the disciplines.		Of equal importance, applying the ideas of organizational theorists such as Sergiovanni, middle level thinkers have additional rationale for creating a special space for their students.	Assessment: (Learners showing their understanding of the agenda): Projects related to themes, journals, portfolios, authentic assessment, demonstrations.

Figure 1.   Ingredients forming the middle level CIA: This figure shows the evolution of founding concepts that became the basis for the Progressive educational movement that in turn grew to support the emerging middle level curriculum, instruction and assessment movement that took center stage starting in the late 1980's.

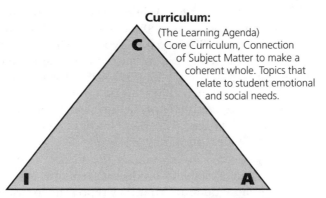

Curriculum:
(The Learning Agenda)
Core Curriculum, Connection
of Subject Matter to make a
coherent whole. Topics that
relate to student emotional
and social needs.

Instruction:
(Communicating the Agenda)
Cooperative learning, Team
teaching, hands-on learning,
thematic units

Assessment:
(Learners showing understanding
of the agenda) Projects related to
themes, journals, portfolios,
authentic assessment,
demonstrations

Figure 2.   The Middle Level CIA Triangle: This figure depicts the middle level
movement's priorities in the three areas of curriculum, instruction and assessment.

Anfara and Kirby (2000) report a very different possibility. Their research
shows the results of a minimally implemented middle level program.

> The literature on curriculum and instructional goals related to middle
> schools includes discussions on the application of the basic skills mastered in
> elementary school, an understanding of the interrelatedness of the core aca-
> demic subjects, the development of higher-order skills, and the availability of
> exploratory opportunities. Instead, the picture painted by the students'
> quotes give one the impression of a curricular wasteland—where imagina-
> tion, creativity, and the love of learning die. (p. 13)

A 1996 NMSA study of trends in curriculum, instruction, and assessment
implementation, titled *America's Middle Schools: Practices and Progress,* measured
over several decades, revealed an equally uncertain picture. The shape of curriculum was mixed. Separately organized core subjects were very much in evidence on one hand while elective trends did show many of the middle level
values described above. Of the required and elective courses outside of the
basic four courses mentioned above, health, computers, and sex education
showed some increase from 1988–1993. According to the same study, results
in instruction showed the same combination of new and traditional practice.
Most schools estimated that they used interdisciplinary instruction between 1
and 20% of the time. About one quarter of the schools said that they used this
approach between 21–40% of the time and 16% used an interdisciplinary

approach 40% of the time or more. While direct instruction and lecture were criticized by middle level advocates, 90% of schools used this approach, 50% used cooperative learning, 33% used inquiry approaches, and 50% used independent study. In assessment, little advance toward the middle level movement's goals was seen in this study. By 1993, 80% of schools used a letter to describe student achievement, making this the most commonly used method. Parent conferences were used 62% of the time while informal written notes were employed in 60% of the cases. Some form of student portfolios were used only 22% of the time.

While certainly some schools embody the ideals of the middle level movement and serve as exemplary models, it seems doubtful that these are the norm and still more doubtful that they represent consistent, pervasive change. In some ways, this substantiates the concerns of some scholars, such as Anfara and Kirby, that the vision is not yet realized. In fact, clear signs indicate that the middle level movement CIA may exist more as a philosophy than as a practice. It is ironic, therefore, that this movement, and the system of schools attempting to follow it faithfully, are under attack.

The Challenge of Countermovements

Contributing to the air of uncertainty raised by the questions surrounding implementation is the rise of a conflicting set of beliefs that take the form of standards, high-stakes testing, and accountability. If the middle level movement was an attempt at a Progressive revolution, these movements represent a counterrevolutionary restoration of tradition. While some attribute the rise of the current conservative movements to the 1983 publication of *A Nation at Risk* (National Commission on Excellence in Education, 1983), the roots go much further back. Just as the middle level movement rests upon earlier ideals that merged into Progressive Education, the countermovements themselves have a long and powerful legacy worthy of discussion. These founding ideas include the Scientific Management of the early 20th century, Essentialism, and Perennialism.

Scientific Management

First felt in the U.S. business world, the concepts of Fredrick Taylor that became Scientific Management soon became an irresistible force in schools. According to Callahan (1962),

> The dominance of businessmen and the acceptance of business values (especially the concern for efficiency and economy); the creation of a critical, cost-

conscious, reform-minded public, led by profit-seeking journals; the alleged mis-management of all American institutions; the increased cost of living: all these factors created a situation of readiness for the great preacher of the gospel of efficiency, Fredrick W. Taylor, and his disciples. And school administrators, already under constant pressure to make education more practical in order to serve a business society better, were brought under even stronger criticism and forced to demonstrate first, last, and always that they were operating the schools efficiently. (p. 18)

Taylor's system emphasized central command and control of all operations, uniform ways of doing work aimed at uniform results measured through constant, imposed monitoring. The current emphasis on standardized, computer-generated and analyzed assessments, cost-cutting direct instruction, and a standardized curriculum all aimed at producing the "best product at the lowest cost," have clear roots in this early 20th-century business model.

Essentialism

Essentialism is often associated with William Bagely, professor at Teachers College, Columbia University, during the early decades of the last century. To Bagely, the schools must prepare students for a harshly competitive world. Curriculum should become much more standardized with little local design and should above all be rigorous. So-called soft subjects like social studies were suspect and "exacting studies" like Latin, algebra, and geometry need to be emphasized. The Essentialist favored an imposed, highly structured curriculum, a tight regime of tests to measure for results and a warning that failure to do so would imperil our social and economic position in the world. These arguments have become common fare in the debates supporting high-stakes testing, accountability, and curriculum standards from the late 1990s to today.

Perennialism

Robert Maynard Hutchins, famed president of the University of Chicago, described an allied but different vision in *The Conflict in Education* (1953). According to Hutchins, education's aim is the improvement of people to know the good, and the education that best fits free people is a liberal education. Therefore, liberal education meant exposure to classics of culture and science for everyone.[5] The origin of the very term "liberal education" refers to one free to pursue higher thoughts. The Perennialists' views can best be seen today in the standards movement and its fundamental concern for perceived high quality content in all traditional disciplines.

An Altered Context

While the genesis of today's conservative education movement did not start with *A Nation At Risk*, that document did act as a catalyst. According to Berliner and Biddle (1995), there has been a constant and consistent empowerment of those who find the movements described above to be a source of inspiration and identification. The chorus of mistrust directed at public education has also coincided with a sense of economic and social uncertainty. These values seem more in harmony with the ethic of justice than with the ethic of critique or the ethic of care (Shapiro & Stefkovich, 2001).

Standards, High-Stakes Testing, and the Accountability Movement

Finding inspiration in earlier movements of scientific management, Essentialism, Perennialism, and current trends criticizing public education, today's counterforces of standards, high-stakes testing, and accountability have grown and cohered. The manifestations of the standards movement (numerous and highly specific curriculum scope and sequence plans from professional societies, foundations, state and local government), high-stakes testing (required, standardized tests for all students in order to pass to the next grade level and/or to be able to graduate from secondary school matched with equally high-stakes testing of the professional teachers and administrators who serve these students) and accountability (attaching consequences in a typically bureaucratic hierarchical fashion to everyone in the system so that the standards and assessments are beyond anyone's ability to ignore) are well known to almost anyone who has worked in the K–12 public school system in the United States over the past half decade. Together, they represent a clear CIA (see Figure 3) with specific content, clear assessment, and pressure to aim instruction at broad coverage (see Figure 4). This is a very different vision than that of the Progressives, but equally part of America's educational history. Not the least difference between the two is the standards, high-stakes testing, accountability movement's deemphasis on inputs from children and classroom teachers in favor of state, national government, and corporate control.

Just as early Progressive ideals influenced core middle level documents in the late 1980s and throughout the 1990s, a parallel case of key Essentialist, Perennialist, and Scientific Management ideals also find their way into

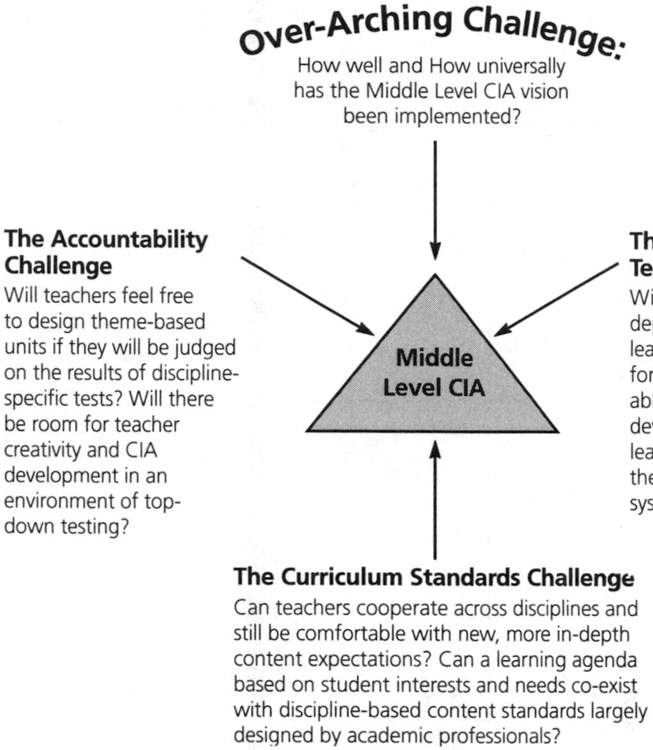

Over-Arching Challenge:

How well and How universally
has the Middle Level CIA vision
been implemented?

**The Accountability
Challenge**

Will teachers feel free
to design theme-based
units if they will be judged
on the results of discipline-
specific tests? Will there
be room for teacher
creativity and CIA
development in an
environment of top-
down testing?

**Middle
Level CIA**

**The High-Stakes
Testing Challenege**

Will there be time for in-
depth units and hands-on
learning and still prepare
for tests? Will teachers be
able to attend to both the
developmental needs of
learners and represent
the state testing
system?

The Curriculum Standards Challenge

Can teachers cooperate across disciplines and
still be comfortable with new, more in-depth
content expectations? Can a learning agenda
based on student interests and needs co-exist
with discipline-based content standards largely
designed by academic professionals?

Figure 3.   The Vulnerability of the Middle Level CIA to Four Important Challenges. This figure shows the forces that now stand in opposition to the middle
level movement.

current core documents. Interestingly enough, the most recent update of
Turning Points, Turning Points 2000, reflects some of these changes. While
not a total about-face, *Turning Points 2000* marks a major shift to emphasize
standards. The idea of rigorous, public academic standards for what students should know and be able to do take the place of prior values found
in the 1989 document. There is also less of an emphasis on interdisciplinary learning, exploratory curriculum, and on portfolio assessment.

CONCLUSION

An example of these two CIAs in conflict may help to illustrate the point.
About four years ago, I started to spend a good deal of time in one model
middle-grades classroom. It was almost the embodiment of the concepts in
Turning Points. There were four large classrooms organized by an interdis-

Early Ideas	Added to:	Current Manifestations
Scientific Management: The idea that efficiency and cost effectiveness. The "best product for the lowest cost." Uniform testing to assure consistent results.	**The traditional ethic of justice:** Application of uniform rules to achieve an equitable process and social development.	**Curriculum Standards Movement:** Specific and numerous academic standards are now established by subject matter experts at the state and national levels.
Essentialism: "Hard," "Demanding" subjects applied universally to all students.	**An atmosphere of uncertainty about the future.** Doubt about economic and political stability.	**High Stakes Testing:** Standardized testing for students and educators are in place. Consequences and rewards include serious implications for professional survival and for graduation.
Perennialism: The belief that a specific body of content is universally important and needed for all educated people to master.	**Serious and sustained criticism of school results.** Rejection by some of child orientation.	**Accountability:** Everyone in the system is evaluated continuously based on their performance or their students' performance on standardized tests designed to measure degrees of mastery of the standards-based curriculum.

Figure 4.   Ingredients of the Counter-Middle Level CIA. This figure demonstrates the evolution of this movement and the founding ideas that undergird it.

ciplinary team of teachers; classes were connected in a new, well-equipped building; students had a good deal to say about their learning and worked in small teams and individually; and multiple intelligences were recognized and built into instruction and assessment. After several visits I began to understand just how complex and rich the middle level program was at this school and for me to appreciate the thoughtfulness and understanding demonstrated by these teachers and the school's administrators. During these months, I observed as one team of student teachers and their cooperating teachers put in place an amazing unit that brought all of the approximately 80 students together to solve a challenge. The student teachers took the part of aliens. One day the students were all brought into the auditorium where these aliens appeared on stage. In convincing and dramatic tones, the space visitors challenged their middle-level students to design a sustainable system of long-range space travel within a month. During that time, teams of students worked with teachers and student teachers. Some built large-scale rockets; others learned about growing vegetables without soil and created greenhouse plants to fit the needs of the mission. Others read relevant literature. Each time I left this classroom, I came away with a sense that the students were learning core subject matter in a meaningful, integrated, and exciting way. At last, the time drew near for concluding the projects. Full class meetings were held, some pointing to great progress, some requiring greater effort.

When the final day arrived, the room seemed electric. Parents came streaming into the large room to see the work of their children and to marvel at their progress on this difficult and imaginative project. I walked around the room to learn how the families would react. Many were thrilled, making comments like, "Can you believe that they were able to build a mock spaceship? Look how close to the space shuttle it looks!" I began to think that these middle level educators were an unqualified hit. Then I watched one mother and her younger daughter stare at one particular poster depicting space travel. To be fair, it was not the most impressive artifact in the room. Frowning as she read the poster, the mother tapped her child on the shoulder and said in a loud, annoyed voice: "Will you look at that! A misspelled word right there! Right there for everyone to see! What kind of school is this?"

My initial shock almost boiled into outrage. How could anyone be immersed in so much obvious creativity and thoughtful, focused learning and not be impressed? Worse, how could anyone simply zero in on one misspelled word in this universe of vital student productivity? Only much later, having considered the contending schools of educational belief, did I see this incident for what it really was: A case of conflicting philosophies each holding fast to their own CIA triangle. The middle level program in general, expressed in the space unit, was a clear instance of Progressive education. School learning was geared to the world beyond school, hands-on activities and individual attention was central, and group cooperation toward shared goals was indispensable. The curriculum was open yet engaging. The instruction was equally flexible, allowing for work ranging from individual to large group and was aimed at a complex project tied to a culminating event. The assessment was equally rich and complex. Projects from groups and individuals were everywhere in sight. Students also worked along specific requirements for individual accountability built upon rubrics. While there was clear coherence among the CIA elements, it did not satisfy at least one parent. Her image of learning was born out of a different vision, one, I would argue, much more along the lines of an Essentialist thinker. Instead of seeing richness in the agenda, she seemed to see confusion and a lack of focus. Rather than being impressed by the diverse ways that learning took place, she seemed peevish about the amount of time all of this took away from more traditional studies. Finally, contrary to my own sense of awe at the quality of most of the students' work, she saw a complete lack of rigor. In the end, the size and the scope of the project seemed a source of frustration to her. The more she saw of this middle level philosophy in action, the less she seemed to like it. I was tempted to think that this was a fluke but soon a neighboring middle school, renowned for its own interdisciplinary, team approach, became a hotbed of angry parent meetings and turbulent board sessions. At one time, hundreds of parents presented the school board with a petition demanding a change in direction and a move toward a more discipline-based curriculum, taught in a more teacher-centered fashion with regularly administered standardized tests.

While no example should be generalized, I think that this case does depict some central conflicts that the innovators of the middle-level CIA need to consider if they wish to retain the essence of the movement in these times. What is at issue is a fairly clear conflict between very different philosophies. On a national scale, new challenges face the Progressive middle-level CIA (see Figure 5). In the eyes of the Scientific Managers, the Essentialists, and the Perennialists, they are the true guardians of equity and a meaningful democratic education. In fact, the conflict represented by the middle-level movement and their opponents favoring accountability, standards, and high-stakes testing may best be seen as an important manifestation of the most central contradiction in U.S. education in the past century. The Progressive middle-level movement and the more essentialist/perennialist standards/accountability movements stand in opposition. The disconnection between them may be severe enough to put them on a collision course.

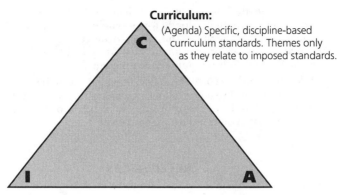

Curriculum:
(Agenda) Specific, discipline-based curriculum standards. Themes only as they relate to imposed standards.

Instruction:
(Communicating the Agenda) Pressure to teach by discipline. Coverage pressure may lead to increase in direct instruction. Diminished time for hand-on learning. Teacher evaluation, pay, promotion, and tenure aligned to externally designed testing.

Assessment:
(Determining Learner) High stakes, standardized testing. Increase of "rigor" in determining success. Annual testing required by state and federal legislation.

Figure 5.   The Emerging Counter-Middle Level CIA. This figure depicts the rival values that the represented by changes in curriculum, instruction and assessment policy shifts. These changes flow from the accountability, high stakes testing and standards movements.

NOTES

1. While Hall's work can clearly be connected to the writing of Rousseau, Froebel, and Pestalozzi, through their common interest in developmental states of childhood, his direct influence on the United States is of particular interest and importance to this discussion.

2. At the same time, teaches of middle year students are themselves dealing with the conflicts appropriate to their stage: young teachers (intimacy vs. isolation), middle-aged teachers (generativity vs. absorption), teachers near retirement (integrity vs. despair). Thus, Erikson's work places all of us in some form of conflict that we need to work out. Those working with middle level students must design curriculum, instruction, and assessment that fits the conflicts of that age and allows them to understand their own conflicts.

3. Spencer's interpretation of Darwin's work on evolution, known as Social Darwinism, made it clear that inequality among people was simply a result of inequality of talent and ability. If survival of the fittest in the forest caused certain animals to thrive while others became extinct, he held that the same applied to the city and its slums.

4.   As we will see, the concept of the project method survives in today's middle level movement both in a literal form—the projects of individuals or groups created as part of the unit—and as it informs the learner's portfolio. Both of these are elements of assessment since they help learners to demonstrate knowledge of the curriculum or learning agenda.

5.   While Hutchins's (1953) emphasis on social participation represented an overlap with the Progesssive's own concern for hands-on interaction with the world beyond the classroom, his focus on a particular content places him somewhat at odds with those concerns.

REFERENCES

Alberty, H. (1953). Meeting the common needs of youth. In *Adapting the secondary school to the youth. 52nd Yearbook of the N.S.S.E.* Chicago: University of Chicago Press.

Anfara, V., & Kirby, P. (2000). *Constructing and deconstructing the middle school: Where are we and how we got there.* In V. Anfara, Jr. & P. Kirby (Eds.), *Voices from the middle: Decrying what is, imploring what could be* (pp. 1–20). Dubuque, IA: Kendall/Hunt.

Bagley, W. C. (1938). An essentialist's platform for the advancement of American education. *Educational Administration and Supervision, 24,* 244–256.

Beane, J. A. (1993a). The case for core in the middle school. In T. Dickenson (Ed.), *Readings in middle school curriculum: A continuing conversation* (pp. 17–20). Columbus, OH: National Middle School Association.

Beane, J. A. (1993b). Re-thinking the middle school curriculum. In T. Dickenson (Ed.), *Readings in middle school curriculum: A continuing conversation* (pp. 41–52). Columbus, OH: National Middle School Association.

Berliner, D. C., & Biddle, B. J. (1995). *The manufactured crisis: Myths, frauds, and the attack on America's public schools.* Boston: Addison-Wesley.

Brown, K. M. (2000). Creating community in middle schools: Interdisciplinary teaming. In V. Anfara, Jr. & P. Kirby (Eds.), *Voices from the middle: Decrying what is, imploring what could be* (pp. 81–116). Dubuque, IA: Kendall/Hunt.

Callahan, R. E. (1962). *Education and the cult of efficiency.* Chicago: University of Chicago Press.

Carnegie Task Force on Education of Young Adolescents. (1989). *Turning points: Preparing America's youth for the 21st century.* Washington, DC: Carnegie Council on Adolescent Development.

Dewey, J. (1916). *Democracy and education.* New York: Free Press.

English, F. (1988). *Curriculum auditing.* Lancaster, PA: Technomic.

English, F., & Larson, R. (1996). *Curriculum management for educational and social service organizations.* Springfield, IL: Charles C. Thomas.

Erb, T. (2000). Do middle school reforms really make a difference? *The Clearinghouse, 73*(4), 194–200.

Erb, T. O. (1993). Preparing prospective middle grades teachers to understand the curriculum. In T. Dickenson (Ed.), *Readings in middle school curriculum: A continuing conversation* (pp. 95–104). Columbus, OH: National Middle School Association.

Erikson, E. (1963). *Childhood and society* (Rev. ed.). New York: Norton.

Faunce, R., & Clute, M. (1961). *Teaching and learning in the junior high school.* San Francisco: Wadsworth.

Gilligan, C. (1982). *In a different voice: Psychological theory and women's development.* Cambridge, MA: Harvard University Press.

Gross, S. J. (1998). *Staying centered: Curriculum leadership in a turbulent era.* Alexandria, VA: The Association for Supervision and Curriculum Development.

Graves, F. P. (1912). *Great educators of three centuries: Their work and its influence on modern education.* New York: MacMillan.

Hall, G. S. (1918). *Youth, its education, regimen and hygiene.* New York: D. Appleton.

Hall, G. S. (1905). *Adolescence: Its psychology and its relations to psychology, anthropology, sociology, sex, crime, religion, and education* (Vol. 2). New York: D. Appleton.

Hechinger, F. M. (1992). *Fateful choices: Healthy youth for the 21st century.* New York: Hill & Wang.

Hutchins, R. M. (1953). *The conflict in education.* New York: Harper & Row.

Jackson, A. W., & Davis, G. A. (2000). *Turning points 2000.* New York: Teachers College Press.

Jacobs, H. (1998). *Mapping the big picture.* Alexandria, VA: The Association for Supervision and Curriculum Development.

Joseph, B., & Kirby, P. (2000). Power in the middle: What's good for the goose. In V. Anfara, Jr. & P. Kirby (Eds.), *Voices from the middle: Decrying what is, imploring what could be* (pp. 81–116). Dubuque, IA: Kendall/Hunt.

Kilpatrick, W. H. (1926). *Foundations of method: Informal talks on teaching.* New York: MacMillan.

Kliebard, H. M. (1986). *The struggle for the American curriculum 1893–1958.* New York: Routledge.

McEwin, C. K., Dickenson, T. S., & Jenkins, D. M. (1996). *America's middle schools: Practices and progress, a 25 year perspective.* Columbus, OH: National Middle School Association.

Morgan, G. (1997). *Images of organization.* Thousand Oaks, CA: Sage.

National Commission on Excellence in Education. (1983). *A nation at risk: The imperatives for educational reform.* Washington, DC: U.S. Department of Education.

National Middle School Association. (1995). *This we believe: Developmentally responsive middle level schools.* Columbus, OH: Author.

Piaget, J. (1952). *The origins of intelligence in children.* New York: Basic Books.

Sergiovanni, T. (1996). *Leadership for the schoolhouse.* San Francisco: Jossey-Bass.

Shapiro, J. P., & Stefkovich, J. F. (2001). *Ethical leadership and decision making in education: Applying theoretical perspectives to complex dilemmas.* Mahwah, NJ: Erlbaum.

Stevenson, C. (1993). You've gotta see the game to see the game. In T. Dickenson (Ed.), *Readings in middle school curriculum: A continuing conversation* (pp. 73–82). Columbus, OH: National Middle School Association.

Taba, H. (1962). *Curriculum development: Theory and practice.* New York: Harcourt, Brace, & World.

U.S. Bureau of Education. (1893). *Report of the committee of ten on secondary education.* Washington, DC: Government Printing Office.

Vygotsky, L. (1978). *Mind in society* (M. Cole, V. John-Steiner, S. Scribner, & E. Sociberman, Eds.). Cambridge, MA: Harvard University Press.

West-Olatunji, C.A. (2000). *Culturally and developmentally appropriate interventions for the alternative middle school.* In V. Anfara, Jr. & P. Kirby (Eds.), *Voices from the middle: Decrying what is, imploring what could be* (pp. 137–162). Dubuque, IA: Kendall/Hunt.

CHAPTER 1

CURRICULUM INTEGRATION

Theory, Practice, and Research for a Sustainable Future

**Billy O'Steen, Pru Cuper, Hiller Spires,
Candy Beal, and Carol Pope**
North Carolina State University

ABSTRACT

For many educators, a tension exists between the theoretical and practical aspects of curriculum integration. What educational theorists and scholars may present as the most effective ideas may not seem feasible to educators who are increasingly evaluated on students' test scores. Consequently, educators may embrace the curriculum-integration approach or not attempt it at all. Such a polarity suggests a value-laden continuum along which degrees of curriculum integration adoption may fall. However, a review of recent research suggests that as teachers implement curriculum integration, they engage in a contextual selection process that is based on contextual constraints and supports. In fact, teachers approximate but rarely achieve full curriculum integration. The nonhierarchical and idiosyncratic selection pro-

Middle School Curriculum, Instruction, and Assessment, pages 1–22
Copyright © 2002 by Information Age Publishing
All rights of reproduction in any form reserved.

cess resists prescribed boundaries and categories yet reflects the phenomenological nature of contemporary educational practice. For curriculum
integration to be fully implemented and sustained as a viable curricular
option for middle level educators, future research should include (1) qualitative and quantitative research, emphasizing grounded theory on the contextual selection process, contextual constraints, and supports to refine current
curriculum-integration understandings; (2) effects of the contextual selection process, contextual constraints, and supports on learning outcomes
associated with curriculum integration; and (3) the relationship between
those learning outcomes and performance on high-stakes tests.

Consider the middle level educator who is handed a set of discipline-specific standards and informed that her students' performance on an end-of-
year assessment (based on those standards) is linked to compensation, promotion, and publicity. Upon surveying this set of directives as to what she
should teach, the educator faces a critical decision of how to go about it.
Unfortunately, her instant reaction may be to approach teaching the standards by "teaching the test." Her attempt to blend personal philosophy and
academic research regarding best curricular methods may buckle under
the pressure to get through the mandated curriculum efficiently. It may
well result in "drill and kill" pedagogy featuring a class of bored, passive,
and uncritical students.

Consider a second middle level educator who is handed the same set of
discipline-specific standards but who has determined she will use a curriculum-integration approach. This educator is also mindful of the mandated
standards but makes a decision to attend to the standards within the context of student-generated inquiry topics. These topics can then lead to the
creation of action-oriented end products whereby students experience a
sense of their own social agency in relationship to the world beyond the
walls of the classroom.

And so the question arises: Is it more prudent to teach to the test in the
hope of improving standardized scores, or is it better to put major emphasis on encouraging student inquiry by working with topics that are relevant
to adolescents? This is one of the most compelling questions facing middle
level educators today. Debate over curricular approach and content is
ongoing and occurs at all levels of education. In the United States, this
debate historically has been focused on *who* determines the approach and
the content. For now, the content area of the debate has been answered
with President Bush's recent approval of the *No Child Left Behind* (Educational Research Service, 2001) legislation that effectively mandates a state
and federal system of standards and testing. While educators will increasingly be told *what* to teach, they will still retain a degree of choice in determining *how* to teach. Fortunately, this is the more critical choice to retain.
Educators' decisions regarding the *how* element within their classrooms

must be informed and supported by a blend of personal philosophy and academic research.

The current high-stakes testing and standards-driven environment leads many educators to adopt a strict, subject-centered delivery of curriculum. To do otherwise in the face of test scores related to school accreditation, personal compensation, and job security appears counterproductive. However, as many educators know from their own classroom experiences, academic preparation, and professional development workshops, other approaches are possible. In fact, alternative approaches, in many cases, are more compatible with the developmental needs of adolescents.

One alternative curricular approach that may offer teachers a means of addressing the developmental needs and interests of adolescents is the established and comprehensive curriculum integration approach that James Beane (1993) defined. The following section examines how Beane's approach is a convergence of the theoretical influences of (1) John Dewey's time-honored ideas on the child and the curriculum, (2) the Scales (1991) and Brazee (1995) frameworks regarding the developmental needs of young adolescents, and, finally, (3) the National Middle School Association's (NMSA) recommendations (1995) for effective middle-school practice.

CURRICULUM INTEGRATION: THE THEORETICAL INFLUENCES

The tenets of curriculum integration are rooted in the convergence of Dewey's ideas on the child and curriculum, the developmental needs of young adolescents, and the NMSA's recommendations for middle level curriculum (see Figure 1.1). While much has been written individually about these theoretical influences, it is important to briefly review how specific aspects of each area converge to provide a theoretical rationale for considering curriculum integration in middle level education.

Dewey' s Ideas on the Child and the Curriculum

In his early examination and discussion of psychology's concept of the *reflex arc* (the separation of stimulus from response rather than the idea of an ongoing interaction between the two), Dewey expressed much of what later became his core philosophy of education and life. In addition to providing a foundation for his later work, Dewey's reconceptualization of psychology's *reflex arc* also represents a clear theoretical connection with curriculum integration. Dewey (1896) sought to revise what was taken for

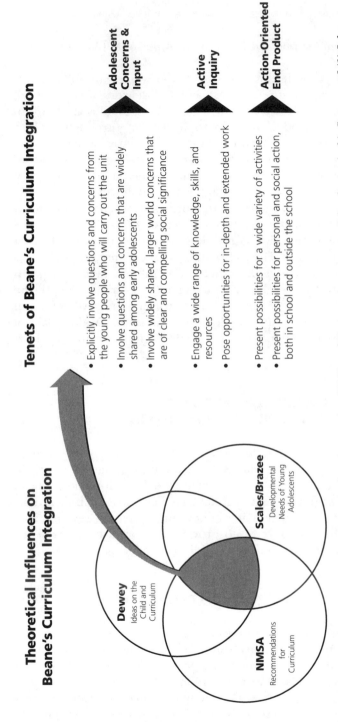

Theoretical Influences on Beane's Curriculum Integration

Tenets of Beane's Curriculum Integration

Dewey
Ideas on the Child and Curriculum

Scales/Brazee
Developmental Needs of Young Adolescents

NMSA
Recommendations for Curriculum

Adolescent Concerns & Input

- Explicitly involve questions and concerns from the young people who will carry out the unit
- Involve questions and concerns that are widely shared among early adolescents
- Involve widely shared, larger world concerns that are of clear and compelling social significance

Active Inquiry

- Engage a wide range of knowledge, skills, and resources
- Pose opportunities for in-depth and extended work

Action-Oriented End Product

- Present possibilities for a wide variety of activities
- Present possibilities for personal and social action, both in school and outside the school

Figure 1.1. The tenets of Beane's curriculum integration (1993, p. 75) as a convergence of the theoretical influences of (1) John Dewey, (2) Scales (1991) and Brazee (1995), and (3) NMSA.

granted in psychology, pedagogy, and philosophy by replacing the reflex arc concept with a *circle of experience*. It was Dewey's perception that separating stimulus from response led to an artificial duality of thought and action. For him, this separation was explicitly evident in a subject-centered curriculum that did not provide students with any opportunities to affect their surroundings in a more dynamic and lifelike circular interaction—a student-centered curriculum.

By extending the basic idea of integrating stimulus and response instead of separating them, Dewey wrote about how best to reconnect the responses of citizens with the different stimuli of American society. Included in his wide range of writings were thoughts about the roles of philosophy, government, and art, but his most prolific writing and speaking focused on the role of education in American society. More specifically, Dewey aimed the majority of his energy and work on expanding his ideas regarding the reflex arc vs. the circle of experience into a theory of experience and education. This theory reflects his belief in the need to integrate life experiences into education.

> The isolation of thinking from confrontation with facts encourages that kind of observation which merely accumulates brute facts, which occupies itself laboriously with mere details, but never inquires into their meaning and consequences—a safe occupation, for it never contemplates any use to be made of the observed facts in determining a plan for changing the situation. (Dewey, 1920, p. 141)

Dewey's work in creating and directing the Lab School at the University of Chicago from 1894 to 1904 clearly provided a "living laboratory" for him to observe, think, and theorize about education. Through a series of essays written during his Lab School tenure, Dewey developed the thesis that the content of education and the structure of school should be reintegrated into society. Because human beings live in communities, Dewey reasoned that their education must originate from the self and concern learning to live with others in a social setting. Furthermore, this education that originates with the self and is rooted in the community must, in fact, be life itself and not intellectualized partitions.

> I believe that the only true education comes through the stimulation of the child's powers by the demands of the social situations in which he finds himself.... The child's own instincts and powers furnish the material and give the starting point for all education. (cited in Dworkin, 1959, p. 20)

For Dewey, to enact this belief requires a reconstruction of the curriculum and school. Instead of putting the school in a building apart from the community, he preferred to have the school become a part of the community. Part of this transformation would involve bringing all parts of the community and its practices into the school and vice versa. His examples of reintegrating the community's practices into the school included having a working kitchen, garden, and shop in which students would have the opportunity to perform "real" tasks and pursue knowledge around those tasks that interested them.

In his final piece of writing during his tenure at the University of Chicago, Dewey sought to reunite and reintegrate two entities that he felt had been wrongly separated—the child and the curriculum. Instead of continuing down the path of traditional education and maintaining "a child versus the curriculum" (cited in Dworkin, 1959) philosophy, Dewey advocated that teachers view subject matter as material for students to use in creating action-oriented end products. In Dewey's opinion, the relevance of subject matter can only be found within the experiences and contexts of the students.

Thus, for Dewey, the teacher's role is not to be a dispenser of knowledge but to be a guide who assists the student in using his or her own experiences and interests toward cocreating an engaging curriculum. Dewey continued to refine these ideas and to focus on the role of experience in education and the need to integrate education with democracy. He believed that the role of education is to teach individuals how to become more interactive with their social environment in order to cocreate that environment. Furthermore, he believed that the educative experience would be achieved only by "making the individual a sharer or partner in the associated activity so that he feels its success as his success, its failure as his failure" (1916, p. 14).

In summary, the main connections between Dewey's concept of experiential education and curriculum integration are (1) a cocreated and flexible course of study based on an integration of subject matter and students' experiences; (2) the educator's responsibility for the integration of cocreation, facilitation, and instruction and; (3) a structural and functional integration of the students' curriculum with community issues.

Brazee's Application of Scales's Developmental Needs of Young Adolescents

Included in Dewey's (1916) ideas for a curriculum that integrates subject matter with students' interests and community issues is an admonition to respect and complement developmental needs. However, as John Arnold (1993) argues, "curriculum designed specifically for middle grades education is paltry" (p. 2). For Arnold, middle level educators must design curricular approaches that address the specific needs of young adolescents as "they have been neglected, misunderstood, stereotyped, and to some extent, exploited. Like all minority groups, they need to be empowered" (p. 1). In stark contrast to a subject-centered curriculum solely focused on covering content, Arnold's "empowering curriculum will help young adolescents understand and counter the forces which are exploiting them and/or hindering their development" (p. 7).

This notion of linking curriculum to students' developmental needs is further advanced and clarified by Brazee (1995). "Even though there are a number of different points which suggest a particular stance toward curriculum, the foundational rationale for middle school curriculum must be young adolescent growth and development" (p. 7). One curricular design that Brazee sees as meeting the needs of young adolescents is curriculum integration because "responsiveness to growth and development of young adolescents is the backbone of integrated curriculum" (p. 20).

To support his argument, Brazee uses Scales's (1991) seven developmental needs as "one particularly useful framework for understanding the complex and continuous changes young adolescents undergo" (1995, p. 9). While working at the Center for Early Adolescence, Scales created a list of seven developmental needs: (1) positive social interaction with adults and peers; (2) structure and clear limits; (3) physical activity; (4) creative expression; (5) competence and achievement; (6) meaningful participation in families, schools, and communities; and (7) opportunities for self-definition. Scales explains that the list of needs is "based on extensive research on successful schools and community-based programs, and on a wide-ranging review of literature" (p. 13), including the work of Erickson, Gilligan, and others.

Brazee (1995) explicitly connects each of Scales's developmental needs with a tenet of curriculum integration in order to illustrate the particular strength of this approach in middle level education. In constructing this connection, he stresses that the traditional, subject-centered approach is not appropriate for middle level curriculum. "Middle-level schools have not lived up to their billing as developmentally responsive schools for young adolescents; they have failed to address the fundamental element of the school—its curriculum" (p. 16). While Brazee notes that adopting curriculum integration is not simply an add-on or an easy undertaking because it "means to fundamentally change the school for students, teachers, and parents" (p. 18), he is adamant that curriculum integration is a necessary move. He asserts:

> Nearly one hundred years after the first developmentally responsive school, the junior high school, it is time for the modern middle school to fulfill its original promise. Appropriately, two elements must work in conjunction—knowledge about (1) young adolescent development and (2) integrated cur-

riculum. Stated simply, we have come as far as we can by changing schedules, organizing teachers and students into teams, and adding on to the already over-crowded curriculum. Now we must turn our attention to crafting the curriculum into what it must be: responsive to the unique and compelling needs of young adolescents. (1995, p. 21)

National Middle School Association's Recommendations for Curriculum

The National Middle School Association has embraced both Dewey's broad concept of an integrated curriculum and Brazee's more specific alignment of middle school curriculum with "the unique and compelling needs of young adolescents" (1995, p. 21). The NMSA's recommendations for curriculum (1995) call for a blending of Dewey's ideas with the developmental needs of adolescents so that "middle level curriculum is distinguished by emphases that stem from the unique characteristics and needs of young adolescents. The curriculum of a developmentally responsive middle level school is challenging, integrative, and exploratory" (p. 20).

In order for a curriculum to be challenging, the NMSA suggests that it must be engaging to young adolescents and "address substantive issues and skills that are relevant or are made relevant to students; be geared to their levels of understanding; and enable them increasingly to assume control of their own learning" (p. 21). Implied and explicit, then, teachers and students will cocreate a challenging curriculum in the attempt to address "students' own questions and concerns" (p. 21). Clearly, the subject-centered curriculum, seen as an efficient approach in the current educational environment, is not consonant with the NMSA's definition of a challenging curriculum.

The challenging curriculum, according to the NMSA, must be integrative in order to "help students make sense out of their life experiences" (1995, p. 22). To implement this, the NMSA recommends that "middle level schools can offer courses and units, taught either by individual teachers or by teams, that are designed specifically to integrate the formal school curriculum" (p. 23). By using mandated curricular standards as means and not ends, "integration...is enhanced when the curriculum is focused on issues significant to both students and adults" (p. 23). To view curriculum within this framework requires a shift for students and teachers to become producers instead of consumers of knowledge (p. 23).

In order to produce knowledge within the middle-school curriculum, the NMSA suggests that "the entire curriculum, not just certain courses or activities, should be exploratory" (1995, p. 23). The NMSA defines exploratory curriculum as that which enables students to discover more about themselves, have opportunities to contribute to society, and become familiar with lifelong enrichment possibilities. Thus, the NMSA curriculum must operate on both personal and public levels.

Beane's Curriculum Integration

According to the tenets of Beane's curriculum integration (1993), students are initially engaged in units of study when teachers are careful to address their concerns and invite their input. In so doing, students are prepared to become active citizens as their questions and concerns will presumably focus on real world issues. For Beane, placing the child at the center and as the creator of her middle-level curriculum forms the foundation for real learning. Beane states that students should explore "questions of values, morals, and ethics in immediate and distant social relationships, and with regard to the form and function of social institutions" (p. 56). By placing the responsibility of curriculum creation with students rather than with educators (from varying levels within the establishment), Beane is calling for a very different model. And to those in favor of mandated standards, Beane's model appears to be the antithesis of what is expected or presumed to work most efficiently in covering content (for a comprehensive, Web-based discussion about assessment and Beane's curriculum integration, see www.nscu.edu/chass/extension/ci/).

Beane (1993) further delineates his model of teaching and learning by explaining how students and teachers should proceed once students' questions have been elicited. During the pursuit of answers to their questions, the walls separating disciplines into defined blocks of study should be eliminated. Using their own questions as the foci of study, Beane suggests that students and teachers will cover academic content by uncovering its relevance and necessity in relationship to their questions. Furthermore, by pursuing real questions, Beane states that students will gain opportunities to develop self-efficacy skills rather than simply memorizing decontextualized content.

> Because "knowing how" and actually "doing" for some purposes are so closely related, it sensibly follows that skills are only worthwhile when they are actually applied to real situations and, further, that they are most likely to be learned when they are so applied. In other words, the learning and valuing of skills are most likely assured if they are placed in a functional context where their application is immediate and compelling. (p. 63)

For students and teachers involved in Beane's curriculum integration, an evaluative benchmark, then, goes beyond the classroom. Instead of study solely devoted to performance measured by an end-of-grade test, study is devoted to and measured by the public application of learned skills to real situations. Obviously, to implement this approach requires an educator to not only rethink traditional models of teaching and learning but to also struggle with an overall, oppositional structure. Beane acknowledges that curriculum integration is not just a model du jour to apply half-heartedly. He states, "the everyday schedule is formed around the activities, problems, or projects that young people are involved with . . . if the curriculum is to change, then so will the usual way of assessing and reporting the schoolwork of early adolescents" (1993, pp. 94–95). To follow Beane's lead requires a commitment based on the belief that his approach addresses the developmental needs of young adolescents, and in so doing, provides the best opportunity for middle level education to serve as a preparation for life and not just a holding place until high school. Beane proposes the following:

> The centerpiece of the curriculum would consist of thematic units whose organizing centers are drawn from the intersecting concerns of early adolescents and issues in the larger world. Within the units, opportunities would be planned to develop and apply the various skills I have described, including those that are often called "desirable" but are typically found only on the periphery of the curriculum. Similarly, such concepts as democracy, human dignity, and cultural diversity would persistently be brought to life in the content of the units and processes used to carry them out. (p. 68)

Thus, the tenets of Beane's curriculum integration appear to represent a converging point of Dewey's ideas on the child and curriculum, the developmental needs of adolescents as presented by Brazee's application of Scales's list, and the NMSA's recommendations. However, the fact that middle-level educators have not universally adopted curriculum integration illustrates a divide between a theory that appears appropriate and a practice that reflects contemporary challenges. To further explore this apparent disconnect between theory and practice, we reviewed research on curriculum integration from the past decade. As an analytical framework for reviewing the research, we have clustered Beane's original seven components of curriculum integration into three overarching categories: adolescent concerns and input, active inquiry, and action-oriented end product (see Figure 1.1).

CURRICULUM INTEGRATION: THE RESEARCH BASE

To include a range of context-specific perspectives and approaches, we examined a 10-year span of literature regarding the application of curriculum integration from a number of sources, including *Middle School Journal,*

Research in Middle Level Education Quarterly, and *The Handbook of Research in Middle Level Education.* We also referred to Stevenson and Carr's (1993) collection of classroom experiences with curriculum integration, Integrated Studies in the Middle Grades: "Dancing Through Walls." Our content analysis of this research yielded two major conclusions: (1) teachers engage in a contextual selection process as they approximate curriculum integration, and (2) this process is directly affected by contextual constraints and supports.

The Contextual Selection Process for Curriculum Integration

To understand and work toward implementing the curriculum integration model, educators should recognize that such implementation is likely to occur gradually and in an idiosyncratic fashion. They should also recognize that a contextual selection process is likely to be involved—a process of making choices. Just as fine dining involves choosing items from the menu that are most palatable and digestible for differing tastes, the same can be said for the process of adopting portions of curriculum integration. From the overarching categories included in the full curriculum-integration model—the full "menu" (see Figure 1.1)—teachers may select what is most appealing and practical for their particular classroom setting.

While major categories include units of study that feature: (1) adolescent concerns and input; (2) active inquiry; and (3) action-oriented end products, we found that teachers rarely initiated all three of these categories simultaneously or in equal degrees. Instead, they chose aspects of each depending upon their particular context—their geographical setting, the expectations of their schools' administrations and parents; their students' backgrounds, interests, and needs; and finally, their own interests and needs. Subsequent implementation occurred recursively in a back-and-forth, adjust-as-you-go contextual selection process, as illustrated by the following classroom examples.

Adolescent concerns and input. One of the initial and most basic tenets within the first category of the curriculum integration model suggests the importance of *explicitly involving questions and concerns from the young people who will carry out the unit.* Pate, Homestead, and McGinnis (1995), two middle level teachers and an associate professor of middle level education, accepted the challenge of developing a year-long curriculum for their eighth-grade students that focused on creating a democratic classroom. Working with 60 students, they created units of study grounded in areas of specific student concern. The combined efforts of teachers and students resulted in four thematic units that addressed state-mandated standards while progressively (but gradually) involving more student decision-making responsibility. "We learned that developing a trusting relationship and a democratic classroom takes time and work and give and take. We learned that the process went more quickly and smoothly when we gave our students something tangible to edit, critique, or vote on rather than asking them to create something from scratch" (Pate et al., p. 125).

Pate and colleagues (1995) concluded that the process of adopting curriculum integration is difficult and students who are used to being more passive in the classroom setting will not necessarily embrace it. Working with students whose previous school experiences consisted of a system that basically handed them a set of plans and behavioral expectations, this group of teachers found that some students "had a difficult time understanding that more time spent on planning and preparation translated into less time fixing problems" (p. 125). In the final analysis, they felt that their venture into curriculum integration was worthwhile, that mutual learning had occurred and, most importantly, that by including "issues relevant to students, curriculum connections [were] successfully made" (p. 125).

A second tenet of curriculum integration within the category of *adolescent concerns and input* calls for *involving questions and concerns that are widely shared among early adolescents*. A four-week study conducted by middle level teachers (Sage, Krynock, & Robb, 2000) can be examined as a counterpoint to Pate's study in terms of student participation in topic selection. Conducted in a suburban community near Chicago, this study involved integrating science and language arts classes "on a problem centering around [maintaining] prairie areas on the school's campus" (p. 149). This group of teachers felt their project included many components of curriculum integration, however, student questions and concerns were not actively addressed. For this reason, the project did not engage students as effectively as the teachers had hoped. One of the students summed up the feelings of the group. "I mean, this class could be fun if it was a problem that we cared about, but what do we care about the prairie?" (p. 163). Fortunately, Sage and colleagues appreciated the many benefits from their undertaking and did not give up on curriculum integration. They spoke of the importance of "encouraging students to see learning as real life, not as a school 'game'"(p. 170). In retrospect, they felt that the active learning, revision of traditional teacher and student roles, and focus on a real-world topic (e.g., maintaining the prairie environment) made their initial foray into curriculum integration a success.

The final consideration under the category of *adolescent concerns and input* calls for *involving widely shared, larger world concerns that are of clear and compelling social significance*. In an effort to integrate eighth-grade social studies and language arts, Canadian teachers Erlandson and McVittie (2001) demonstrated that focusing on larger world concerns, in their case "conflict with the environment," is not always perceived as an effective learning experience by all students. At the close of their unit of study, two interviewed students felt that the experience would have been more meaningful and they would have become more involved if they could have had more say in the focal topic. Despite their intentions to approach the mandated curriculum in an integrated and relevant manner that centered on the very compelling issue of environmental protection, the topic was admittedly not student selected. The teachers noted the value of the personal/subject integration that took place in their combined classes, but candidly stated, "These students are issuing a challenge to us teachers to listen to what is important to them and to act on that information" (p. 35). In this case, as in the Sage and colleagues (2000) study, teachers selected only certain aspects of curriculum integration. They took their first steps into new teaching territory and experienced a resulting mix of positive and critical reactions.

Active inquiry. The second major category within the curriculum integration model suggests using inquiry-based learning with students. A key consideration within this category involves *students engaging a wide range of knowledge, skills, and resources.* Vermont middle school teachers Smith, Mann, and Steadman (1993) took a unique approach to engaging a group of 65 fourth through eighth graders in such an inquiry-based process through a unit of study they called "Adopt a Business." While this project featured contextual selection of multiple facets of the full curriculum-integration model, most noteworthy was its emphasis on developing student knowledge through extended work.

The goals for this unit of study were to relate in-school learning to real-life application as students interacted with adults in their community and learned the details of owning and running small businesses. While the teachers were instrumental in planning the unit of study, the students took the lead in researching businesses of interest to them and then planning their own small business ventures. Their engagement with a wide range of skills included research methods such as taping interviews with local business owners (and later transcribing those tapes), documenting their daily experiences in journals, and serving as participant observers as they each worked with local business owners. For their culminating activity (another key category within the full curriculum-integration model this group of teachers opted to include), the students prepared an open-house presentation for their classmates, parents, and the local business community to demonstrate what they had learned.

The overall reaction to this unit of study was extremely positive. Everyone involved appreciated the opportunity to conduct real-world research and to work through the reality of business ownership. One of the teachers summed up the project. "For some kids, this was the first opportunity to spend meaningful time with an adult outside their family structure. For others, it was a chance to explore connections between education and success in later life" (Smith et al., 1993, p. 107).

A second area of *active inquiry* also focuses on *posing opportunities for in-depth and extended student work.* In a qualitative study of a group of Brown Barge Middle School graduates, Powell and Skoog (1995) found 9th and 10th graders comparing their high school experience of "changing topics every time you go to a new class" to their Brown Barge integrated-curriculum experience where you "changed classes but you were still on the same topic" (p. 96). The curriculum-integration emphasis on in-depth and extended student work resulted in student perceptions of having "learned more" when all of their classes revolved around one topic. At Brown Barge, students felt that their content and topic knowledge was deeper when they concentrated on one overarching theme and when they addressed this theme continuously over a 12-week period.

Action-oriented end products. The final category in the full curriculum-integration model calls for *presenting possibilities for a wide variety of activities.* Through a 6-week unit titled "A View from the Park—Studying Our Town" (Brown & Eaton, 1993), two eighth-grade teachers from Vermont combined their reading and science classes for an integrated learning experience that culminated in a town-wide presentation of varied student products. The unit revolved around researching 10 historic buildings within walking distance of the school—when the buildings were constructed, who built them, their original purpose, architectural style, and materials used. Research included visits to the local library and interviews with the present building residents. Students' products included booklets, videotapes and photographs, drawings and posters, and a reenactment of a historic event related to their building. Through this varied choice of culminating activities, students gained a rich and novel appreciation of their town. One student expressed the feelings of the entire group. "[We] found out that our town was a lot more complex than the skimpy little town we thought it was. . . . We met new people and felt like citizens rather than just students" (p. 97).

Also within the category of *action-oriented end products,* teachers are encouraged to *present possibilities for personal and social action, both in school and outside the school.* Kesson and Oyler (1999) described the work of students and teachers as they connected an in-class reading of *An Enemy of the People* with a real-life situation in their community. The Oklahoma homeland of these students was heavily polluted with residue from lead and zinc mining, asbestos waste from an abandoned tire plant, and acidic ashes from a solid waste incinerator. Through curriculum integration, the students researched the sources of pollution; wrote a book about the situation; conducted toxic tours of the area; and created *The Legacy,* a collection of poetry, prose, autobiographies, and songs about the effects of living on poisoned land. As a result of their efforts, students and teachers raised community and governmental awareness of the problem so that areas were declared EPA Superfund sites. Kesson and Oyler expressed their satisfaction with this unit of study: "There was a lot of denial in the community before the students started the Tar Creek project .... But, you know, to me, the students are the key to getting Tar Creek ... cleaned up or improved or whatever is going to happen. They're the ones that are going to do something about it" (p. 139).

Reviewing this decade-wide and geographically broad sampling of curriculum integration projects, both teachers and students appear to have much to gain from implementing such approaches to the extent possible within their particular settings. While both teachers and students in the highlighted studies voiced certain concerns, the majority of attempts at curriculum integration registered positive reactions. Even in their voicing of concerns, teachers and students as partners in the education process weighed and considered new approaches to learning. With potential for such positive classroom interactions, it is natural to question why there isn't more widespread adoption of this model (partial or full), and further, what it would take in the way of structural and systemic educational change to ensure more widespread adoption.

Contextual Constraints and Supports for Curriculum Integration

Beane (1997) describes the difficulty involved in integrative curriculum reform by positing that a progressive philosophy of education is "not for the professionally faint-hearted—not when the road to high pedagogy is paved with tough politics" (p. 84). Specifically, this complexity occurred in the research we reviewed due to the presence or absence of site-specific structural supports. For example, for curriculum integration to be implemented successfully, administrators must be willing to devote time and effort to sustaining the implementation. Additionally, teachers must have support from their colleagues as they accept the challenges involved in adopting this intensive curricular approach.

An example of strong internal support comes from studies conducted at Brown Barge Middle School (Powell & Skoog, 1995; Powell, Skoog, & Troutman, 1996). The entire school had adopted curriculum integration by creating thematic units, or "streams," chosen by students. These streams sought to incorporate real issues with academic content through a nonlinear system that eliminated separate disciplines. This approach appeared to succeed within the school and teachers reported increased student engagement. However, because students entered a more linear-oriented curriculum in high school, they perceived themselves as being "behind" peers who had attended a traditional middle school. "I learned how to work in a group. I learned things that will probably benefit me later in life, but not right now [in high school]" (Powell & Skoog, 1995, p. 98). Thus, they concluded that students were not making the connections between what they had learned within a curriculum-integration approach and later experiences within a more traditional approach. While the internal support was present at the middle school, the students found that there was a disconnect between their middle school and high school experiences.

In another study by Powell and Skoog (2000), teachers role playing the part of students also observed the disconnection between curriculum integration and traditional learning. In this study, teachers attended a workshop in which they completed an environmentally based curriculum-integration project. They were interviewed before and after the experience. The data demonstrated that while the teachers may have experienced the benefits of curriculum integration, they did not adopt the approach due to the competing demands from state-mandated standards and tests. Additionally, the teachers observed that without sustained support from school administrators and colleagues, implementation of the workshop ideas was impossible. As one teacher asserted, "Integrative curriculum will only work if the whole school changes" (p. 27).

Further evidence of the need for administrative support was demonstrated through a study conducted in 400 Missouri middle, junior, and senior high schools (Arredondo & Rucinski, 1995). This group of researchers found that teachers in schools with a high degree of curriculum integration, an interdisciplinary curriculum, or a multidisciplinary curriculum tend to have greater teacher involvement in decision-making processes. In these curriculum integration "user" schools, principals and central office administrators reported being a key part of the initiation process. They explained the need to offer ongoing support through frequent classroom visits, observation of classes, supportive conferences with teachers in which they listened to success stories and problems, staff development on curriculum integration, and the need to offer common planning time for teachers.

In a final study, Weilbacher (2001) examined the apparent "waning of interest" in curriculum integration via interviews with four experienced middle level teachers who moved from using a full curriculum-integration model to a more modified model. The teachers also identified several constraints that discouraged full curriculum-integration implementation. The main factor of concern to the teachers was that of time, specifically, the inordinate amount of time needed for unit planning and maintenance and other school-related demands. Curriculum-integration time demands also interrupted teachers' personal and family time. Additionally, teachers were troubled by the fact that they often made promises to their students in terms of allowing for student input on the generation of curricular activities that they knew they wouldn't be able to fulfill. They also tired of the defensive posture they had to maintain in response to criticisms from administrators, parents, and coworkers. Finally, there was the ongoing matter of high turnover in teacher-partners who were willing to implement the full curriculum-integration model with them.

DISCUSSION AND DIRECTIONS FOR FUTURE RESEARCH

As illustrated in the first section of this chapter, clear and compelling theoretical support and rationale exist for using curriculum integration in middle level education. However, practicing educators are experiencing mixed results as they apply this curricular approach in their classrooms. Additional research is needed for curriculum integration to be fully implemented and sustained as a viable curricular option for middle level educators. Within this context, we propose the following research agenda.

First, we need a combination of quantitative and qualitative research, including grounded theory to further depict the contextual selection process that curriculum-integration teachers use. Although most of the reviewed studies of curriculum integration are qualitative and anecdotal in nature, a "thick description" (Lincoln & Guba, 1985, p. 125) that enables the reader to see potentially transferable components is rarely employed. Too often, the descriptions lean more toward first-person testimonials, which provide believers in curriculum integration with useful anecdotes but may appear too localized for nonbelievers as they attempt to comprehend transferability or viability. Thus, sustained, in-depth, and qualitatively rigorous views of curriculum integration in action are needed.

Of particular interest within the qualitative research area is the development of grounded theories. In the case of curriculum integration, we believe such theories would revolve around the contextual selection process, constraints, and supports to refine current curriculum-integration understandings. In their explanation of the value of grounded theory, Lincoln and Guba (1985) posit that "mutual shapings found in a particular context may be explicable only in terms of the contextual elements found there." Furthermore, they claim that grounded theory is "more likely to be responsive to contextual values and not merely to investigator values" (p. 41). Thus, grounded theory has the potential to produce new insights as it examines accepted theoretical understandings (e.g., "grand theories" such as Beane's full curriculum integration model) within contemporary settings.

That most of the reviewed studies of curriculum integration are qualitative and anecdotal in nature is not surprising. Because the tenets of qualitative research roughly parallel those of curriculum integration, it appears to be the most appropriate methodology for analyzing this approach. "Realities are multiple, constructed, and holistic. All entities are in a state of mutual simultaneous shaping. Inquiry is value-bound" (Lincoln & Guba, 1985, p. 37), it appears to be the most appropriate methodology for analyzing this approach. However, for educators practicing in the current educational environment, more quantitative research is also needed. To adopt curriculum integration, contemporary educators need outcome-based information that suggests, at the very least, that this approach provides students with the means to survive academically.

Of the reviewed studies, only the work of Hough and St. Clair (1995) employed a traditional quantitative methodology of pretest, intervention, and posttest. To distinguish their study, Hough and St. Clair examined documented outcomes from prior empirical integration studies and found numerous design flaws. These flaws centered on (1) unclear definitions of interdisciplinary teaching, and (2) the inability to isolate interdisciplinary teaching from other closely related variables that affect student learning. However, in their study, the intervention's brevity (a 4-week unit) and a lack of "thick description" about the unit hinder broader interpretations about the effects of curriculum integration.

The need for both types of research was most clearly illustrated by a participant's comments from one of the reviewed studies. As quoted previously but worthy of revisiting, a student at Brown Barge Middle School stated, "I learned how to work in a group. I learned things that will probably benefit me later on in life, but not right now [in high school]" (Powell et al., 1996, p. 98). There is a need for both educators and students to explicitly know how the learning outcomes associated with curriculum integration "translate" into performance on high-stakes tests, which is valued in the current standards-driven environment. Not to provide this translation through both qualitative and quantitative research will leave educators and students in the position the Brown Barge student described, whereby learning outcomes are perceived to be devoid of immediacy and relevancy.

Second, we must further examine effects of the contextual selection process, constraints, and supports on learning outcomes typically associated with curriculum integration. The words of qualitative researchers Lincoln and Guba (1985) are once again applicable. "Interpretations depend so heavily for their validity on local particulars" (p. 42). With curriculum integration, "local particulars" center on how teachers determine which features of curriculum integration are most appropriate for their classrooms. Future research needs to examine these "local particulars" in more detail. For example, research questions may ask, Are there certain features within the curriculum integration process that are more robust than others? In a particular instructional context, does it make a difference whether the teacher or the student selects the issue for inquiry? Or, does the emphasis on an action-oriented end product overshadow the necessity for issues and concerns originating from the students? To further assist educators to make decisions during the contextual selection process, these questions should be answered, thereby examining the specific relationships between individual curriculum-integration components and desired learning outcomes.

Third, we need to assess the relationship between these curriculum integration learning outcomes and performance on high-stakes tests. Mandated high-stakes testing is a major threat both to curriculum integration and to the middle level school's commitment to meet the needs of young adolescents (Vars, 2001). Vars is confident that curriculum integration can be retained and that the most important state and district standards can be taught. However, this confidence must be bolstered by research that clearly illustrates that learning results from curriculum integration are connected to performance as measured by state-mandated tests. Until that research is available, both educators and students are in the precarious position of using an approach that is theoretically appropriate but lacks the evidence that it is effective in the high-stakes testing environment.

Securing a sustainable future for curriculum integration requires that theorists, practitioners, and researchers undergird their good intentions with focused actions to influence the curricular debate. We firmly believe that the viability of curriculum integration depends on how future research unfolds. This research must be conducted in a politically savvy manner to address aggressively the questions of educators as well as evaluators. Curriculum integration obviously addresses the developmental needs of middle level students and the pedagogical interests of many educators. The current challenge, however, is also to address the political needs of the larger educational community, as well as the practical concerns of a demanding and discriminating public.

REFERENCES

Arnold, J. (1993). A curriculum to empower young adolescents. *National Middle School Association Midpoints, 4*(1), 1–11.

Arredondo, D., & Rucinski, T. (1995). The use of integrated curriculum in Missouri middle schools. *Research in Middle Level Education Quarterly, 19*, 27–35.

Beal, C., Grable, L., & Robertson, A. (2001). *Curriculum integration: Middle school educators meeting the needs of young adolescents* [Online]. Available: http://www.ncsu.edu/chass/extension/ci/ [2002, March 11].

Beane, J. (1993). *A middle school curriculum: From rhetoric to reality.* Columbus, OH: National Middle School Association.

Beane, J. (1997). *Curriculum integration: Designing the core of democratic education.* New York: Teachers College Press.

Brazee, E. (1995). An integrated curriculum supports young adolescent development. In Y. Siu-Runyan & C.V. Faircloth (Eds.), *Beyond separate subjects: Integrative learning at the middle level.* Norwood, MA: Christopher-Gordon.

Brown, C., & Eaton, M. (1993). A view from the park. In C. Stevenson & J. Carr (Eds.), *Integrated studies in the middle grades: Dancing through walls.* New York: Teachers College Press.

Dewey, J. (1896). The reflex arc concept in psychology. *Psychological Review, 3*(4), 357–370.

Dewey, J. (1916). *Democracy and education.* New York: Free Press.

Dewey, J. (1920). *Reconstruction in philosophy.* Boston: Beacon Press.

Dworkin, M. S. (Ed.). (1959). *Dewey on education.* New York: Teachers College Press.

Educational Research Service. (2001). *No child left behind: A special reprint of President George W. Bush's education plan with relevant discussion questions education leaders should ask.* Arlington, VA: Author.

Erlandson, C., & McVittie, J. (2001). Student voices on integrative curriculum. *Middle School Journal, 33*(2), 28–36.

Hough, D., & St. Clair, B. (1995). The effects of integrated curricula on young adolescent problem solving. *Research in Middle Level Education Quarterly, 19*, 1–25.

Kesson, K., & Oyler, C. (1999). Integrated curriculum and service learning: Linking school-based knowledge and social action. *English Education, 31*(2), 135–149.

Lincoln, Y. S., & Guba, E. G. (1985). *Naturalistic inquiry.* Newbury Park, CA: Sage.

National Middle School Association. (1995). *This we believe: Developmentally responsive middle level schools.* Columbus, OH: Author.

Pate, P. E., Homestead, E., & McGinnis, K. (1995). Student and teacher co-created integrated curriculum. In Y. Siu-Runyan & C. V. Faircloth (Eds.), *Beyond separate subjects: Integrative learning at the middle level.* Norwood, MA: Christopher-Gordon.

Powell, R., & Skoog, G. (1995). Students' perspectives on integrative curricula: The case of Brown Barge Middle School. *Research in Middle Level Education Quarterly, 18*, 85–114.

Powell, R., & Skoog, G. (2000). Middle level integrative curriculum reform: A study of teachers' epistemological theories. *Research in Middle Level Education Annual.*

Powell, R., Skoog, G., & Troutman, P. (1996). On streams and odysseys: Reflections on reform and research in middle level integrative learning environments. *Research in Middle Level Education Quarterly, 19*, 1–30.

Sage, S., Krynock, K., & Robb, L. (2000). Is there anything but a problem? A case study of problem-based learning as middle school curriculum integration. *Research in Middle Level Education Annual, 23*, 149–179.

Scales, P. (1991). *A portrait of young adolescents in the 1990s: Implications for promoting healthy growth and development.* Carrboro, NC: Center for Early Adolescence, University of North Carolina at Chapel Hill.

Smith, C., Mann, L., & Steadman, W. (1993). Adopt a business. In C. Stevenson & J. Carr (Eds.), *Integrated studies in the middle grades: Dancing through walls.* New York: Teachers College Press.

Stevenson, C., & Carr, J. (Eds.). (1993). *Integrated studies in the middle grades: Dancing through walls.* New York: Teachers College Press.

Vars, G. F. (2001). Can curriculum integration survive in an era of high-stakes testing? *Middle School Journal, 33*(2), 7–17.

Weilbacher, G. (2001). Is curriculum integration an endangered species? *Middle School Journal, 33*(2), 18–27.

CHAPTER 2

EXPLORATORY EDUCATION IN A SOCIETY OF KNOWLEDGE AND RISK

Leonard J. Waks
Temple University

ABSTRACT

Exploration has been an important theme in the education of adolescents since the beginning of the 20th century. Early in the century exploratory education focused on adjustment to adult occupational roles. In the 1960s exploration was moved from the junior high to the middle school and focused on individual talents and preferences. In today's society of knowledge and risk, some argue that exploratory education should be refocused on the act of exploration itself, as adult life will continue to change and require readjustments in unfamiliar circumstances. Exemplary practices in exploratory education at the middle school should confront learners with ill-structured problems requiring knowledge inputs in the central, but ever-shifting domains of adult life, including work, personal relationships, and civic commitments.

"Exploration" has throughout the 20th century been an important theme in the education of adolescents and has been especially prominent as a keynote

Middle School Curriculum, Instruction, and Assessment, pages 23–40
Copyright © 2002 by Information Age Publishing
All rights of reproduction in any form reserved.
23

in the philosophy of the middle school. Recently, however, it appears to have receded to the margins as academic subject-matter standards and high-stakes tests have taken center stage. Why has exploration been devalued?

In the emerging "knowledge economy," some argue that neither the need nor the time exists to devote to exploration prior to "serious" academic learning—there is simply too much to learn, and *only* those with solid postsecondary academic preparation can get a decent job. Routine jobs—for example, as health care aides, fast food workers, and machine assemblers—will not provide a living wage, job security, or fringe benefits. Thus, it is more important than ever that all learners acquire a rigorous academic education. Presecondary exploration is no longer needed because a significant choice of high school tracks is no longer available— all students will need to prepare for college.

But at the same time, today's young people are also said to be entering a "risk society" where occupational futures are more uncertain than ever, and where, as a result, exploration of the unfamiliar and uncertain could be an especially relevant educational theme. Two questions thus arise: Does exploration have a significant role in the education of today's adolescents, and if so, what is it?

In this chapter, I examine the concept of "exploration" and its shifting role in the education of early adolescents at different points in the past century. I then characterize the situation of adolescents in today's society of knowledge and risk and ask whether exploratory learning has a distinct role for them. I conclude that exploration, suitably interpreted, may be more important today than in the past.

THE MEANING OF EXPLORATION

We can begin the analysis of exploration by noting that the verb "to explore" has *two* distinct senses or meanings in English. According to the *Oxford English Dictionary*, the earliest, introduced in the late 16th century, is "to investigate, to seek to ascertain or find out (a fact, a condition of anything)," and closely related, "to look into closely, to examine or scrutinize." This first investigative sense is a *convergent* sense of "explore" because the act of exploration *zeroes in* on a specific fact or concrete detail. In this sense, we might explore a haystack to locate a needle.

A second sense, from the 17th century, is "to search into or examine (a country, place, etc.); to go into or range over for the purpose of discovery." This second, ranging or scanning, sense is more *divergent* because in this sense exploring is scanning or ranging over some space, area, or domain to set boundaries around it or to characterize it as a whole. In this sense we explore the haystack not to locate the needle but just to find out what might be in a haystack. (My distinction here is similar to the one suggested by Berlyne [1960] between "specific" and "diversive" exploration.) A survey of contemporary dictionaries and thesauri confirms the persistence of this basic distinction. *The American Heritage Dictionary*, for example, distinguishes two meanings: (1) to investigate systematically, and (2) to travel into or range over (an area) for the purpose of discovery. Synonyms listed in the *Random House Thesaurus* are distinguished into the same two groups: (1) to examine, research, scrutinize, investigate, plumb, analyze, probe; and (2) to scout, range over, travel to observe, survey, traverse.

The first sense associates exploration with a *point*, the second with a *space* or *area*. Exploration in the first sense involves *zeroing in*, as for example, upon the determinate needle in the haystack. Exploration in the second sense involves *going into* an indeterminate space or zone, that is, an area or region distinguished from adjacent parts by distinctive features or characteristics or set aside for specific purposes (e.g., a residential or commercial zone).

The purpose of exploration in the first sense is to determine a specific fact or answer to a specific question; the purpose of exploration in the second sense is to determine the defining boundaries of, or conceptual categories of objects within, a heretofore-indeterminate area or region. The first is successful when it locates the specific object or determines the specific fact, the second when it makes an indeterminate region more determinate for the explorers, *orienting* them to the region and the sorts of objects it contains.

Exploration and Adolescence

Which sense of "exploration" is most closely associated with exploratory education in the middle school? Compton and Hawn (1993) define exploration as used in middle level education as "the act of looking into, closely examining, investigating" (p. 16); that is, they choose the first or convergent sense. The decisive problem with this choice is that exploration in that sense has an equally important place in education at *all* levels, and thus has no specific link to adolescence. Children *and* adults, from elementary *through* professional school, do a lot of "looking into," and "closely examining" and "investigating." If this is what has been meant by "exploration," the junior high and middle school would not be "exploratory schools" in any *distinct* sense. Investigating history, or fractions, would count as exploratory education, and the concept of "exploration" would not offer *any* distinctive guidelines for middle level curriculum.

By contrast, the second sense is tied closely to the central meaning of adolescence. The term "adolescent" is derived from the Latin *adolesens*, meaning "growing towards." Dictionaries provide both a general definition of "adolescent" as "no longer a child but not yet an adult," and a more biological definition, as "from the onset of puberty to maturity." Unlike puberty, maturity is a social concept and is reached at different ages in different kinds of societies. In agricultural societies adult responsibilities are assigned at the onset of puberty if not before, so there is no distinct period of adolescence. In industrial societies some variation exists in the age defined as maturity, and the stage of adolescence generally extends from puberty until the socially assigned age is reached. However, all these societies have a prolonged period of adolescence, during which young people attend school and prepare for adult roles. To the psychologist and educator, the basic concept of adolescence is the stage of learning to be a mature, independent adult.

Thus adolescents by definition are leaving childhood behind and standing at the threshold of adult life, to them an unknown region with its own specific elements: autonomy, individual identity, economic independence, sexuality, moral and ethical responsibility. Their overarching developmental task at this stage is to achieve an orientation to the realm of adulthood and its constituent elements. They cannot yet be held to adult norms and standards—they have not yet attained adult status. They stand on the threshold of adulthood and their challenge is not to act like adults but to search the realm of adulthood to select and shape adult selves, to discover what acting like adults *means* for them.

The Explorer as "Stranger in a Strange Land"

Exploration in the relevant sense thus involves journeying into the adult lifeworld on analogy with journeying into an unknown land. The significant knowledge to be attained is orientation knowledge, not knowledge organized, as in the academic disciplines, for adult uses but knowledge organized to focus and facilitate the journey through the essential dimensions of adult life.

The phrase "stranger in a strange land" here is meant to point to the two reciprocal poles—subjective and objective—of exploratory situations and experiences. On the subjective side, the explorers are strangers. They are from another land, foreign, alien. They are out of place; they feel strange and disoriented. They do not know their way around or what is expected of them. On the objective side, the world they encounter is itself strange, unfamiliar, foreign, disorienting. It contains few cues to guide behavior. The situation is thus one of *reciprocal strangeness*. As exploration progresses, the unfamiliar world becomes more familiar and the stranger more like a native.

The central focus of exploration is typically the external, objective pole. Effective explorers set their sights on the new world to be explored, not on their uneasy selves or their activities of exploration. But exploration is typically undertaken for some end. Newcomers explore not merely to *discover* but also to *adjust;* they familiarize themselves with the new situation in order to live and act effectively within it. The conquistadors came not merely to discover but to plunder and convert, the Puritans to settle. So in this process of *mutual* accommodation, explorers must, on occasion, turn their attention inward, from the objective world to themselves, to examine whether changes in their reactions and habits or methods of exploration might help them to adjust. When we speak of adolescents as "exploring themselves and their worlds" it is useful to understand that although two targets of exploration are mentioned, the phrase indicates one integrated process of adjustment—learning to see oneself in terms of the adult world and the adult world in terms of oneself. While this adjustment is the enduring challenge of adolescence, its specific problems and emphases (objective or subjective) change as adolescents themselves and the distinct adult worlds they enter change.

EXPLORATORY EDUCATION

We may now turn to exploration as an evolving theme in adolescent education. In colonial Massachusetts, district schools provided children with the rudiments of education, while grammar schools provided preparatory training in classical languages for the very few students destined for college, most of whom would never attend the district schools. Most youngsters began to take on adult roles after a few years of district schooling and had no specific period of adolescence.

Early in the 19th century some school districts instituted public high schools that, unlike grammar schools, were genuinely *secondary* schools providing studies organized in academic disciplines—history, literature, mathematics, and science—for students who *had* attended and completed the district school's course of study. The elementary school, influenced in the 19th century by the child-centered ideals of reformers like Horace Mann, and the high school constituted two distinct levels of an educational "ladder" providing a complete education at public expense.

By the turn of the 20th century some prominent educators were already casting doubt on this neat elementary-secondary scheme, recognizing that the increasing numbers of youngsters in the upper elementary and lower secondary grades formed a group in need of a distinct kind of school. They were no longer children, and hence child-centered methods of instruction were no longer suitable to their needs. But they were also not yet adults and hence could not readily be motivated to acquire knowledge as organized within academic disciplines for adult uses (Caissy, 1994). Instead, these learners, for the first time labeled "adolescents," needed schools that could specifically address transitional needs during their passage from childhood to adulthood.

As participation in the upper elementary and secondary grades rapidly expanded after the turn of the century, youngsters who did not fit into this established two-level distinction became more visible. After G. Stanley Hall's (1904) famous book on the topic of adolescence, the concept became firmly established as a stage of human development, with its own distinct developmental tasks and educational requirements, including achievement of (1) more mature relations with age-mates of both sexes, and masculine or feminine social roles; (2) emotional independence from parents and other adults and shaping a personal system of ethics and values as a guide to responsible behavior; and (3) assurance of economic independence, including selection of possible occupations and courses of preparatory study (see Blair & Jones, 1964, pp. 5–6).

It was then frequently stated for the first time that adolescents required a school program specially shaped to facilitate these developmental tasks—one providing a time, space, and structure of activities to explore their new selves and worlds. Thus a strong intuitive link was established between adolescence as a life stage and exploration as a distinct kind of learning experience.

Adolescence in the Early Industrial City

The origins of the junior high, of adolescence as a defined life stage, and of the perceived need for a distinct exploratory stage of schooling correspond with the maturing of the American industrial city. At the turn of the 20th century, the nation experienced rapid industrialization, urbanization, and (not coincidently) increasing participation in formal education. In the prior, proto-industrial society of small farmers and merchants and craftsmen, occupational know-how was acquired on the job; on the whole, school contributed little to work, and the large majority of citizens attended for only a few years. By contrast, the industrial society was marked by the dominance of two large groups of workers: a steadily growing group of college-educated professionals and a still larger group of industrial workers including both skilled artisans and unskilled factory operatives.

In this occupational structure, secondary education gradually became the gateway to adult life—to both the industrial workplace and, through college, to the professions as well as to life as adults in the industrial city.

What did "exploration" mean in this situation? The pre-high school years became the *customary* time to come to grips with one's likely future work options, to learn society's expectations for adult behavior, and to choose an appropriate track in the secondary school. The comprehensive high school provided vocational tracks for future industrial and commercial workers and academic or college-prep tracks for the minority going on to college and the professions. Transitions from these curriculum tracks to the industrial workplace or to college were more or less straightforward, as were those from the various professional curricula of the college to professional situations.

This relative occupational clarity also shored up traditional family and gender roles. Professional men and working men alike could expect to support a family on their income. Women faced barriers entering both the professions and the skilled trades, but many found roles as housewives and mothers that the popular media both shaped and applauded. The pathways from childhood to adult status were thus well marked. As a result, the exploratory aim of the pre-high school experience was also clear: to facilitate youngsters' orientation to their available life options and their associated curricular pathways. To achieve this aim, all students were to be guided through academic *and* vocational or domestic experiences to facilitate acceptance of, and adjustments to, their destined places in adult society.

Origins of the Junior High School

The junior high school was developed to serve the children who previously attended Grades 7 and 8 in the elementary school and Grade 9 in the high school, and the exploratory theme became prominent in early statements of its aims. The Commission on Reorganization of Secondary Education (1918) saw the junior high as helping students explore their attitudes and make provisional choices about occupational aims and hence secondary school courses of study. Subjects like industrial arts (for boys), home economics (for girls), and high-school subjects in mathematics, science, and foreign languages in a preliminary way became exemplars of exploratory education in the junior high school.

Significantly, many adolescents at this time were children of immigrant families from rural villages, or migrants from America's rural areas. These youngsters were the "first adolescents;" they made up the first generation in their families to adjust to the adult roles of industrial society during a standard period of school years. The youngsters' challenge was to "explore themselves and their world" to discover where they fit in the industrial occupational order and then to choose an appropriate secondary-school track. Their parents and grandparents had neither attended post-elementary schools nor prepared for industrial and professional jobs, and thus they did not provide adequate models of adulthood.

To simplify, we may say that in this early 20th-century situation only a small number of pegboard holes (professional, industrial, commercial, agricultural, domestic) existed, each with a corresponding curriculum track. Exploration *meant* discovering the shape of the holes and of oneself as a peg, and then choosing a curriculum track that would further shape one to the hole where one fit best. The great strength of this conception, with exemplars such as industrial arts and home economics, was that it assigned exploration to definite subject areas and specifically trained teachers.

Adolescence and Exploration in the 1960s

Exploration continued to be a central theme of the junior high school until the 1960s. For example, a classic textbook on the junior high (Van Til, Vars, & Lounsbury, 1961) included an entire chapter on exploratory programs. The Council on Junior High School Administration (1964), in its policy statement "Ten Tenets of Jr. High Administration," stated that "the junior high age is an especially fruitful time for exploration" (p. 330).

But there was a new twist. Partin (1965), for example, offered a somewhat typical definition of exploratory education for this time, one that was richer and more subjective than earlier formulations. A junior high student, he said, needs to explore the world and become aware of himself as a person. This student is concerned with questions of identity and with obtaining objectives of personal significance. Thus, the junior high should offer an exploratory program that provides adolescents with the opportunity to find their way, to scan the world of work and the world of values. Junior high should provide a time, a place, and a group where they can feel esteemed. Notice that here the subjective pole of the exploratory situation is emphasized, with terms like "aware of himself as a person," "personal significance," "personal identity," "world of values," being "esteemed." This emphasis suggests that adolescents of this period faced a new challenge of adjustment.

Indeed, important changes were taking place in both adolescence and adult life. The number of industrial jobs had peaked and was beginning to decline. The professional jobs demanding college preparation were becoming more differentiated, and a larger proportion of careers required specialized training beyond secondary school. With the American economy dominant in the world, working families (from both working class and professional class) were doing well enough that they could aim to send their children to college, and post-secondary education expanded greatly.

The period of adolescence, from the onset of puberty to full-adult status, was thus considerably prolonged.

Older "holdover" exemplars of exploratory education such as industrial arts and home economics were becoming less relevant, however, as the proportion of industrial jobs was declining and women were rejecting housewife roles and claiming occupational equality with men. For early adolescents the problem was no longer choosing between a few simple occupational alternatives: industrial, commercial, professional, or domestic work, and their respective secondary curriculum tracks. More youngsters were headed for postsecondary education, but now they had to make curricular and extracurricular choices throughout high school, based on their assessment of their occupational destinations, to prepare for appropriate secondary electives and postsecondary educational tracks.

The differentiated culture of the college-based professions and technical trades provided opportunities for those of every talent and interest. The challenge for many early adolescents of this period was no longer to choose a specific adult occupational role—adult life was too far away. It was rather to get to know enough about *themselves* to guide them through their many choices in preparing for post-secondary education. The exemplars of exploratory education shifted from preparatory subjects offering virtual equivalents of future adult worlds (e.g., industrial arts and home economics) to experiences revealing current talents and feelings of the participants—adolescent versions of human potential workshops. Exploration came to emphasize discovering oneself as a distinct individual. The subjective emphasis suggested experiences involving unstructured or open-ended problems freely chosen by learners, as opposed to routine subject matters that were highly structured and presented didactically.

Alexander and Kealy (1969), for example, advocated a "personal development area" for exploration, clearly distinguished from activities aimed directly at development of cognitive abilities. Brazee (2000) later reported that exploratory activities of the middle schools—also called "encores," or "specials"—were often provided outside the regular curriculum, in short courses outside the regular school day. In this way 'exploration' became increasingly separated from the regular curriculum.

This less structured and more personal acurricular approach to exploratory education never thrived as a practice in the junior high. Alexander and Kealy (1969) found that few junior highs actually had extensive exploratory programs. Smith (1966) explained why: He investigated the attitudes of junior high school principals and found that few favored any decrease in the academic subject-matter requirements for junior high teachers, whom they perceived as secondary educators. True to their name, the junior high schools remained in practice junior versions of secondary schools, with curricula organized, like those of the high school, around academic disciplines.

Origins of the Middle School

Two other developments in the 1960s brought about changes in exploratory education: the recognition of the earlier onset of puberty in American youth and the initial establishment of middle level schools. Educators and psychologists argued that the decreasing age of puberty in contemporary youth implied a redefinition of early adolescence, beginning at age 10 rather than 12 or 13. This implied the need for an earlier transition away from the elementary school than was provided by the junior high. At the same time, middle schools were being established—largely for reasons of administrative convenience—to serve youngsters from grades 5 or 6 through 8 rather than 7 through 9. The "baby-boom" generation led to overcrowding in the elementary schools in the early 1960s. By moving ninth graders from the junior high to the high school, and fifth and sixth graders to join the seventh and eighth graders in what was now a middle level school, districts could avoid the expense of constructing new schools. By doing so they could also achieve a greater degree of racial integration, by moving children from racially segregated elementary schools to more integrated schools earlier in the school sequence (Beane, 1993). The two trends merged as the new middle schools came to be seen as more appropriate settings for these more rapidly maturing early adolescents.

Early onset of puberty is not of course accompanied by any corresponding early onset of adult social status or responsibilities. Youngsters who had outgrown child-centered modes of instruction by age 10 were even less ready for secondary-school knowledge, organized in academic disciplines, than previous cohorts of 12- and 13-year-olds. In fact, now a longer period of years separated the onset of puberty and the use of disciplined knowledge in adult occupational roles. The middle school, as a distinct institution rather than as a junior version of secondary school, thus appeared to offer an especially promising venue for exploration as self-discovery. Advocates claimed that middle-level education could be shaped to facilitate this sort of exploration because, unlike the junior high, the middle school could be free from pressure to organize its curriculum around academic disciplines.

Leading junior-high experts including Lounsbury and Alexander became prominent advocates of the middle school, and transferred the exploration theme to the middle level. Curtis (1967) made exploration of individual student interests central to the rationale for the middle school. McQueen (1972) emphasized exploratory education as *the* distinguishing mark of the middle school as *contrasted* with the junior high. Some research confirmed the validity of this contrast. Onofrio (1971) found that middle-school principals, unlike the junior-high principals that Smith (1966) studied, favored extensive exploratory programs spanning required and elective courses in the curriculum as well as extracurricular activities. By the 1980s exploration was central to the middle-school philosophy, as stated in such influential reports as *This We Believe: Developmentally Responsive Middle Level Schools* (NMSA, 1982) and *Turning Points: Preparing American Youth for the 21st Century* (Carnegie Council on Adolescent Development, 1989).

But the less structured, more personal approach to exploration did not flourish in the middle school either. Kindred, Wolotkievicz, Mickelson, Coplein, and Dyson (1976) found little evidence that the middle school curriculum was facilitating exploration. Researchers in the 1980s and 1990s found exploratory programs to be unrelated to other areas of the curriculum, shaped by teacher interests rather than adolescent's developmental needs and imbalanced by an academic emphasis (see Anfara & Brown, 2000, p. 60). Today's middle school principals find selling exploratory programs to teachers difficult, while teachers, far from viewing exploration as the central function of the middle school, resent pressures to implement exploratory programs as "added responsibilities." Middle level educators still agree that exploration is important but translating this consensus into "concrete curricular and instructional practices" continues to be "difficult" (Anfara & Brown, 2000, p. 65).

Exploration at the Margins

In sum, exploration, once considered the central purpose of schools for adolescent learners, has been pushed to the margins—if not beyond. Junior high schools and middle schools were conceived as distinctively exploratory *schools* (e.g., Lounsbury, 1985). Because they served early adolescents starting a once-in-a-lifetime transition from child to adult status, such schools were aimed at addressing the developmental needs inherent in this transition, providing a rich opportunity for exploring the self and the world. They thus required an exploratory *curriculum* (see, e.g., Compton & Hawn, 1993, who conceive of exploration as the "total" middle school curriculum).

But in practice exploratory *programs* have become increasingly peripheral to the middle-school curriculum or relegated entirely to the extracurriculum, or eliminated, and middle school theory is now following suit. *Turning Points 2000* (Jackson & Davis, 2000, p. 23) *replaces* the exploration theme of the middle school with a curriculum "grounded in rigorous public standards for what students should know and be able to do." The language of "academic standards" and "excellence" is adopted explicitly to highlight the prominence of teaching and teacher-directed instruction in academic disciplines (p. 48), rather than student-directed exploratory learning. The heart of middle-level education, as conceived in *Turning Points 2000*, is no longer *exploration* (which, as we will see, involves uncertainty and the tentative movement into the unknown), but "academic *excellence*" (see p. 33 and throughout), the attainment of academic objectives that curriculum experts already agreed upon in advance. Significantly, the *only* recommendation about exploration in *Turning Points 2000* is one addressed not to educators but to *parents*—to provide for explorations *outside* of school (p. 24).

"RISK SOCIETY" AND THE POST-INDUSTRIAL CRISIS OF YOUTH

To understand whether exploratory education continues to have an important role for today's adolescents, we must consider the new situation they face. Throughout the industrially developed world, adolescents confront a new problem of adjustment brought on by the transition to the global, high-technology, knowledge-based economy, with all its associated risks.

High technology communications have enabled jobs to be outsourced globally from large, vertically integrated "flagship" firms to smaller "partner" firms. In this process most routine tasks have been shifted to low-wage workers in the developing nations or to new immigrants or contingent workers drawn from disadvantaged minority groups, working part time, without benefits, at or near the minimum wage. Even high-skilled technical and managerial tasks can now be assigned to well-trained but low-cost networked professionals working for overseas partners. In every work sector, skilled work requires flexible and adaptive use of new flows of knowledge and information. Much is organized in multifunctional, multidisciplinary teams pulled together only for the duration of the project.

The implications of this occupational reorganization are now becoming clear. The industrial society's division of adult work into careers of college-based professionals and those of organized industrial workers is mostly a thing of the past. In its place, there is the new post-industrial division of knowledge workers and routine workers. The former, with or without diplomas, must have flexible cognitive skills and must constantly acquire new knowledge and skills. The latter, with or without diplomas, cannot earn a living wage or employment security and thus cannot sustain full-adult status.

Unlike the career pathways of industrial society, pathways to post-industrial knowledge work roles in this so-called "risk society" are not well marked, and formal education prior to the period of adult work no longer plays the same decisive role. No formal curriculum, in itself, provides the full portfolio of skills and dispositions needed for today's knowledge work. New skills must constantly be acquired through both adult continuing education and on-the-job experiences in cutting-edge work. Today the slogan is no longer that education is the necessary preparation for work, but that cutting-edge work is the necessary preparation for that further education needed for the next job.

This process of continuous reinvention of one's occupational role in 'risk society' implies the growing irrelevance of the diploma orientation—of occupational identities defined in terms of professional diplomas and single, narrowly defined professions. Celente (1997, p. 18) puts this bluntly: "opportunity," he says, now "misses those who view the world only through the eyes of their own profession." Boyett and Conn (1991) note that professional employees who possess, process, and analyze information to make routine decisions are being replaced in reengineered firms by workers at lower levels aided by computer networks and intelligent software. While these lower-level employees become networked knowledge workers, many of the "downsized" higher-level employees now either move to smaller firms, start their own firms (as consultants or freelancers), or establish new startup operations within their prior firms.

Because of the volatility of these situations, Boyett and Conn (1991) predict the average American will work in 10 or more jobs in five or more firms prior to retirement. Flexibility and creativity are more valuable for success than endurance, loyalty, or proficiency in specialized tasks. "The real opportunities...will lie in the ability to creatively identify these small business opportunities that can be exploited either within the organization (via a new 'business unit') or outside (as an entrepreneurial startup)" (p. 4).

Along similar lines, Gorman (1996, pp. 27–38) views flexible and creative knowledge workers as "multipreneurs," who can (a) form short- to midterm goals and identify others with complementary goals, (b) work independently or as part of a team, (c) move across professional cultures, (d) develop a portfolio of skills applicable in various settings, and (e) tap into resources to get the job done. Such workers, he says, need broad, inclusive occupational identities; they need to be able to define themselves as "conceptual thinkers," or "planners and facilitators," or "communicators," rather than as bearers of "off-the shelf" identities like "lawyer," "accountant," "engineer," or "manager" derived from professional or technical curricula and diplomas. These broad, pragmatic identities permit shifts across occupational boundaries and professional cultures and encourage constant updating of knowledge bases and skills useful in projects across many fields.

This shift to knowledge work has also had broad implications for the other core aspects of adult life. Becoming an adult was until recently more or less a matter of fitting into conventional work, relationship, and residential niches but is now an improvisation, a continuous "work in progress." Bateson (1990, p. 2) says that "Today, the materials from which a life is composed are no longer clear. It is no longer possible to follow the paths of previous generations. Our lives are subject to repeated re-direction.... Many of the most basic concepts we use to construct a sense of self...have changed their meanings: work, home, love, commitment." Models of ordinary successful lives held up to young people involve early decisions and commitments, often to educational preparations launching an ever more successful career. Biographies from the past are misleading for those now entering adulthood because they present journeys toward a specific end already apparent at the beginning. These pictures are "increasingly inappropriate today" (Bateson, 1990, p. 6).

In this situation the transition from school to work is problematic and nonlinear. It is marked by a to-and-fro process—times in and times out of school, times in and times out of the workforce, times of full-time work and school. The distinct transition *event*, the time of assuming adult status, is being replaced by an indistinct and erratic *process*. This process of adjustment imposes an even more prolonged period from the onset of puberty to the achievement of full-adult status. This extended period of "identity work" (engaging in the tasks that shape an adult identity), which may stretch until the mid-20s or even beyond, is now leading young people to form new kinds of identities that are more fluid and pragmatic and less tied to the adult roles of job and marriage that are difficult to sustain.

Young people now must actively construct, deconstruct, and reconstruct identities, inventing and reinventing new future orientations and life narratives to make sense of this "to-and-fro" process of coming of age. Even as they assume adult work responsibilities, they cannot overcommit to any established adult identities, to permanent career plans or personal relationships. So instead of adolescence being a distinct life phase, it is becoming a longer but less distinct phase marked by a blurring of the lines on both sides of the child–adult divide: adults in their 30s still acting "young" and preteens prematurely acting "old." This allows for greater time for and freedom in exploration of adult roles, but with potentially negative fallouts (Furlong, 2000; Wyn & Dwyer, 2000).

For this reason the received conception of exploratory learning as appropriate for a phase of education preparatory to adult life, as facilitating selection from among curricular and career options, is now woefully inadequate. No "exploratory" experiences during the presecondary school years or at any other time can facilitate the "right" career or curriculum choices. Instead adult life is an exercise in continuous exploration. Tom

Peters (2001, pp. 90–92), author of *In Search of Excellence*, says he is no longer interested in excellence, because today what is interesting keeps changing, and excellence is too static a notion. Today, he says, he would write *In Search of the License to Explore.*

Exploratory Education for Today

Exploratory education in the early junior high schools aimed at making the adult world familiar so that young people could adjust to one of the limited number of stable options and choose one of the standard secondary school tracks. Exploratory education today also aims to make the adult world more familiar. But today's adult world is very different; it is increasingly marked by change, disruption, uncertainty, and readjustment. Today's mature adults remain more or less "strangers in strange lands" throughout life, entering new fields, acquiring new knowledge bases, pragmatically adjusting their self-definitions. (This nagging sense of remaining somewhat disoriented is what accounts for the success of those amusing how-to books for "Dummies" and "Idiots"). Exploratory education, to put my point paradoxically, now should aim at making the sense of strangeness or unfamiliarity itself more familiar, to assist learners in adjusting to, and thriving in, conditions of more or less permanent strangeness. This is not an occasion for elaborating this conception of exploration in detail, but I will close by indicating five important elements of such a conception.

Our 20th-century history with exploratory education has taught us that for any approach to exploratory education to be implemented, it needs a definite place in the institutional scheme of things. Thus exploration needs, first and foremost, a *specific curriculum niche* marked as clearly as other school subjects, a niche like industrial arts and home economics and unlike *ad hoc* short courses, seminars, and add-ons. It is appealing to speak of exploration as affecting the total climate of the middle school, but in itself this will not address the curriculum problem. Once a clear niche is established we can go on to concern ourselves about the proper diffusion of exploratory learning throughout the entire curriculum. But without such a niche, exploratory education will remain peripheral and *ad hoc*. If necessary, we could invent a name for a core exploratory course sequence, "pragmatics" or "epistemics" or some other name derived from Greek, to make it sound official and deserving of time and attention.

Second, the exploration niche should contain *well-defined standard content*, whatever adjustments are made to suit the needs or preferences of individual learners or particular teachers. Algebra and geometry, logic and rhetoric, history and literature have core topics and so should the course in exploration. This standard content should be organized around approaching ill-structured problems in key domains of adult life and around obtaining and using knowledge resources to address them, individually and in groups. Standard topics could include finding and defining problems, obtaining knowledge resources (from libraries, Internet databases, interviews), assessing and validating knowledge and information, documenting (in notebooks or logs) the knowledge and information acquired and the processes involved, setting goals and seeking team members with complementary goals, shaping the knowledge and information acquired for use in addressing the problems as defined, documenting one's issues and concerns related to knowledge acquisition and use in personal journals, shaping the results of exploration into products, evaluating the process and results and reporting the results to peers in oral reports, newsletters, videos, and websites. Careful documentation and reporting permits learners to reflect upon their exploratory processes in order to improve them.

Third, it would be helpful if *exemplary practices* of exploratory education became widely recognized and adopted. The kinds of ill-structured problems selected for study should be drawn from essential, but now unstable, dimensions of adult life-work, home, community, technology, environment, relationships. Industrial arts had its stock learning activities (e.g., making pump lamps). Many excellent exploratory activities can be found in the middle-school literature (e.g., designing a recreational facility for children living in a homeless shelter, subject to budget limitations, time deadlines, and space constraints (see Pate, 2001). It would be useful if some of these became stock kinds of middle-school activities—widely used, discussed, and researched.

Fourth, as Brazee (2000) emphasizes, exploratory learning experiences should be shaped—and promoted—as *complementary, rather than as opposed to, disciplined academic learning*. Linkages between knowledge and information resources used by learners and the academic disciplines—mathematics, science, history, and social studies, literature and language arts—should be explicitly and repeatedly brought home to learners. Perhaps web-based manuals of useful concepts and materials from these disciplines formulated in terms that 10- to 12-year-olds can read and understand could be prepared and updated for just-in-time learning. As high schools and colleges become linked to the Internet through broadband connections, searches in databases for knowledge and information resources and just-in-time learning are becoming more standard features of discipline-based education. And these resources are standard features of knowledge work in today's workplaces. So the connections between exploration, systematic disciplinary learning, and adult knowledge use are actually becoming more definite and easier to explain, even to early adolescents.

Finally, if exploration is truly to become the hallmark of the middle school, then teachers must be oriented to exploratory learning, not to basic cognitive skills or academic disciplines. The middle schools, as Smith (1966) argued a third of a century ago, will require their own trained and certified body of exploration-focused teachers rather than instructors oriented to elementary school skills or to the domain of academic disciplines—the hallmark of the secondary schools.

REFERENCES

Alexander, W., & Kealy, R. (1969). From junior high school to middle school. *High School Journal, 53*(3), 151–163.

Anfara, V., Jr., & Brown, K. (2000). Exploratory programs in middle schools. *NASSP Bulletin, 84*(9), 58–67.

Bateson, M. (1990). *Composing a life.* New York: Plume.

Beane, J. (1993). *A middle school curriculum: From rhetoric to reality.* Columbus, OH: National Middle School Association.

Berlyne, D. (1960). *Conflict, arousal, and curiosity.* New York: McGraw-Hill.

Blair, G., & Jones, S. (1964). *Psychology of adolescence for teachers.* New York: MacMillan.

Boyett, J., & Conn, H. (1991). *Workplace 2000: The revolution reshaping American business.* New York: Dutton.

Brazee, E. (2000). *Exploratory curriculum in the middle school.* (ERIC Document Reproduction Service No. ED447970)

Caissy, G. (1994). *Early adolescence: Understanding the 10 to 15 year old.* New York: Plenum Press.

Carnegie Council on Adolescent Development. (1989). *Turning points: Preparing American youth for the 21stcentury.* Washington, DC: Carnegie Corporation of New York.

Celente, G. (1997). *Trends 2000: How to prepare for and profit from the changes of the 21st century.* New York: Warner Books.

Commission on Reorganization of the Secondary School. (1918). *Cardinal principles of secondary education* (Bulletin 1918 #35). Washington, DC: U. S. Department of the Interior, Bureau of Education.

Compton, M., & Hawn, H. (1993). *Exploration: The total curriculum.* Columbus, OH: National Middle School Association.

Council on Junior High School Administration. (1964). Ten tenets of junior high administration. *Clearing House, 38,* 329–333.

Curtis, T. (1967, Winter). Rationale for the middle school. *Impact on Instructional Improvement,* pp. 6–10.

Furlong, A. (2000). Introduction: Youth in a changing world. *International Social Science Journal, 164,* 125–133.

Gorman, T. (1996). *Multipreneuring.* New York: Fireside.

Hall, G. (1904). *Adolescence: Its psychology and its relations to physiology, anthropology, sociology, sex, crime, religion and education.* New York: Appleton.

Jackson, A., & Davis, G. (2000). *Turning points 2000: Educating adolescents in the 21st century*. New York: Teachers College Press.

Kindred, L., Wolotkievicz, R., Mickelson, J., Coplein, L., & Dyson, E. (1976). *The middle school curriculum, a practitioner's handbook*. Boston: Allyn & Brown.

Lounsbury, J. (1985). *Critical issues in middle level education: Exploratory programs at the middle level*. Reston, VA: National Association of Secondary School Principals.

McQueen, M. (1972). Rationale of the middle school: Not just another name for junior high. *Educational Digest, 37*, 10–13.

National Middle School Association. (1982). *This we believe: Developmentally responsive middle level schools*. Columbus, OH: Author.

Onofrio, J. (1971). *The evolving middle school in Connecticut: Principal's opinions concerning uniquecharacteristics and recommended trends* (Doctoral dissertation, Fordham University). Proquest Digital Dissertations #AAT7127016.

Partin, C. (1965). To sample—or to explore? *Educational Leadership, 23*(3), 194–199.

Pate, E. (2001). Students, standards and exploration: Creating a curriculum intersection of excellence. In T. Dickinson (Ed.), *Re-inventing the middle school* (pp. 79–95). New York: RoutledgeFalmer.

Peters, T. (2001). Tom Peters's true confessions. *Fast Company, 53*, 78–92.

Smith, M. (1966). The case for teachers specifically prepared to teach in junior high school. *Journal of Teacher Education, 17*, 438–443.

Van Til, W., Vars, G., & Lounsbury, J. (1961). *Modern education for the junior high years*. New York: Bobbs-Merrill.

Wyn, J., & Dwyer, P. (2000). New patterns of youth transition in education. *International Social Science Journal, 164*, 147–160.

CHAPTER 3

DEVELOPMENTAL APPROPRIATENESS VERSUS ACADEMIC RIGOR

An Untenable Dualism in Middle Level Education

Vincent A. Anfara, Jr.
University of Tennessee
Leonard J. Waks
Temple University

ABSTRACT

Middle schools are on the defensive for a lack of rigor in the curriculum. Drawing on the insights of John Dewey, this chapter explores the untenable dualism that presently exists between "developmental, student-centered" and "academic, subject-centered" approaches to teaching and learning. The question remains: Is attention to the developmental characteristics of middle school students really the cause of their academic problems? The authors call upon those involved in middle schools to (1) operationalize the notion of

Middle School Curriculum, Instruction, and Assessment, pages 41–55
Copyright © 2002 by Information Age Publishing
All rights of reproduction in any form reserved.

logical rigor, and (2) build a research base on the developmental needs of young adolescents and the knowledge resources that can assist them in meeting their needs. Only when we recognize that learning can demonstrably be both developmentally appropriate and academically rigorous can we stop the pendulum that relentlessly swings an uncritical conception of both.

The teachers became more distant and uncaring throughout my middle school career. The teachers would come to class, lecture, and go home. Students had very little contact with the educators as class curriculum shifted from hands-on learning to textbook/lecture style. At this point, many students started disliking school because the school environment was closed, cold, and very boring. As I entered sixth grade...I quickly discovered that the school I had once loved was falling further into my memories. (student reflecting on her middle school experience, 1998)

INTRODUCTION

Middle schools are on the defensive. The Southern Regional Education Board in March 1998 called middle schools a "weak link" in the K–12 education chain. In April 1998 "Muddle in the Middle," an article in *Education Week*, characterized middle schools as "the wasteland of our primary and secondary landscape." Significantly, it asserted that the middle school is "supplanting academic rigor with a focus on students' social, emotional, and physical needs" (Bradley, 1998, p. 38). This complaince about academic preparedness is reiterated in a recent newspaper article: "U.S. students stagnate in seventh and eighth grades, leaving them unprepared and unmotivated for the stiff high school...classes looming ahead" (Whitmire, 1998, p. A-1).

Indeed, academic problems in the middle years are real and conspicuous. The 1994 National Assessment of Educational Progress (NAEP), for example, indicated that only 29 percent of eighth graders in the United States scored at the proficient level. U.S. eighth graders scored below the international average (41 countries participating in testing) in math and science according to the 1995 Third International Math and Science Study (TIMSS).

The question remains: Is attention to developmental characteristics of middle school students really the root cause of their academic problems? In this chapter we revisit the original concepts that motivated the founding of middle schools and the current proposals for middle level reform, keeping this dualism between "developmental, student life-centered" versus "academic, subject-centered" pedagogy front and center.

The emotive terms used to state the academic versus developmental dualism ("hard" vs. "soft," "tough" vs. "tender," "rigor" vs. "ease") bring to mind the image of a pendulum. "Reformers vacillate," Cuban (1990) notes, "between teacher-centered and student-centered instruction, academic and practical curricula..." (p. 4). What keeps the pendulum swinging is the antithesis of two opposed value concepts, neither based on solid empirical ground, each appealing to certain groups. As Wise (1989) reminds us, "many of the proposed 'solutions' to current problems have little...empirical grounding" (p. 36). Because the reforms associated with each of the poles reflect opposing values, public opinion shifts as economic, social, and demographic changes create social strife. Perennial but recently deemphasized value positions receive renewed attention and get translated into a new wave of policies and programs—with insufficient attention to the facts at hand. The developmental versus academic conflict in the middle schools displays just this sort of logic of conflicting values, each rising, then falling, and then rising again.

Drawing upon the insights of John Dewey, we hope to demonstrate that the contrast between developmental appropriateness and academic rigor is an "untenable" dualism, requiring a fresh examination of both concepts. Our argument points to specific new directions for middle school renewal which are explored in a concluding section.

THE STORY OF THE MIDDLE SCHOOL

Concerns about developmental needs were central to the founding of middle schools. Middle schools were created in the 1960s as a replacement for junior highs when the literature on junior high schools showed that they were turning into "miniature senior highs" (Johnson, Dupuis, Musial, & Hall, 1994). Cuban (1992) writes, "Junior highs, introduced in the first decade of the twentieth century, went from dropout preventing, job market preparing, adolescent saving institutions to miniature high schools heavily criticized for improperly educating teenagers" (p. 230). In an attempt to explain the failure of the junior high, Lewis (1992) offered that a knowledge base was not available to sustain the uniqueness of the movement and the focus gradually moved toward a subject orientation. Aubrey Douglass, an early advocate of the junior high, wrote in 1945 that the junior high had persistent problems, including a curriculum that was too subject-centered, teachers who were inadequately prepared to teach that level of schooling, a curriculum that was characterized as teacher or textbook controlled, and students who were tracked. In short, the junior high was tarred with the brush of an overemphasis of teacher-centered, academic, and disciplinary approaches. A more developmental emphasis was prescribed.

The primary reason given for the creation of the middle school was that the specific psychosocial, physical, and cognitive needs of young adolescents were not being addressed concretely with the traditional K–8 and 9–12 configuration or the junior high of Grades 7–9. "Developmentally appropriate" became a key phrase for talking about what happens inside the walls of our middle schools. The agreement was that middle schools needed to be organized differently, with different curriculum and different instructional strategies, adjusted specifically to these developmental needs.

To achieve this goal, a number of established educational organizations created special committees or councils to focus on the middle level. The Association for Supervision and Curriculum Development (ASCD) established the Council on the Emerging Adolescent Learner in 1969. The National Middle School Association (NMSA) was formed in 1973. In 1975 ASCD released *The Middle School We Need*, which supported the call to reform middle schools around the needs and characteristics of young adolescents. Reports or position papers like *This We Believe* (National Middle School Association, 1982) and *Turning Points* (Carnegie Task Force on the Education of Young Adolescents, 1989) were later issued to guide the work of reformers.

While the middle school had modest beginnings in the early 1960s, incredible growth in numbers of middle schools began in the late 1960s and early 1970s. From less than 11 before 1960, middle schools jumped to 499 in 1965 to 2,298 in 1970. The growth continued throughout the 1970s to reach 4,088 in 1980. By 1987, the number of middle schools reached 5,466 (Cuban, 1992, p. 244).

Middle School Reforms and the Developmentally Appropriate School

In *This We Believe* (1982, revised in 1995), the National Middle School Association acknowledged that "in order to be developmentally responsive, middle schools must be grounded in the diverse characteristics and needs of these young people" (p. 5). In that position paper six characteristics and six components were identified that would help define what was meant by the term "developmentally responsive."[1] In 1985 the National Association of Secondary School Principals released *An Agenda for Excellence in Middle Level Education*, which focused on 12 areas (i.e., school culture and climate, student development, curriculum, learning and instruction) deemed important to reforming middle schools. In 1989 the Carnegie Council on Adolescent Development issued *Turning Points* which identified eight challenges for our middle schools, including the creation of small learning communities, ensuring success for all students, staffing middle schools with teachers who are specifically trained to teach at this level, and re-engaging families in the education of their children. *Turning Points* proclaimed that "a volatile mismatch exists between the organization and curriculum of middle grade schools and the intellectual and emotional needs of young adolescents" (pp. 8–9). In short, the middle school represented a shift from a discipline-based, teacher-centered focus to one based on students' developmental needs.

The Middle School and Curriculum

In *This We Believe* (1982, revised 1995), the National Middle School Association acknowledges that "curriculum is the primary vehicle for achieving the goals and objectives of a school" (p. 20). NMSA characterizes a developmentally responsive curriculum as "challenging, integrative, and exploratory" (p. 20). A challenging curriculum "actively engages young adolescents, marshaling their sustained interest and effort" (p. 20). An integrative curriculum "help students connect school experiences to their daily lives outside the school, and ...encourages them to reflect on the totality of their experiences" (p. 22). Lastly, an exploratory curriculum "enables students to discover particular abilities, talents, interests, values, and preferences,... reveals opportunities for making contributions to society, and... acquaints students with enriching, healthy leisure-time pursuits" (pp. 23–24). According to NMSA, this curriculum should be delivered within the context of varied teaching and learning approaches with assessment and evaluation that promotes learning. *Turning Points* (1989), likewise, addresses the issue of curriculum in the middle school. While acknowledging that "every middle school should offer a core academic program" (p. 42), middle-grade educators are to fashion a full academic program for all students that integrates English, fine arts, foreign languages, history, literature and grammar, mathematics, science, and social studies.

Following these reports, a surprisingly consistent picture of the "good middle school" emerged. As early as 1991, George announced that the national debate about the characteristics of the exemplary middle school was over. Indeed, ask someone today to identify the components of a developmentally appropriate middle school and the response will most likely include advisory programs, interdisciplinary teaming, flexible scheduling, and an exploratory curriculum: precisely those components that distinguish the middle school from "miniature high schools" with their disciplinary curricula.

While there has been general agreement as to what structures or components should be operating in middle schools, translating these structures into concrete curricular and instructional practices has been slow. Supporting this point, Manning (1993) writes: "While developmental psychologists have offered insightful theories about physical, psychosocial and cognitive development, the process of translating them into practice has been somewhat slow, especially beyond the elementary school years" (p. iii). In a recent study of 73 middle schools in the northeastern United States, only 14 (19%) had advisories, 6 (8%) organized their teachers into interdisciplinary teams, 5 (7%) utilized flexible scheduling, and 0 (0%) described their curriculum as exploratory (see Anfara & Brown, 2000). Additional research (Alexander & McEwin,1989; Cawelti, 1988) supports the finding that the practices universally acknowledged to be essential to good middle level education are not frequently practiced in our middle schools. This empirical finding calls into question whether middle schools ever concretely embraced these originating ideas as concrete operating principles. Developmentally appropriate middle schools appear to remain more an ideal than a reality.

Nonetheless, developmentally appropriate middle school has provoked a subject-centered reaction in the 1990s. The pendulum that swung in the direction of middle schools is swinging back again. Recent reform efforts again emphasize core academic content and complain of the lack of rigor in "developmentally oriented" middle schools. The problem is clear: Blaming the academic failures of middle level education on developmental features of middle schools may be pointing to a cause that does not even exist!

DEVELOPMENTALLY APPROPRIATE VERSUS SUBJECT-CENTERED CURRICULUM: AN UNTENABLE DUALISM?

The insights of John Dewey offer a pathway beyond the pendulum swing of this persistent dualism. For Dewey this sort of dualism always grows out of a genuine problem—a situation where elements, as they stand, are conflicting. The solution can be found only by "getting away from the meanings of terms that is already fixed upon" to see the situation in a fresh light (Dewey, 1902, pp. 3–4).

And Dewey himself attacked this very problem of developmental appropriateness versus academic rigor in many of his educational writings. His formulations, as we will demonstrate, point to a clearer, more discriminating analysis of the term "academic rigor" that dissolves the conflict. Interestingly, his analysis points to three distinct stages in the growth of knowledge utilization, appropriate to early primary, middle, and secondary educational levels. For this reason his formulations have a surprisingly direct relevance to today's situation in middle school criticism.

Academic Knowledge as the Goal of School Learning

Dewey's analysis begins by establishing a goal for the process of schooling considered as a whole. It may surprise those whose understanding of Dewey's thought is gleaned from secondary sources that for Dewey the goal of school learning is indeed rigorous, disciplined knowledge in its mature form. While Dewey always emphasizes this goal, he does not merely take it at face value, but seeks a deeper understanding of (a) what knowledge in this sense is, and (b) how in this sense it can be achieved through a sequence of school experiences—a curriculum. His answers to these questions point to his resolution of the dualism.

For Dewey the curricular sequence must always start where the child is—school subject matter is selected from materials at hand in "ordinary life experiences." But the selection is guided by our aim, the development of adult knowledge. This "far-away point" is of value to us in interpreting children's ordinary experiences in terms of their potential pathways of development to adult life (Dewey, 1902, pp. 13, 19). So the very next step after selecting some material of child experience for use in school is always to guide it "into a fuller and more organized form, a form that gradually approximates that in which subject matter is presented to the skilled, mature person" (Dewey, 1938, pp. 73–75). For the more mature student, in the secondary school, school subject-matter knowledge is organized in a rigorous disciplinary form: extensive, accurately defined, and logically related. But to get to this goal we must for younger students begin with knowledge as something fluid, partial, and connected through objects and activities in their childhood worlds. This knowledge is hardly unorganized—but it is organized around the lives of children, unified by personal and social interests, rather than those of adults (Dewey, 1902, p. 5; 1916, pp. 183–184).

Knowledge in the "Having" Mode versus Knowledge in Use

Adult knowledge as a goal is itself hardly something fixed and finished, perfect and inert. It is rather something evolving, to be used flexibly in the intelligent conduct of evolving life. Knowledge is killed when conceived as an object abstracted from life, to be possessed and worshiped. Rather, knowledge is a tool in various social roles: scientist, engineer, technician, teacher. As a goal of education, knowledge is not a possession but a means of increasing intelligence in the life of the group by being put to use.

To achieve this goal of mature-knowledge-in-use, it is necessary always to have in mind not merely the given knowledge content but also its underlying practical logic. Educators must keep in mind how the content and mature organization of knowledge grows out of the practical demands of social life, and how that content is used, tested, and modified in use. The series of curricular activities gradually must approximate mature knowledge-in-use just as the young people themselves gradually approximate maturity in their life roles and consequent knowledge needs. But the crucial point is this: Subject-matter content can only be learned for intelligent use as it is learned in the context of intelligent use. Dewey is uncompromising in this demand and bears quoting at length:

> there is all the difference in the world whether the acquisition of information is treated as an end in itself, or is made an integral portion of the training of thought. The assumption that information that has been accumulated apart from use in the recognition and solution of a problem may later on be, at will, freely employed by thought is quite false. The skill at the ready command of intelligence is the skill acquired with the aid of intelligence. (1933, p. 163)

Knowledge Content Evolves but Logical Organization Remains Stable

Knowledge content in the curriculum is thus always relative to its intelligent use; to be learned *for* use it must be learned *in* use. And the uses of knowledge vary both at different stages of life and over time, even for mature knowledge users. On the one hand, the young are involved in different roles than adults; they have different developmental tasks and, for this reason, different cognitive needs. For knowledge to enter effectively into their mental life, it must be developmentally relevant. On the other hand, even adult practices evolve over time and impose ever new knowledge requirements; yesterday's medical or engineering knowledge would hardly suffice for today's practitioners.

But though the content of knowledge is fluid, the practical logic of knowledge is stable both over the course of a life and through historical time. There is an "innate disposition to draw inferences and an inherent desire to experiment and test." Thus the mind "at every stage of its growth. . .entertains suggestions, tests them by observation of objects and events, reaches conclusions, tries them in action, finds them confirmed or in need of correction or rejection" (Dewey, 1933, p. 181). Even little babies do this much, while research scientists and science-based professionals continue to modify the organization and content of knowledge whenever existing knowledge fails as a resource for effective action.

This distinction between the content and the logic of knowledge is the turning point in Dewey's analysis as it points to two distinct objects that can be assessed in terms of academic rigor: (a) the organization of knowledge content and (b) the consecutiveness and connectiveness of logic in practical thinking—deliberation leading to the selection and employment of means. We return to this distinction after considering academic disciplines as organizing patterns of knowledge content.

Academic Disciplines as Patterns of Knowledge for Generic Adult Uses

The academic disciplines are organizing patterns for knowledge, forms for the composition and arrangement of information for generic purposes of adult life in societies that have established specialized institutions for knowledge. The content of disciplined knowledge is constantly being renewed under the pressure of new developments in industry, engineering, the military, and other branches of knowledge. The knowledge content of these generic disciplines is then made specific to adult uses: hence courses in economics for managers, biochemistry for health professionals, statistics for educators. Adult occupations furnish the "stabilizing axis" about which disciplined knowledge is organized (Dewey, 1933, p. 151).

Because knowledge as a goal of education is relative to occupations, "the scheme of a curriculum must take account of the existing social life" (Dewey, 1916, p. 191). Any conception of academic disciplines and the curriculum sequence must presuppose a background of representative roles of knowledge users at different stages of social maturity—child, youth, and adult.

School Subject Matter and Adult Knowledge

Subject matter in school learning cannot be restricted to the content of academic disciplines, for this would mean narrowing the content of school experiences of even young students to the materials of adult occupations and concerns. In education, subject matter is more usefully conceived as any content that comes into the field of interest of students or teachers, in relation to solving problems, or relieving tensions, or satisfying needs. As matter, subject-matter content is something moved around, tried out, tested, used to perform operations, and so on. Put simply, subject matter is any stuff of life experience entering the educational situation.

On Dewey's account, life experiences involve actions—taking means in pursuit of ends and undergoing consequences as these pursuits succeed or fail. Having an experience is being involved with the materials of a situation marked by tension and carrying the situation to a successful close. Some elements of the situation are taken as means while others point to ends to be reached. Subject matter as the stuff of experience is always relative to interests, which Dewey says are in between points or links of means and ends. Interests are spotlights pointing to means—to the solutions of problems or the resolutions of tensions.

Some people can take a direct interest in subject-matter knowledge, and thus cognitive learning can be interesting in itself. But knowledge is of interest in different ways to scholars, technicians, and teachers—adult knowledge users—on one hand, and to students on the other. To scholars, disciplined subject matter is bracketed off from the rest of life and treated as self-contained. The problems and goals of scholarship reside in the knowledge itself. The scholar draws on some available "on-the-shelf" knowledge to test and modify other knowledge contents. To the science-based professional and the technician, knowledge is an "on-the-shelf" resource for solving problems, resolving tensions, and meeting needs in various spheres of practical life. For the teacher, disciplined knowledge is of interest as a suggestive field of ideas and materials (Dewey, 1916) and provides a vision of the end of the curricular process. It is a resource for activating the intelligence of the students and for interpreting the potentialities inhering in their present activities. Thus "the subject matter of science and history and art serves to reveal the real child to us" (Dewey, 1902, p. 16).

But young learners are connected to social life through child and youth roles, not those of adults. Their interests—their linkages of means–ends—thus cannot be identical with "the formulated, the crystallized, and systematized subject matter" of any of these representative adults (Dewey, 1916, p. 182).

Rather, cognitive interests develop through three stages in school students. For the youngest, knowledge is mere familiarity. What is known are home, neighborhood, and family members. For more mature youth in the middle stage, knowledge is connected to youth roles in social life outside the immediate family, for example, sports, cars, music, and parties. It is information asked for and received, picked up from friends and family, teachers and the media. This knowledge per se is not a matter of interest, but rather a more or less ad hoc resource for use within problematic realms of young life. It is spotlighted as interesting not in and for itself, but as it aids effective action. Only as youth move toward adult roles and can conceive themselves as occupying these can they see knowledge in the form organized for adult roles as potentially useful. Only then can knowledge become an object of interest in itself, as something discriminated within the flow of experience as linking needs and acquirements, problems and solutions, tensions and their resolutions. At each stage knowledge is used to augment the operation of intelligence in ends-directed activity, but only at the last stage does it approximate the form in which subject matter is presented to the skilled, mature person.

Development and the Real Problem of Cognitive Education

To summarize to this point, at each stage of development, children have assigned roles, and distinct social expectations are imposed upon them. For this reason each child has a concrete social life with its felt problems and needs, and these in turn establish varying requirements for cognitive learning. Knowledge utilization in a stage-specific form is thus a goal at every phase of the educational process. And because child life is continuous with adult life and grows into it, adult knowledge organized in disciplinary form provides a "far-away" end that is nonetheless useful in interpreting child achievements throughout the curricular sequence.

The knowledge that comprises the educational goal is knowledge-in-use, not knowledge as a possession. While knowledge content changes at different stages in the student's life, the practical logic of knowledge-in-use remains the same and so forms the stable backbone of cognitive education. The teacher's job is not to convey or transmit knowledge, for only knowledge in the "having" mode can be conveyed or transmitted. Rather, the teacher's job is first to obtain an intimate working knowledge of both adult subject matter and the life-stage specific problems of young people and then to establish learning situations that (a) quicken these youth problems—make them felt more acutely; (b) indicate knowledge resources relevant to their solution; and (c) compel consecutive thought—rigorous, practical logic—in using them.

At the first two stages of child-knowledge use, these resources are simply not always going to be in a form that would satisfy adult knowledge users. And the organization of subject matter that young people achieve in their learning activities, while demonstrably useful for their own youthful purposes, will not always be the organization useful to adults. But what can be assessed in more or less constant terms throughout the curriculum—and can provide the focus of assessment—is the rigor of logical connection, of inference, of intelligent knowledge-in-use.

This prepares us to resolve the untenable dualism of development versus academic rigor. We can state that the disciplinary organization of knowledge content, as a body of propositions, is rigorous in that it is extensive, accurately defined, and logically connected. However, the youth's practical thinking can also be more or less rigorous when evaluated against academic criteria—sufficiently extensive and defined for the problem at hand and logically connected. Developmentally appropriate knowledge-in-use may thus be academically rigorous in a robust and even determinate sense even when it fails to mimic the academic disciplines.

Adult Knowledge as Proximate Goal

Knowledge approximating the form in which it is presented to the young learner is the "far-away" goal that nonetheless illuminates activities and achievements at every stage. But when possession of adult knowledge becomes prematurely the proximate goal in educating the young learner, three immediate evils result. First, knowledge becomes eviscerated, losing all contact with real life at both of its natural points of contact—those of its generation and its use. Knowledge shows up in the curriculum, predigested, canned, and conveyed to students who have no idea where it came from, who made it, or why they went to all the trouble. Because this occurs, students in turn can form no clear ideas about what the knowledge might be used for or what they themselves are expected to make of it. Second, students lose all motivation for learning because the subject matter is not interesting to them—it has no power to link available means to their youthful ends. To make it interesting we are forced to dress it up with humor or showmanship, which are not integral to it and distract attention from what is. Third, because adult knowledge employs terms and forms of organization specific to adult uses and foreign to the child's life, the material must be "watered down." This means that features integral to the subject matter as adult knowledge must be eliminated—the material is entirely robbed of what it needs to be put to any use whatsoever, so the child loses use of both his own logic and acquaintance with that of adult knowledge users.

These lead to a final evil: we come to think of "good students" as those who can absorb and even love all this dead stuff, the little "know-it-alls" proud to show off their attainments and primed to compete for academic honors awarded on the basis of inauthentic measures—the kids rightly despised by schoolchildren with any life remaining in them.

CONCLUSION

Will the current call for stiffer curriculum get rid of the "crack in the middle?" Will a subject-centered curriculum transform "the wasteland of our primary and secondary landscape" into some sort of oasis? Simply answered, no.

It is understandable that what we are presently doing in middle schools looks "soft," especially when the results of tests like TIMSS and NAEP are released. It follows that dissatisfaction will result in some communities of value, new pressures will be applied, the reform pendulum will swing, and middle schools will be placed on the defensive. But the problems cannot result from the developmental reforms, for these were never sufficiently implemented on a grand scale. And the solution cannot be found in what current reformers are calling for, a curriculum that robs young adolescents of all motivation for learning because it makes no connection between knowledge and the real world. This kind of "academic rigor" would merely force our middle schools to once again become the very "miniature junior highs" whose manifest failures they were invented to rectify.

On the other hand, failure to reflect on the underlying assumptions and implications of this current indictment will leave the very conspicuous problems revealed by NAEP, TIMSS, and other sources unaddressed. Middle-level educators will then be missing an opportunity to provide a more adequate, empirically grounded base for middle school curriculum renewal. The "good" middle school will remain an ideal that has never even been tried.

The next two steps forward are intimately connected. They are (1) operationalizing the notion of logical rigor, and (2) building a research base on the developmental needs of middle level youth and the knowledge resources that can assist them in meeting their needs.

The first tool would allow middle school teachers to design and implement curriculum activities that provide appropriate opportunities for students both to learn appropriate content and to demonstrate their knowledge acquisition and utilization. What is needed are less generic, more content-specific, tests of critical thinking than those provided by current "critical thinking" tests. We want good measures of critical-thinking-in-use to apply to actual products of middle school student thinking to determine their logical rigor—the extent and validity of logical connections. Then such products could be evaluated as "hard" and demanding a standard as provided by standardized tests, not merely by the informal, unreliable, and easily biased judgments of individual observers.

Additionally, we need to know more about the developmental tasks and roles of middle-level students. Until we know what these students are up against, we cannot have an empirically grounded basis for selecting curriculum content that is relevant to their lives. As Dewey argued, such students rarely have needs that demand the conscious bracketing of knowledge as something organized in distinct academic "disciplines." For these students, knowledge is for the most part a resource pool providing collections of materials relevant to needs. For middle school teachers, on the other hand, the academic disciplines are consciously distinguished—as organizing tools for storing and connecting materials that can nourish the problem-solving and decision-making thinking of their students. Children facing different tasks and challenges will find different funds of knowledge relevant and useful. Organizing knowledge with an eye to potential uses for middle level students can simplify the knowledge acquisition and curriculum development process. Although the concrete thought processes of every child are different, their concerns are similar enough to point to academic content that will fly as relevant and useful. Testing of curriculum content based on empirical determination of these concerns frees teachers from the need to "reinvent the wheel."

We have argued that developmentally appropriate knowledge-in-use may be academically rigorous even when it fails to mimic the more "adult-like" academic disciplines. It is possible to develop developmentally appropriate curriculum content, and to measure the academic rigor of learning outcomes without relying upon achievement tests grounded in academic disciplines. Only when we recognize that learning can demonstrably be both developmentally appropriate and academically rigorous can we stop the pendulum that relentlessly swings between uncritical conceptions of both.

ACKNOWLEDGMENT

Used with permission from the National Middle School Association. Material originally appeared in November 2000 and January 2001 issues of *Middle School Journal.*

NOTE

1.   The six characteristics include: (1) educators committed to young adolescents, (2) a shared vision, (3) high expectations for all, (4) an adult advocate for every student, (5) family and community partnerships, and (6) a positive school climate. Program components include: (1) curriculum that is challenging, integrative, and exploratory; (2) varied teaching and learning approaches; (3) assessment and evaluation that promotes learning; (4) flexible organizational structures; (5) programs and policies that foster health, wellness, and safety; and (6) comprehensive guidance and support services (p. 11).

REFERENCES

Anfara, V., & Brown, K. (2000). In their own words: Have our middle schools responded to the needs of young adolescents? *Research in Middle Level Education Annual, 23*, 65–84.

Alexander, W., & McEwin, C. (1989). *Schools in the middle: Progress 1968–1988. NASSP schools in the middle: A report on trends and practices.* Reston, VA: National Association of Secondary School Principals.

Association for Supervision and Curriculum Development. (1975). *The middle school we need.* Washington, DC: Author.

Bradley, J. (1998, April 15). Muddle in the middle. *Education Week*, pp. 38–42.

Carnegie Task Force on the Education of Young Adolescents. (1989). *Turning points: Preparing American youth for the 21st century.* Washington, DC: Carnegie Council on Adolescent Development.

Cawelti, G. (1988). *Middle schools, a better match with early adolescent needs, ASCD survey finds. ASCD Curriculum Update.* Alexandria, VA: Association for Supervision and Curriculum Development.

Cuban, L. (1990). Reforming again, again, and again. *Educational Researcher, 19*(1), 3–14.

Cuban, L. (1992). What happens to reforms that last? The case of the junior high school. *American Educational Research Journal, 29*(2), 227–251.

Dewey, J. (1902). *The child and the curriculum.* Chicago: University of Chicago Press.

Dewey, J. (1916). *Democracy and education.* New York: Macmillan.

Dewey, J. (1933). *How we think: A restatement of the relation between reflective thinking and the educative process.* Heath. (Pagination to the 1986 edition, in John Dewey, *The later works,* Vol. 8, Jo Ann Boydston, Ed., Carbondale, IL: University of Illinois Press).

Dewey, J. (1938). Experience and education. *Kappa Delta Phi.* (Page references to Collier Books edition, 1963).

Douglass, A. (1945). The persistent problem of the junior high school. *California Journal of Secondary Education, 20,* 112–120.

George, P. (1991). Student development and middle level school organization: A prolegomenon. *Midpoints, 1*(1), 1–12.

Johnson, J., Dupuis, V., Musial, D., & Hall, G. (1994). *Introduction to the foundations of American education.* Needham Heights, MA: Allyn & Bacon.

Lewis, A. (1992). Middle schools come of age. *Education Digest, 58*(2), 4–7.

Manning, M. (1993). *Developmentally appropriate middle level schools.* Wheaton, MD: Association for Childhood Education International.

NASSP Council on Middle Level Education. (1985). *An agenda for excellence at the middle level.* Reston, VA: Author.

National Education Association. (1899). *Journal of proceedings and addresses.* Denver, CO: Author.

National Middle School Association. (1982). *This we believe.* Columbus, OH: Author.

Whitmire, R. (1998, March 21). Middle schools targeted as weak link in education chain. *The Reporter,* pp. A1, A4.

Wise, A. (1989). Calling for "National Institutes of Education." *Education Week, 9*(7), 36.

CHAPTER 4

CULTURALLY RESPONSIVE INSTRUCTIONAL PROCESSES

Dave F. Brown
West Chester University

ABSTRACT

The extensive changing cultural demographics of American classrooms create a need for the implementation of specific instructional processes to help diverse students succeed academically. America's teachers are primarily European-American, many who may be unaware of or perhaps reluctant to implement culturally responsive instruction. Young adolescence is a particularly crucial developmental period to respond to the ethnic and cultural characteristics of students due to their advancing social and cognitive awareness. This chapter provides a description of specific ethnic and cultural instructional processes that positively influence diverse students' learning, including collaborative learning processes, inductive learning, contextual instruction, and communication processes.

Few of us...would care to admit that the way we teach compromises the learning of members of certain cultural groups. Yet, to avoid or remain insensitive to the cultural issues and influences within our teaching situations under the guise, for example, of maintaining academic standards or treating everyone alike is no longer acceptable. (Wlodkowski & Ginsberg, 1995, p. 8)

Middle School Curriculum, Instruction, and Assessment, pages 57–73
Copyright © 2002 by Information Age Publishing
All rights of reproduction in any form reserved.

Changing demographics across America, particularly in urban centers, have created the need for teachers to possess extensive knowledge on effective instructional strategies for culturally and ethnically diverse learners. Both university and K–12 educators require and frequently seek resources to create and maintain classroom environments that provide for the learning needs of ethnically and culturally diverse students. Despite educators' interests in culturally responsive teaching, time constraints constantly create challenges for teachers as they seek a quick fix to meet their students' needs while simultaneously attempting to appease those who judge their efforts through high-stakes test scores. Many instructional strategies and curricular decisions that positively affect diverse learners are incongruous with some of the teaching processes specifically used to prepare students for externally imposed standardized tests (Gay, 2000; Kohn, 1999, 2000). Faced with a difficult choice, educators are apt to choose more traditional instructional processes to satisfy the demands for higher test scores, particularly in urban districts where state and federal funding is directly linked to students' scores. This decision to ignore culturally responsive curriculum and instruction may be particularly damaging to young adolescents who become increasingly aware of the mismatch between their own ethnic and cultural needs and the attitudes and processes that middle-level teachers demonstrate.

Many teachers may develop an understanding of the philosophy of culturally responsive teaching but are unaware of the strategies for enacting instructional structures that support the theory. Nieto (1999) stated, "The chasm between multicultural education defined as critical pedagogy by scholars and actual school practices defined as multicultural by teachers in schools is wide indeed" (p. 107). Teachers' lack of practical knowledge is supported by Bennett (2001): "There is a small but growing body of research, primarily dissertations, that points to a gap between multicultural curriculum theory and classroom practice" (p. 182). A critical dimension of culturally responsive learning is *equity pedagogy* (Bennett, 1990). Teachers who promote equity pedagogy create learning environments that support the talents of all children, assist all students in reaching their potential, and implement instructional processes that reflect students' "cultural socialization" (Bennett, 2001, p. 183). Bennett added, "In contrast to curriculum reform, the dimension of equity pedagogy is often overlooked as an essential component of multicultural education" (p. 190).

Teachers feel a genuine sense of frustration when they are unaware of how to meet students' learning needs (Darling-Hammond, 2001). Teachers' failure to succeed with students often leads to student frustration followed by each one blaming the other for their failures (Weiner, 2000; Wlodkowski & Ginsberg, 1995). However, the academic achievement of African, Hispanic, Native, and Asian Americans as well as other immigrant students can be increased when "Teaching strategies and activities build upon the cultural and linguistic strengths of students and when teachers have cultural competency in the cultures of their students" (Parkay & Hass, 2000, p. 257).

NONWHITE, YOUNG ADOLESCENTS' CULTURAL IDENTITY DEVELOPMENT

Teachers whose culturally responsive actions are limited may produce the most damaging circumstances for nonwhite, young adolescents. These children are aware of cultural and ethnic differences and the impact of those differences on their learning. Nonwhite, young adolescents experience challenges in identity development as they struggle to understand how and if they should become a part of the Eurocentric culture (Gay, 2000; Rice, 1999). Necochea, Stowell, McDaniel, Lorimer, and Kritzer (2001) describe the ethnic-identity development of young adolescents:

> A second aspect of identity and ethnicity is how middle level students come to think about others based on ethnicity. Quintana (1998) points out that middle level students are operating on a level where they develop a social perspective of ethnicity. For middle level students, this means an understanding of subtle aspects of ethnicity beyond food, fashion, and folklore to deeper aspects of differences in values, world-view, and especially socioeconomic connections to ethnicity. Perhaps what is more important, it means an awareness that ethnicity is a key factor in social relations and an awareness of ethnic-based discrimination and prejudice. (p. 167)

Bennett (2001) described one particular study (Katz, 1999) that demonstrates the effects of young adolescents' growing awareness of ethnic and cultural differences. Katz (1999) discovered in closely monitoring the social growth of eight Latino immigrant students that despite fairly good academic progress and social development as elementary students, they all became alienated from school during their three years in middle school. These eight students described their teachers as uncaring and discriminatory toward Latinos. Only two of these eight students made it to their senior year of high school perhaps as a result of these feelings of alienation. Geneva Gay (1994) provides a powerful comment to support developing practices to meet the needs of culturally and ethnically diverse students, especially during young adolescence:

> If ethnic identity development is understood as part of the natural "coming of age" process during early adolescence, and if middle level education is to

be genuinely client-centered for students of color, then ethnic sensitivity must be incorporated into school policies, programs, and practices. (p. 153)

The results of ignoring the differing learning needs of ethnically and culturally diverse students is staggering considering the following statistics:

- More than 1,000 students from foreign countries enter American schools every day (Rong & Preissle, 1998).
- 70 to 80% of students in urban centers are either Latino or African American (Henry & Kasindorf, 1997).
- Non-native English speakers are the fastest-growing population of students in the United States (Marcias & Kelly, 1996).
- The Hispanic American high school dropout rate is 22% and the African American rate is 18% (National Education Association, 2001). (cited in Brown, 2002)

The general public may inaccurately believe that Asian students fare much better academically; however, Asian Americans include a broad range of immigrant students from places such as the Philippines, Indonesia, Laos, Cambodia, and Vietnam who with other Asian students experience many challenges in adjusting to American classrooms. Rong and Preissle (1998) described the challenges:

Despite the academic success of some, many Asian students continue to experience feelings of inferiority, alienation, and social isolation in school. Psychologists and sociologists have reported severe problems in development of ethnic identity and ethnic attitude among Asian youth. (p. 146)

Think about how middle school teachers have the power to affect the social and emotional transition of immigrant students into schools. It is unfathomable that teachers with appropriate knowledge of their students' cultural and ethnic learning needs would ignore that information as they plan and deliver instruction if they realized the impact on the future academic and social competence of their students.

WHO WILL TEACH DIVERSE LEARNERS?

Teachers of diverse learners ideally would share similar cultural backgrounds as their students—especially those students who are second language learners (SLL). Reality indicates, however, that no balance between diverse learners and teachers with similar backgrounds will occur soon. Thousands of new teachers are hired in the large urban centers every year (Jennings, 2001; Ladson-Billings, 2001). These new hires, recent college graduates, and the veteran teachers in all of America's schools are primarily white European Americans—88% as reported by Ladson-Billings.

These demographic facts do not have to result in dire circumstances for culturally diverse students. However, many students are currently experiencing academic difficulty because teachers are unable to recognize and respond to their cultural learning needs. Bennett (2001) noted, "When the personal or cultural knowledge of students and teachers differs, uninformed teachers may lower their expectations for student success" (p. 181). White teachers, in essence, need to develop a clear understanding of the philosophy associated with culturally responsive teaching and must begin to implement the accompanying instructional strategies and curricular changes required to deliver meaningful learning experiences for African, Hispanic, Native, and Asian American students as well as for other immigrant students.

ALTERING TEACHERS' ATTITUDES

Altering teachers' beliefs about teaching and learning in America is similar to chopping at the roots of the family's favorite century-old, 150-foot oak tree on the side of the grandparents' driveway. Like the roots of the old oak tree, teachers' beliefs about education are built upon deep and protected structures. If someone sees you chopping at that oak tree, you might even be labeled un-American. Similar negative feelings are often reserved for those who espouse a different way of viewing students, teaching, and learning in American classrooms. Many noneducators, perhaps many who are legislators, may not understand the need for culturally responsive instruction and curriculum. This lack of awareness may produce less support for educators to adopt culturally responsive teaching. Sleeter (1992) discovered in an extensive study that teachers were willing to make changes in pedagogy, but they were not as accepting of making critical changes in their general teaching philosophies. Frustration results for students and their parents when teachers fail to comprehend the value of culturally responsive instruction, ignore the information that is available, or are unaware of how to implement strategies to assist students.

The first step in altering instructional processes is to help teachers realize that other, more effective instructional strategies are needed to help culturally and ethnically diverse students learn. Helping teachers realize the need for a different set of strategies is especially challenging for teacher educators because most preservice teachers are European American. Whites have been drowning in a culture of how to do schooling that they are immersed in—much like fish in water—without noticing it (Howard, 1999). Frequently reinforced egocentric and Eurocentric views of how teaching and learning should occur make it difficult to encourage teachers to examine their beliefs to understand that these Eurocentric actions also represent a cultural teaching perspective: one that is severely limiting for many students.

Several strategies exist for helping European American teachers identify their own culture of teaching. I suggested that educators identify their cultural schooling perspective by reflecting on the following questions:

1. What should the social relationship be between students and teachers; that is, how are students expected to respond to you as a teacher? Should they look into your eyes when they speak to you? Are they permitted to challenge your authority? Is laughing with you permitted?

2. What is the role of students during recitations? Students may wonder about the following: Am I supposed to raise my hand when a question is asked? Can I collaborate with others when the teacher asks a question? Am I expected to use my books to respond to questions? Is it acceptable to question another student's answer?

3. What is the best way to help students improve their language so that they speak and write standard and formal English? Should I permit students to speak their language in class and correct them later? Should I correct them every time they use Black English Vernacular or part of their Spanish language in a sentence with mostly English words? How long should I allow them to continue to use Spanish (or other foreign languages) in my room? How should I correct their writing so that they learn to write standard English?

4. How much of my students' culture should I recognize, since I want them to succeed economically in America? Can I use part of their background experiences in my curricula, or should I ignore their culture so that they learn enough about American culture? How important is it to use books and other curricular materials that my students recognize as being a part of their cultural experiences?

5. How quickly should I move through the curriculum? Is it better to cover all the content in the book or move more slowly so that all students learn the principles well before we move to other topics? Can I leave out certain parts of the curriculum if it doesn't interest my students as much as it does me?

6. How much collaborative learning should I permit in my room? Shouldn't I encourage them to work alone most of the time? Wouldn't competition among students motivate them to work harder? Would some of my students learn better if they were allowed to work with a partner or in a group?

7. Which instructional strategies will work best for most of my students? Should I use less lecture? Would discussion groups work better for some of the class activities? Should I use less individualized work and more cooperative learning type of assignments?

8. Is there a better way to group students during independent activities? Should I group students by ability or allow all ability levels to work together?

9. How do the books that I use in my class influence the views of my students? Do the stories and pictures represent the lives of these children or adolescents? What are the other sources of diverse literature and historical books that I can use that will better represent my students' lives? (Brown, 2002, pp. 21–23)

The learning experiences of most American teachers would create responses to these questions that reflect traditional classroom social structures and instructional processes—practices that have little relevance to the learning needs of many culturally diverse students. Yet, without asking these questions of most teachers, they are unlikely to identify or question instructional processes that create considerable obstacles for culturally diverse learners. A specific case in point is the story told by two middle level teachers who took turns observing one another to provide feedback on cultural teaching effectiveness. One of those teachers was white, and she unknowingly responded inappropriately to her African American students' comments, behaviors, and reactions to her teaching (Obidah & Manheim Teel, 2001). The white teacher would never have realized how her responses to some cultural nuances of African Americans were perceived negatively by students without receiving specific feedback from her colleague. Wlodkowski and Ginsberg (1995) describe how teachers unwittingly enforce teaching strategies that discourage culturally diverse learners:

> If we teach as we were taught, it is likely that we sanction individual performance, prefer reasoned argumentation, advocate impersonal objectivity, and condone sports-like competition for testing and grading procedures. Such teaching represents a distinct set of cultural norms and values that for many of today's learners are at best culturally unfamiliar and at worst a contradiction to the norms and values of their gender and their racial and ethnic background. (p. 7)

My intent within this chapter is to provide readers with a specific set of instructional processes that support culturally and ethnically diverse learners while describing the value of these strategies for young adolescents.

CULTURALLY RESPONSIVE INSTRUCTIONAL PROCESSES

Inductive Teaching and Learning

Geneva Gay (2000) described the need for more active instructional processes for culturally and ethnically diverse learners. Using the inductive approach for studying new concepts and principles is one approach that matches the needs of African, Hispanic, and Native American students. Principles that are taught from a whole-to-parts process provide a better understanding for students than a parts-to-whole approach. Traditional instructional processes at the middle school level such as teaching the parts of a volcano, the steps to solving mathematical equations, or introducing vocabulary out of context before demonstrating the whole process can cause confusion for many culturally and ethnically diverse students. Some culturally and ethnically diverse learners may need to view experiments, videos, and demonstrations prior to being given specific details to understand new principles.

Inductive teaching may be especially necessary for second language learners who are introduced to many new vocabulary words during daily lessons.

During traditional instruction, teachers might ask students to look up words in a dictionary or glossary of a text and attempt to define them individually without prior explanation. These short introductions to vocabulary prevent students from genuinely understanding new concepts. Visual representations of ideas and words are needed to ensure greater understanding.

Contextual Experiences

As concepts and principles become more advanced in middle school, middle school teachers may frequently provide abstract information to students without making explicit connections to their background knowledge. Imagine the challenges many students experience in imagining or picturing the following principles with words only:

- a solar eclipse
- how antibodies attack cells
- convection
- the size of a milliliter
- how pistons work
- side–angle–side
- the perimeter of a polygon

These principles are part of the science and mathematics curricula for fifth graders in many urban schools. If asked to merely look up these words in a glossary and read text with few pictures independently, students are unlikely to comprehend these words. Delpit (1995) and Gay (2000) indicated that it is highly ineffective to use decontextualized teaching with Hispanic and African American students. Students require more explicit and teacher-directed instruction of new vocabulary associated with abstract principles and concepts. Students should be engaged in the following instructional activities:

- telling stories
- having students share experiences related to story topics
- engaging students in kinesthetic reenactments of historical events
- using pictures, films, diagrams, and videos to provide clarity
- designing graphic organizers that clarify confusing topics
- encouraging students to design physical models of new principles
- inviting guest speakers to provide accurate descriptions and explanations of topics studied
- establishing field trips as frequently as possible to any site (even on school grounds) to provide clarity to students on unfamiliar topics (Brown, 2002, pp.149–150)

Collaborative Learning

Teachers in many American classrooms rely on individualized and competitive learning situations. Research from numerous studies has provided overwhelming support for collaborative versus competitive learning (Lipsey & Wilson, 1993; Slavin, 1991; Walberg, 1999). Kline (1995) stated, "Only in U.S. classrooms are individuals asked to find every answer, solve every problem, complete every task, and pass every test by relying solely on their own efforts and abilities" (p. 23). A glance at the job section of the local newspaper reveals that employers are interested in hiring "team players." Schools must shoulder some responsibility for helping students develop these group skills; however, using collaborative learning situations is also preferred among Asians, African Americans, and Latinos (Gay, 2000). The cognitive abilities and social needs of young adolescents make middle school classrooms a highly appropriate place for instruction that utilizes collaborative discussions, group problem solving, and team research activities. Immigrant students facing the challenges of learning English would also benefit from collaborative learning. Two researchers noted that mathematical achievement was much higher among African and Hispanic American students when they modeled the group learning processes used by Chinese Americans (Fullilove & Treisman, 1990). Several meaningful collaborative learning activities for middle school include

- writing workshop including collaborative brainstorming, peer revision, and editing
- literature circles for the discussion of commonly read books
- team book talks where partners make oral presentations of trade books they have read
- group investigations of hypotheses developed in science or history
- reader's theater in which small groups of students present scenes from stories read
- groups of students working together at stations to complete mathematics problems or science experiments
- paired reading partners who read text orally to one another (Brown, 2002, p. 152)

Young adolescents must be taught how to learn collaboratively for it to have a meaningful impact. Teachers must explicitly explain and demonstrate effective use of peer revision in writing workshop, students' roles in literature circles, and the specific responsibilities for each student in cooperative learning situations. Although many teachers may occasionally enjoy designing collaborative instruction, teachers must prioritize collaborative learning in situations in which it may not commonly be used, such as mathematics and in homework assignments, to ensure that culturally and ethnically diverse students' learning needs are addressed.

Culturally Responsive Instructional Communication

Effective instruction naturally involves the ability of teachers to communicate congruently with students. Teachers' social behaviors—including nonverbal and verbal communication—affect students' desire to cooperate and engage in learning activities. The value of communicating effectively with culturally and ethnically diverse students is emphasized by Saravia-Shore and Garcia's (1995) finding: "The aspects of culture that influence classroom life most powerfully are those that affect the social organization of learning and the social expectations concerning communication" (p. 57). Howard (2001) discovered, "The achievement of students is increased when teachers modify their instruction to make it more congruent with the cultures and communication styles of culturally diverse students" (p. 183). Educators will have a more meaningful impact on students if they are aware of and respond to the preferred discourse patterns of their culturally and ethnically diverse students.

Saravia-Shore and Garcia (1995) described how communication affects learning:

> When the norms of interaction and communication in a classroom are very different from those to which the student has been accustomed, students experience confusion and anxiety, cannot attend to learning, and may not know how to appropriately seek the teacher's attention, get the floor, or participate in discussions. By acknowledging students' cultural norms and expectations concerning communication and social interaction, teachers can appropriately guide student participation in instructional activities. (p. 57)

Traditional classroom discourse and how it affects culturally diverse students may be unnoticeable to teachers and students who have spent the majority of their lives in American classrooms. Some educators may need to view a videotape of their teaching and discuss the interaction patterns that define a traditional classroom in order to begin to identify alternative possibilities.

Social interaction patterns naturally vary according to the culture and ethnicity of students. A large percentage of African American students, for instance, often speak in the dialect of Black English Vernacular (BEV). Other nonstandard forms of English are spoken by a few Americans such as Hawaiian Creole and Appalachian English (Ruddell, 1999). It may be common for teachers, particularly at the middle and high school level, to correct students' language when they use one of these alternative forms of English, particularly BEV. Standard English should not be viewed as a replacement for African American students' use of BEV, but instead, as an alternative dialect that should be used in specific contexts of school and work (Ruddell, 1999). Howard (2001) clarified the problem, "Teachers should recognize that any attempts to invalidate or denigrate the use of nonstandard English might have detrimental effects on the academic prospects for African American students. A teacher's response to students' use of BEV should be one of acceptance without providing correction or passing judgment on the students' language. To overly correct or dismiss students' use of BEV denigrates young adolescents' ethnic and cultural background while creating negative feelings between students and teachers.

Middle level teachers can model standard English while recognizing that BEV is an acceptable variation. Teachers, in addition, should specifically design lessons that demonstrate the appropriate use of and context for using standard English writing and conversation. Dwyer (1991) noted that no evidence exists that proves permitting the use of BEV negatively affects academic achievement.

Gay (2000) noted the following African American students' communication styles that contributed to their academic success:

- dramatic presentation styles
- conversational and active participatory discourse
- gestures and body movement
- rapidly paced rhythmic speech
- metaphorical imagery (p. 87)

These processes involve a great deal of oral communication, such as class discussions rather than the use of lecture methods or other teacher-directed instruction. The use of literature circles, plays, book talks, simulation activities, and reader's theater are all examples of instructional processes that may benefit ethnically and culturally different students (Brown, 2002).

Gains in students' literary skills were noted when they were encouraged to use *signifying* or *sounding* during class discussions (Lee, 1993). Gay (2000) described *signifying* as using insults, insinuation, and exaggeration during class discussions. *Sounding* is a communication pattern in which students may brag in a demonstrative manner, use exaggerated phrases, and speak loudly as if arguing. One other ethnic communication pattern is *call-response*, during which students may provide encouragement, compliments, or loudly disagree while teachers are lecturing. These communication patterns run contrary to many teachers' views of how classroom discussions should be held. Due to young adolescents' gradual movement into the advanced cognitive stages of concrete and formal operational thought, accepting and encouraging these patterns may be an effective avenue for some culturally and ethnically diverse students to more quickly reach these higher cognitive levels.

Assisting Second Language Learners

The influx of second language learners (SLL) into American classrooms creates immense challenges for general education, middle level teachers who may have no experience with or knowledge of the native language of their students. An added stressor for young adolescent immigrant students is their social need to become a part of the mainstream culture of their peers. Middle level teachers must be especially cognizant of immigrant students' social and emotional mindsets to ensure that SLL students find classrooms safe and emotionally comfortable. Middle schools can be socially cruel places since students may commonly ridicule, embarrass, and bully fellow students.

Teachers can be powerful allies of SLL students by demonstrating a genuine interest in the backgrounds of these students, from their language to their previous homeland geography to their family traditions. SLL students may experience feelings of respect when teachers explicitly ask about their interests and previous experiences and use that information as a part of the curriculum.

The greatest challenge may be helping young adolescent SLL students feel comfortable speaking English. School is the primary environment where students will learn English, and as such, teachers must create experiences for SLL students to experiment with language in a risk-free environment. Effective teachers conduct personal research to learn about the rules, vocabulary, and other structures of SLL students' languages. Teachers may discover the challenges that SLL students face learning English if they understand their native language pronunciation patterns, discourse styles, or syntax (Cary, 2000). Personal interviews with SLL students will help teachers identify students' attitudes about entering America and the challenges of adjusting to a new culture since attitudes affect students' efforts, interests, and motivation.

SLL students' oral involvement in class may be quite limited due to their need to listen to the language for awhile before beginning to speak it since they may not know many English words. Young adolescent SLL students may be highly reluctant to attempt to speak during class for fear of being ridiculed for saying words incorrectly or for *code switching*. *Code switching* occurs when students speak orally using some English words that they know interlaced with words from their native language. Anyone who has tried to communicate in a foreign country would naturally do the same if not fluent in the language. It is imperative for teachers to establish classroom policies that protect SLL students from being ridiculed while encouraging code switching so students actually practice speaking the language. Small group social learning is another standard instructional strategy middle school teachers with SLL students should regularly use. Small groups encourage the social acceptance of SLL students with other students, provide a forum for SLL students to listen and speak English, and help develop a trusting classroom atmosphere for young adolescent immigrant students. Constant correction of SLL students' misuse of English words or pronunciation is also detrimental to students' development of English as it is with correcting African American students' use of BEV. As Cary (2000) noted of SLL students, "Giving students permission to get language wrong went a long way in helping them to get it right" (p. 59).

Garcia (1999) suggested these instructional strategies to increase SLL students' learning opportunities:

- increase wait time following your questions and after their responses to promote elaboration and more processing time
- simplify your language—don't speak louder; rephrase comments or questions instead

- don't force students to speak
- pair SLL students with proficient English speakers
- adapt instructional materials to make them more comprehensible
- build on students' prior knowledge bases
- support the student's home language and culture (cited in Brown, 2002, p. 178)

Discussion Discourse Patterns

Many teachers claim that they use a great deal of discussion in their classrooms when they are actually using recitations. *Recitation* involves the use of a pattern of questioning directed by the teacher with little if any actual discussion. A recitation instructional pattern involves three constantly repeated events: (a) the teacher asks a question, (b) a student responds, and (c) the teacher responds to that student's answer. This pattern can be and is usually repeated for several minutes or perhaps an entire classroom period. Many students will not become engaged in the learning process when this pattern of questioning is used. Culturally and ethnically diverse students may be even more reluctant to engage in a recitation due to their views of how to respond to teachers' questions, how to respond to other students' responses, and how to respond to the types of recall questions with known answers that are commonly asked in recitations (Brown, 2002).

African, Hispanic, and Native American students generally use more conversational discourse in their homes than the question/answer/response format used in recitation and in many American classrooms (Gay, 2000). Recitations are passive learning situations for students and may be quite unproductive in encouraging learning among culturally and ethnically diverse students. Culturally responsive instructional processes for many learners should be designed to encourage spontaneous verbal reaction to statements made by teachers and fellow students. Many students should be permitted to speak simultaneously in a discourse pattern referred to as *talk-story* or *co-narration*. Gay (2000) suggested using instructional activities that permit students to "work collaboratively, talk together, create an idea, or tell a story," as more effective strategies for meeting the learning needs of culturally and ethnically diverse students (p. 92). These strategies, as do several culturally and ethnically responsive strategies, prioritize collaborative learning, open oral discourse, and active student-directed learning activities.

CONCLUSION

Young adolescence is an intense time of cognitive, social, cultural, and ethnic awareness. Schools are the breeding grounds for either healthy or unhealthy development of young adolescents' attitudes, feelings, and acceptance of their cultural and ethnic heritage. Middle level educators have a major impact on how young adolescents come to accept their heritage based on how effective teachers are at demonstrating respect for and reacting appropriately to the needs of ethnically and culturally diverse students.

Teachers' acceptance of culturally responsive instruction depends on an understanding of the learning needs of culturally and ethnically diverse students, positive attitudes toward the acceptance and need for differing strategies, and a clear awareness of how changing instruction can impact the learning of diverse students. Despite good intentions of university professors of preservice and inservice teachers and school administrators, genuine classroom practice will not change to meet the needs of culturally and ethnically diverse students until teachers understand and implement the instructional processes supported by research that create success for students. The strategies that teachers must implement to help culturally diverse students succeed are not merely as many teachers perceive "effective strategies for all learners." African, Hispanic, Asian, and Native American students as well as other immigrant students have distinct needs that must become a part of the culture of teaching in American classrooms that all teachers accept and implement. More ethnically and culturally diverse young adolescents will succeed and excel as learners in American classrooms as responsive instructional strategies become standard operational procedure for middle level teachers. Until that time, middle level teachers and students will continue to blame each other for the failure of culturally diverse learners, a failure that rests primarily with the adults who control classroom events and environments. This failure doesn't need to occur if teachers can adopt and continue to add to this list of culturally responsive strategies.

REFERENCES

Bennett, C. I. (1990). *Comprehensive multicultural education: Theory and practice* (2nd ed.). Needham Heights, MA: Allyn & Bacon.

Bennett, C. (2001). Genres of multicultural education. *Review of Educational Research, 71*(2), 171–217.

Brown, D. F. (2002). *Becoming a successful urban teacher.* Portsmouth, NH, & Westerville, OH: Heinemann and National Middle School Association.

Cary, S. (2000). *Working with second language learners: Answers to teachers' top ten questions.* Portsmouth, NH: Heinemann.

Darling-Hammond, L. (2001). The challenge of staffing our schools. *Educational Leadership, 58*(8), 12–17.

Delpit, L. (1995). *Other people's children: Cultural conflict in the classroom.* New York: New Press.

Dwyer, C. (1991). *Language, culture, and writing* (Working paper no. 13). Berkeley: University of California, Center for the Study of Writing.

Fullilove, R. E., & Treisman, P. U. (1990). Mathematics achievement among African American undergraduates at the University of California, Berkeley: An evaluation of the mathematics workshop program. *Journal of Negro Education, 59*(3), 463–478.

Garcia, E. (1999). *Student cultural diversity: Understanding and meeting the challenge* (2nd ed.). Boston: Houghton Mifflin.

Gay, G. (1994). Coming of age ethnically: Teaching young adolescents of color. *Theory Into Practice, 33*(3), 149–155.

Gay, G. (2000). *Culturally responsive teaching: Theory, research, and practice.* New York: Teachers College Press.

Henry, T., & Kasindorf, M. (1997, February 27). Testing could be *the* test for Bush plan. *USA Today,* p. 2A.

Howard, G. R. (1999). *We can't teach what we don't know: White teachers, multiracial schools.* New York: Teachers College Press.

Howard, T. C. (2001). Powerful pedagogy for African American students: A case study of four teachers. *Urban Education, 36*(2), 179–201.

Jennings, P. (2001, March 7). *World News Tonight.* New York: American Broadcast Company.

Katz, S. R. (1999). Teaching in tensions: Latino immigrant youth, their teachers, and the structures of schooling. *Teachers College Record, 100*(4), 809–840.

Kline, L. W. (1995). A baker's dozen: Effective instructional strategies. In R. W. Cole (Ed.), *Educating everybody's children: Diverse teaching strategies for diverse learners* (pp. 21–45). Alexandria, VA: Association for Supervision and Curriculum Development.

Kohn, A. (1999). *The schools our children deserve: Moving beyond traditional classrooms and "tougher standards."* Boston: Houghton Mifflin.

Kohn, A. (2000). *The case against standardized tests: Raising the scores, ruining the schools.* Portsmouth, NH: Heinemann.

Ladson-Billings, G. (2001). *Crossing over to Canaan: The journey of new teachers in diverse classrooms.* San Francisco: Jossey-Bass.

Lee, C. (1993). *Signifying as a scaffold to literary interpretation: The pedagogical implications of a form of African American discourse* (National Council of Teachers of English Research Report No. 26). Urbana, IL: National Council of Teachers of English.

Lipsey, M. W., & Wilson, D. B. (1993). The efficacy of psychological, educational, and behavioral treatment. *American Psychologist, 48*(12), 1181–1209.

Marcias, R F., & Kelly, C. (1996). *Summary of the report of the survey of the states' limited English proficient students and available educational programs and services, 1994–1995.* Washington, DC: National Clearinghouse for Bilingual Education.

National Education Association. (2001, March 19). The bottom line. *National Education Association Today.*

Necochea, J., Stowell, L. P., McDaniel, J. E., Lorimer, M., & Kritzer, C. (2001). Rethinking middle level education for the 21st century. In V. A. Anfara, Jr. (Ed.), *The handbook of research in middle level education* (pp. 161–181). Greenwich, CT: Information Age Publishing.

Nieto, S. (1999). *The light in their eyes: Creating multicultural learning communities.* New York: Teachers College Press.

Obidah, J. E., & Manheim Teel, K. (2001). *Because of the kids: Facing racial and cultural differences in schools.* New York: Teachers College Press.

Parkay, F. W., & Hass, G. (2000). *Curriculum planning: A contemporary approach* (7th ed.). Needham Heights, MA: Allyn & Bacon.

Quintana, S. M. (1998). Children's developmental understanding of ethnicity and race. *Applied and Preventive Psychology, 7,* 27–45.

Rice, F. P. (1999). *The adolescent: Development, relationships, and culture* (9th ed.). Needham Heights, MA: Allyn & Bacon.

Rong, X. L., & Preisssle, J. (1998). *Educating immigrant students.* Thousand Oaks, CA: Corwin Press.

Ruddell, R. B. (1999). *Teaching children to read and write: Becoming an influential teacher* (2nd ed.). Needham Heights, MA: Allyn & Bacon.

Saravia-Shore, M., & Garcia, E. (1995). Diverse teaching strategies for diverse learners. In R. W. Cole (Ed.), *Educating everybody's children: Diverse teaching strategies for diverse learners* (pp. 47–74). Alexandria, VA: Association for Supervision and Curriculum Development.

Slavin, R. E. (1991). Synthesis of research on cooperative learning. *Educational Leadership, 48*(5), 71–77, 79–82.

Sleeter, C. E. (1992). *Keepers of the American dream: A study of staff development and multicultural education.* London: Falmer Press.

Walberg, H. J. (1999). Productive teaching. In H. C. Waxman & H. J. Walberg (Eds.), *New directions for teaching: Practice and research* (pp. 75–104). Berkeley, CA: McCutchen.

Weiner, L. (2000). Research in the 90s: Implications for urban teacher preparation. *Review of Educational Research, 70*(3), 369–406.

Wlodkowski, R. J., & Ginsberg, M. B. (1995). *Diversity and motivation: Culturally responsive teaching.* San Francisco: Jossey-Bass.

CHAPTER 5

EVERY STUDENT AND *EVERY* TEACHER

Crossing the Boundaries of Middle Level, TESOL, Bilingual, and Special Education

Ellen Skilton-Sylvester
Temple University
Graciela Slesaransky-Poe
Arcadia University

ABSTRACT

Drawing on sources from the middle school reform, language education and special education literatures, and interviews with teachers and administrators in Philadelphia, the authors propose an integrated, holistic, and dynamic model for meeting the instructional needs of linguistically diverse students with disabilities. This vision requires thinking about more than language (but also culture and community) and creating not only the least restrictive environment but also the most inclusive environment for instruction. In particular, we argue that teacher collaboration, cross-fertilization, and inquiry are central to meeting the needs of this population and that the needs of

Middle School Curriculum, Instruction, and Assessment, pages 75–102
Copyright © 2002 by Information Age Publishing
All rights of reproduction in any form reserved.

these students are the responsibility of all teachers. A central part of this vision is the belief that finding ways to improve education involves the insights and ideas of teachers who are in the process of teaching students each day and of administrators who are working to improve instruction from within the current system.

For several years, we have been reflecting about the intersection of Teaching English to Speakers of Other Languages (TESOL), bilingual, and special education. We have been looking forward to finding ways to investigate formally where our scholarly interests intersect. As language and special education scholars, our own training has been separated by disciplinary boundaries. This chapter is an attempt to cross these boundaries, not only for us but also for these fields. Our interest is personal and professional. Skilton-Sylvester's area of expertise is language education, and she has been particularly interested in special education issues as a result of having seen friends and family members separated from their general education peers due to their learning disabilities. On a professional level, these issues became important in her work with the School District of Philadelphia as a result of a class-action suit filed on behalf of Asian students because many had been erroneously placed in self-contained special education classrooms. Slesaransky-Poe speaks Spanish as her first language and specializes in special education. On a professional level, she has been aware and concerned with the overrepresentation of students, especially boys, of diverse cultural and linguistic backgrounds in special education. What unites our interest and inquiry is our belief (a) in the possibility and potential of an integrated model for teaching linguistically diverse students with disabilities, and (b) that this will only be accomplished by listening to teachers and administrators and ensuring that teachers are involved in the process of creating solutions.

More specifically, with regard to the middle grades, our inquiry and discussions have made us realize that the needs of these students at this stage require in-depth consideration. English for Speakers of Other Languages (ESOL), bilingual, and special education teachers and administrators often discuss the increased language and content demands as students enter the middle grades and the social, academic, and linguistic struggles that occur at this moment even when students have previously been finding success in school. These concerns are echoed more generally in the current focus of the middle school reform movement on meeting the needs of *every* student. As stated in *Turning Points 2000*, "[The] vision... includes every student in the middle grades, even English language learners and those who may have substantial disabilities or who receive special education services" (Jackson & Davis, 2000, p. 22). Although the needs of both English language learners and students with disabilities are included in this vision, the particular needs of English language learners with disabilities.[1] are not often discussed in the middle school reform literature. This is not only true in relation to middle school reform, but also in terms of most other reform efforts. As Thurlow and Liu (2001) state, "None of the rhetoric of reform has recognized the group of students with disabilities who are also students with limited English proficiency (LEP)" (p. 64).[2] If meeting the needs of *every* student in the middle grades is a priority, we need to explore the particular experiences and needs of this student population.

LEARNING FROM LOCAL TEACHERS AND ADMINISTRATORS[3]

The data on which this chapter is based come from our interactions and interviews with teachers and administrators, many of whom are members of the English Language Learners/Special Education Steering and Planning Committees of the School District of Philadelphia. The purpose of this Steering Committee is advocating "for equity in education and support services for children who are English Language Learners and eligible for special education or gifted programs and services in partnership with all stakeholders, especially families and communities" (School District of Philadelphia, 2002).

In our search for "best practices" in this area, several teachers were recommended to us as examples of those who are finding success in crossing boundaries to build new kinds of instruction for this group of students. In the end, we interviewed eight teachers (see Table 5.1) who work or have worked with young adolescents and cross the boundaries of middle level education, TESOL, bilingual, and special education either as individuals or as members of a team (see the Appendix at the end of the chapter for interview questions). These interviews were starting points for identifying issues, concerns, and best practices and for identifying the beliefs and ideologies that are at the foundation of current institutional and instructional structures and those that might guide future research and practice concerning middle level linguistically diverse students with disabilities.

In addition to these teachers, we interviewed the cofacilitators of the English Language Learner/Special Education Steering Committee, one a special education administrator and the other a language education administrator. Finally, we observed and participated in monthly meetings of the ELL/Special Education Coordinating Committee over a six-month period. Data were analyzed using inductive analytic strategies or what LeCompte and Schensul (1999) call "analysis from the bottom–up."

Table 5.1.   Teacher Positions and Educational Backgrounds

Teacher[4]	Position	Educational Background
Cindy	ESOL teacher	BA in English/Reading & French; Certification in High School English & French; Masters in English Education
Jennifer	ESOL teacher	BA in Elementary Education; Masters in Bilingual/Bicultural Studies
Naomi	Bilingual teacher	BS in Spanish Education; Masters in Elementary Education; Principal's Certificate; Reading Specialist; Doctoral student
Marina	Special education teacher (bilingual)	BA in English; Masters in Special Education
Lori	ESOL teacher (has also bilingual teacher)	BA in Spanish (K–12); Masters in TESOL; In-Service Professional Development in Special Education
Pamela	ESOL teacher	Certified in Elementary Education; Masters in TESOL
Valeria	Special educational teacher (bilingual)	BA in Psychology; Masters in Special Education (for bilingual teachers)
Elena	Apprentice teacher/special education	BA in Social Work; Currently attending Special Education Master's Program

Middle Level Education for English Language Learners with Disabilities

Much of the literature on middle level education has addressed the multiple changes that students experience during these grades. In the following quote, Eric (age 13) discusses some of these issues:

> Being a young adolescent is very cool because you are going through lots of changes—like, your body is changing, and your voice is cracking, and it is a new environment. And I am meeting lots of people I never met before and switching class. I don't have recess anymore. (Knowles & Brown, 2000, p. 8)

In addition to the physical, social, emotional, and environmental changes that students experience when entering middle school, there is also sometimes a shift from student-centered to subject-centered approaches. As it is commonly said, "Elementary teachers teach children, middle school teachers teach subjects."

These shifts present specific challenges for linguistically diverse students with or without disabilities and their teachers. As one ESOL teacher explained, "In fifth and sixth grade, there's just a shift in English demands" (fieldnotes, May 11, 2001). One bilingual special education teacher explained,

> I have recently learned that most students who drop out do so in the seventh grade. (formerly it was ninth grade). This indicates how important it is to provide interesting and motivating programs—a great challenge for students with poor literacy skills, and an even greater one when students who are not literate in their first language are trying to acquire English. (Marina, personal communication, 1/21/02)

One ESOL teacher said: "I perceive that middle school-age students are more sensitive to the social implications of their learning 'different-ness'" (Pamela, personal communication, January 28, 2002). In addition to English demands, the social implications of "different-ness" in the middle grades, and physical and emotional changes, teachers also discuss the academic demands for English language learners with disabilities. In discussing these issues, teachers also indicate uncertainty about how to address the particular needs of middle level English language learners with disabilities. They also discuss a frustration that much of the published research does not address their particular concerns about these students (fieldnotes, May 11, 2001).

Administrators also recognize the academic challenges of middle schools for these students. They are concerned with the behavior problems that appear in this level and the implications for referrals to special education. For example, a special education administrator expressed,

> That's when dramatic behaviors develop.... It's the middle years where the discipline office has the most requests for transfers.... So that's probably the biggest [issue].... I mean it's a cultural shock for kids...especially if it's a special ed kid. They probably in elementary school were treated very differently and then all of a sudden, they're in a building that's three or four times the size it was before. And so I can imagine what it's like. (personal communication, February 1, 2002)

A language education administrator added to this comment, saying:

Yeah, it would be those issues magnified because of the sociolinguistic issues on top of that.... You know, the cultural differences, everything, expectations and then not having English proficiency. (personal communication, February 1, 2002)

These comments from teachers and administrators about middle level English language learners with disabilities illustrate commonalities with the experiences of 13-year-old Eric (and millions of other students who speak English as their primary language), in terms of the complex emotional, social, and academic changes that middle school engenders.

In addition, their insights about linguistically diverse students with disabilities at this level show this population's distinct and diverse needs related to language, culture, and disability. Imagine, for example, the demands that are placed on a student who recently immigrated to the United States, has a disability, is attending middle school, and had little previous schooling in his or her country of origin. As compelling as this example is, however, it is also important to remember the depth of diversity found among students with disabilities who are English language learners. The child sitting next to that child may also be bilingual but may have had extensive schooling in his or her primary language. Even if they share the same disability, their needs would be quite different in the classroom.

THE LEGAL BASIS OF CURRENT STRUCTURES: WHAT *EVERY* TEACHER NEEDS TO KNOW

At present, two separate systems address the needs of English language learners with disabilities. These systems are special education and language education programs. The educational legal system has reinforced the separateness of these two systems and has supported the notion that what is important is tangible and functionally related to school success. As a result, administrators must provide appropriate education services that come from two separate systems with different priorities, allocations, resources, and expertise. Students who are English language learners with disabilities, families, and teachers are often all caught in the middle, pulled in two different directions. We contend that even though the legal system separates them, ESOL, bilingual, and special education services cannot be seen as separate for linguistically diverse students with disabilities. Even so, all educators need to know the legal imperatives for meeting the needs of these students. The antecedents to more recent legal imperatives date back to *Brown v. Board of Education* (1954). In this case, the U.S. Supreme Court ruled that it was unlawful to discriminate arbitrarily against any group of people and that separate education is not equal.

Legal Foundations for Special Education

Even though many laws shape the education of students with disabilities, including Section 504 of the Vocational Rehabilitation Act (1973) and the Americans with Disabilities Act (1990), the Individuals with Disabilities Education Act is the single most central federal law that determines the basis of educational polices and practices for these students. Signed in 1975 under the name of Education of the Handicapped Act (P.L. 94–142), changed to the Individuals with Disabilities Education Act (IDEA, P.L.101–476) in 1990, and reauthorized in 1997, this act mandates that Free Appropriate Public Education (FAPE) for students with disabilities should be provided in the Least Restrictive Environment (LRE). According to IDEA,

> To the maximum extent appropriate, children with disabilities, including children in public or private institutions or other care facilities, are educated with children who are nondisabled; and that special classes, separate schooling or other removal of children with disabilities from the regular educational environment occurs only if the nature or severity of the disability is such that education in regular classes with the use of supplementary aids and services cannot be achieved satisfactorily. (IDEA §300.550 (a))

When education in the general education classroom, even with supports, cannot be attained satisfactorily, two options are presented by the law: (a) to provide a continuum of placement options for students receiving special education services to meet the unique needs of each child with a disability (this continuum includes instruction in general education classroom, special education classroom, special education schools, home instruction, and instruction in hospitals and institutions); and (b) to provide for supplementary services (such as resource room or itinerant instruction) to be provided in conjunction with regular class placement (IDEA §300.551(a)).

Each student receiving special education services should have an Individualized Education Program, or IEP. The term "individualized education program" means a written statement for each child with a disability that is developed, reviewed, and revised that includes (a) the child's present levels of educational performance, including a statement of measurable annual goals, benchmarks, or short-term objectives; (b) the special education and related services and supplementary aids and services to be provided to the child; an explanation of the extent, if any, to which the child will not participate with nondisabled children in the regular class and in the activities; and (c) any individual modifications in the administration of state or districtwide assessments of student achievement that are needed in order for the child to participate in such assessment (IDEA §300.340(a)).

Legal Foundations for ESOL and Bilingual Services

Unlike special education, no federal law specifically addresses the linguistic rights of students. The foundation of court decisions concerning acquisition policy in the schools has come not from the 1968 Bilingual Education Act, but from the 1964 Civil Rights Act and the 1974 Equal Education Opportunities Act. The Civil Rights Act (Title VI) does not specifically address the language issue but instead focuses on race and national origin as the basis of discrimination. The Equal Education Opportunities Act, however, "incorporated the *Lau* mandate. This led in turn to further precedents, such as *Castaneda v. Pickard*, which established a legal standard for 'appropriate action' by schools: programs for LEP students must be sound in theory, provided with sufficient resources in practice, and monitored for effectiveness, with improvements made when necessary" (Crawford, 1996). The Equal Educational Opportunities Act includes "the failure by an educational agency to take appropriate action to overcome language barriers that impede equal participation by its students in its instructional programs" (August & Garcia, 1988, p. 59) as a criterion for determining the denial of equal educational opportunity in the schools. What this means is that language issues in K–12 schools have been made based on the question of whether students' civil rights are being met and whether or not schools have done what they need to do to provide equal educational opportunity.

In *Lau v. Nichols*, the Supreme Court set policy and precedent addressing the needs of linguistic minority students. In this case, "The Court found that Title VI was violated when there was the *effect* of discrimination, although there was no *intent*" (Malakoff & Hakuta, 1990, p. 34). Providing the same services, books, and facilities for linguistic minority students as for others was simply not enough. One outcome of the Lau decision was the *Lau Remedies*, which have directly influenced many subsequent cases *but have not mandated particular types of instruction* (i.e., ESOL, bilingual, sheltered, etc.). These guidelines were published in 1975 by the U.S. Department of Health, Education, and Welfare to assist school districts in developing programs for linguistic minorities. These guidelines specified procedures for evaluating language skills, developing appropriate educational programs, deciding when students could be mainstreamed, and identifying professional standards for teachers (Lyons, 1990, p. 66).

Because of the general nature of the legal guidelines, states often have more specific legal mandates for what is required for adequately providing education for English language learners. For example, the state of Pennsylvania further clarifies the requirements by discussing the fact that the education of students whose dominant language is not English and/or are English language learners is the responsibility of every school district/charter school in the Commonwealth. Title 22, Chapter 4, Section 4.26 of the Curriculum Regulations requires that the school district/charter school provide a program for every student who has limited English proficiency (LEP) or is an English language learner (ELL). The regulation states: "Every school district shall provide a program for each student whose dominant language is not English for the purpose of facilitating the student's achievement of English proficiency and the academic standards under §4.12 (relating to academic standards). Programs under this section shall include appropriate bilingual-bicultural or English as a Second Language (ESL) instruction" (Pennsylvania Department of Education, n.d.). To comply with this requirement, a school district must provide the student with a planned program of English as a second language instruction to facilitate the acquisition of English language skills and provide an instructional program appropriate to the student's developmental and instructional level.

Interestingly, special education is based on specific legislation whereas language education is based on litigation (stemming from more general legislation that protects students' civil rights). This makes the guidelines for providing special education services much more specific and uniform than those for providing language-related services. Table 5.2 provides a comparison and contrast between mandates by the Individuals with Disabilities Act and recommendations of the Lau Remedies.[5] Because the *Lau Remedies* have never been "enforced" and are not law, many of the remedies have not been implemented (Crawford, 1996).

Table 5.2. Key Aspects of IDEA and Lau Remedies

	IDEA	*Lau Remedies*
Education plan	Individualized Educational Program (IEP)	No individualized language plan required; no formal language education plan required at the district level unless school district is found to be "out of compliance" with the Lau Remedies.
Initial evaluation	Parents can deny permission for initial assessment	Mandatory to assess for English language level; also requires assessment in the primary language.
Reassessment	At least every 3 years unless diagnosis is cognitive disability	Timing determined by individual school districts; criteria for when a student can "exit" language services required.

Table 5.2.   Key Aspects of IDEA and Lau Remedies (Cont.)

	IDEA	*Lau Remedies*
Parental role	Consent required for all assessment and placement decisions; parents are part of the IEP team	Appropriate assessment and placement decided by school personnel; parents can deny services and must be notified by the school in their primary language (if necessary) with any information that goes to other parents.
Involvement of multiple educational personnel	Individualized education team (for initial evaluation) should include the following members: student's parent(s), Local Education Agency (LEA) representative (principal or designee), referring teacher (generally the general education teacher), school psychologist, special education teacher, any other(s) determined necessary by the LEA, and student, when possible	Not required.
Placement	Least restrictive environment; Continuum includes general education classroom, resource room, self-contained classroom (students must also be able to participate in other school activities such as clubs, sports, etc.); placement should be reviewed annually	"Appropriate" placement with access to content (can be provided through ESOL, bilingual, or sheltered content instruction; students must also be able to participate in other school activities such as clubs, sports, etc.); the Lau Remedies officially state that ESL instruction alone is not enough (and that native language instruction must be available if there are more than 20 students who speak a particular language within the school district). However, this is monitored only on a case-by-case basis.
Monitoring program success	IEP should be reviewed at least annually	Determined by local schools and school districts; required for schools found to be "out of compliance" for 3 years after plan is submitted.

In this section we have described the lack of integration in the legal foundations for meeting the needs of linguistically diverse students with disabilities. Now, we present the aspects in which the boundaries of both systems intersect.

According to IDEA, procedures for evaluation and determination of eligibility for special education services should be free of cultural and linguistic bias.

> Tests and other evaluation materials used to assess a child … are selected and administered so as not to be discriminatory on a racial or cultural basis; and are provided and administered in the child's native language or other mode of communication.… Materials and procedures used to assess a child with limited English proficiency are selected and administered to ensure that they measure the extent which the child has a disability and needs special education, rather than measuring the child's English language skills. (IDEA, §300.532(a))

In order for a child to be assessed to determine eligibility, IDEA mandates parental consent (see Table 5.2). When parents are not able to communicate in English either orally or in writing, IDEA has created procedural safeguards that require that the parents (a) be fully informed in their native language about the procedures and (b) communicate in their native language about their consent (IDEA, §300.500(a)).

In spite of the fact that IDEA has created these safeguards, in some cases they are not implemented. Such is the example of the class action suit, *Y.S. v. School District of Philadelphia*, in which the original plaintiff was a Cambodian student who was erroneously receiving special education services in a self-contained classroom. In this case, the school district was not in compliance with the two procedures addressed by IDEA and discussed above: assessment and consent.

In spite of the clear benefits of the legal system in providing a framework for addressing the needs of students who are often seen as on the margins of the U.S. educational system, relying on the legal system also reinforces an instrumental orientation to education (Skilton-Sylvester, in press). This orientation can ignore the curricular and instructional aspects of schooling that cannot be mandated by law but require engaged educational professionals working with particular students in particular contexts. It is to this issue that we now turn. In addition to knowing the law, educators need to take ownership of the education of linguistically diverse student s with disabilities. This will, we believe, require rethinking some of the basic assumptions behind the current system.

TOWARD A HOLISTIC, INTEGRATED MODEL

One of the striking aspects about the teacher interviews is the extent of the differences in orientations and practices that exist across schools and classrooms. At one end of the continuum, a teacher discussed the former principal who decided that students could receive *either* ESOL or special education support but not both. This teacher's concept of an ideal situation included:

> [Having] enough teachers to *divide students by ability in language, age and math* [italics added]. Students have been grouped by ability in language in my school, which means there may be eighth graders (13 years old) mixed with fifth graders (10 years old). Targeting interests for both groups may then be a challenge. (Cindy, personal communication, February 6, 2002)

This vision is one where those with like interests and abilities are grouped together and taught separately. She raises interesting questions about the degree to which heterogeneous grouping can work when linguistic, academic, and age-related differences are present. On the other hand, a teacher at another school describes the ideal situation in a different way. She said:

> There would be adequate resources for testing for any and every child who presented significant needs, and adequate resources to meet the needs, once documented. [There would be] resources for in-depth and continuous staff development and *staff support around both ESOL and special education needs in the regular classroom* [italics added]. Adaptive technology would be widely available. (Pamela, personal communication, January 28, 2002)

What is interesting about the visions of these teachers is that they differ quite substantially in terms of what the solution would be. One is envisioning how to increase the benefits of separate services in separate contexts, whereas the other is envisioning what it would take to improve instruction within the general education classroom for all students. Improving services for these students will require complex solutions grounded in local considerations of resources within particular schools and school districts. Solutions will also involve rethinking the tradition of separating students due to their linguistic and disability differences, increasing supports for students and teachers in heterogeneous classrooms, separating students only when absolutely necessary, and finding ways during or after the school day to give students opportunities to connect with others who share their language, culture, and disability.

What we are proposing in this chapter is geared toward all teachers in their work to meet the needs of all students. In particular, this chapter focuses on the ways that middle level content area teachers can work in concert with specialists to address the needs of linguistically diverse students with disabilities in their classrooms. Many reform movements, including middle school reform, focus on meeting the needs of *every* student. We believe that this requires not only the specific knowledge of specialist teachers, but also the common core of knowledge and expertise of *every* teacher. The audience for this chapter is each and every teacher who interacts with culturally and linguistically diverse students with disabilities for any part of the school day.

As mentioned earlier, the current structure consists of two parallel systems for addressing the needs of these students. Having separate systems reinforces the image of ESOL, bilingual and special education as places, when in reality they are services that could be provided in multiple settings. Several researchers (Gallegos & McCarty, 2000; Valles, 1998) suggest that it is only through moving beyond traditional disciplinary boundaries that we can hope to address the real and pressing needs of both teachers and students. Both teachers and administrators in Philadelphia support this idea. As one special education administrator in Philadelphia says,

> [Special education teachers] think "I am a part-time LS [learning support] teacher; I am a full-time LS teacher, I am an emotional support teacher," and I say, "There is no such thing. You're a special ed teacher." And then I say to all the regular ed teachers in the room, "You are all special ed teachers too! Whether you know it or not, you just don't have a degree in it, but *everybody in Philadelphia is a special ed teacher as far as I am concerned*" [italics added]. And a special ed teacher is a regular ed teacher. (personal communication, February 1, 2002)

Similarly, an ESOL teacher discusses the need for all teachers to see themselves as English teachers. He says,

> In some cases, we may encounter content teachers who are receptive to input from ESL professionals. On the other hand, many of them don't think teaching language is their job (even though movements like "reading in the content areas" and "writing across the curriculum" and their advocates have been saying for years that *every teacher is a teacher of English* [italics added]). (listserv discussion, February 22, 2002)

One of the bilingual special education teachers we interviewed also echoed this vision. She explained,

> Anyone considering a career in education today should be prepared to work with culturally and linguistically diverse students. Emphasis needs to be placed on strategies that promote communication and comprehension, attention must be paid to students' emotional development, and programs need to be designed in a way that encourages students to feel connected to institutions that develop strong academic skills. In addition, we need to rec-

ognize those who speak languages other than English as resources to us all. (Marina, personal communication, January 21, 2002)

Our point is very much in line with what these educators are saying: although we need specialists, we also believe that every teacher is both a special education teacher and an English teacher. In addition, although all teachers may not be bilingual, it is possible to encourage bilingualism and see students' languages as resources regardless of teachers' own linguistic repertoires (Cummins, 2000).

A metaphor that may be helpful in thinking through what we are proposing has to do with more recent views of how a bilingual mind works. Traditionally, people have thought about bilinguals as having two separate language systems rather than one complex system that includes two languages. However, as Cenoz and Genesee (1998) suggest, "The language competence of bilinguals should not be regarded as simply the sum of two monolingual competencies" (p. 18). Grosjean (1989, 1992) and Cook (1992, 1993, 1995) discuss a "holistic" view that sees the multiple languages of multilingual speakers as part of a single, complex, and ever-changing system. Cook (1992) has suggested the notion of "multicompetence" to highlight the positive benefits of knowing more than one language, the fact that one might not know all languages in one's linguistic repertoire to the same degree, and the fact that knowledge of multiple languages is part of an integrated system rather than separate systems. In our work on this chapter, we have come to see this as a useful metaphor for a new way of thinking about meeting the needs of culturally and linguistically diverse students with disabilities.

To move toward a holistic, integrated, and dynamic system for meeting the needs of linguistically diverse students with disabilities, both philosophical and practical changes will need to take place. In the following sections, we talk about some of the ways our thinking and our practices will need to change to accomplish this vision. In addition to a paradigm shift in the ways we think about the needs of linguistically diverse students with disabilities, we also believe that we need to take practical steps to change the ways we think about the professional development of teachers. Changes in both our orientations and our actions will be needed to move toward an integrated system for meeting the needs of these students.

MORE THAN LANGUAGE, CONTENT, AND DISABILITY: FROM LEAST RESTRICTIVE ENVIRONMENT TO MOST INCLUSIVE ENVIRONMENT

The New London Group (1996) has suggested that difference has become a core, mainstream issue in our current world. As a result, teaching in heterogeneous classrooms has also become the norm rather than the exception (Cohen & Lotan, 1997). Understanding how to address linguistic, cultural, learning, and behavior differences in the classroom in creative and productive ways is an essential part of the future of education and requires complex rather than simple answers. Central to this shift is working hard to see the strengths of all students and their families.

In basing our instructional decisions on the legal system, part of what has gotten lost are the less instrumental aspects of the education of linguistically diverse students with disabilities. In legal provisions, research literature, and teacher and administrator comments, the focus is on language, access to content instruction, and the nature of the disability (as measured by tests). What gets much less attention are the variety of cultural beliefs of students, families, and schools about language culture, disability, and the purposes of education as well as what it takes to create classroom and school communities that value and respect all students. Moving beyond an exclusive emphasis on language, content, and the nature of the disability is a key step in creating an integrated, holistic, and dynamic system.

In reading *Turning Points 2000*, it seems clear that thought is being given to the linguistic and curriculum-related needs of middle level English language learners and students with disabilities. However, mentioned previously, these groups are addressed separately. An example of the emphasis on language and content can be seen in the following statement: "At the middle grades level, the focus should be on getting students to read in English as quickly as possible and ensuring that they have access to appropriate-level content in the meantime" (Jackson & Davis, 2000, p. 93). Although this statement is in line with commonplace assumptions about the role of other languages in the classroom, it does not take into consideration several aspects: (1) the value of the student's primary language; (2) the fact that research suggests that bilingual instruction may be particularly useful for English language learners with learning disabilities (Baca & Cervantes, 1998); (3) the reality that cultural diversity (and not just linguistic diversity) is central to the experiences of these students in school; and (4) that relationships between parents and schools are crucially connected to cultural expectations about home–school relationships. Lara's (1995) case study of English language learners at a middle school going through the reform process illustrates some of the challenges teachers face in addressing cultural and linguistic diversity during the middle years:

> The instructional design and staffing pattern at Vista prevents the staff from tapping into the linguistic knowledge of the students, even though some of the classrooms incorporate primary languages.... These efforts to use primary languages are commendable, though they are not teacher initiated and are inconsistent. Consequently, the impact on student learning is minimal....

One teacher mentioned that he uses multicultural literature in his language arts class; but most responses reflected a different message: The cultural heritage of the students is not openly recognized as a resource for enrichment. Teachers' references to cultural diversity were almost always made in the context of the problem that it presents to the school, rather than its possibilities. (pp. 22–23)

In spite of a caring and dedicated staff, the orientation is toward seeing this kind of diversity as a problem to be overcome rather than a resource for the school.

Like the language field's primary emphasis on language and access to content, the special education field has had a primary emphasis on the education of students in the "least restrictive environment" and the accurate assessment of disabilities. The IDEA defines "least restrictive environment" in this way:

To the maximum extent appropriate, children with disabilities, including children in public or private institutions or other care facilities, are educated with children who are not disabled, and special classes, separate schooling, or *other removal of children with disabilities from the regular educational environment* [italics added] occurs only when the nature or severity of the disability of a child is such that education in regular classes with the use of supplementary aids and services cannot be achieved satisfactorily. (IDEA Sec. 612.(5)(B)

Here again, it is possible to see an emphasis on the instrumental functions of the classroom, and on the place where education happens. As a local special education administrator says,

The...big problem I think we have here in Philadelphia is the way we use teachers...whether they're ESL teachers or special ed teachers. They tend to be in their own space; kids go to them. And that's, I think, the biggest barrier we need to break down. Those people should live in the building and not in a place so that...unless it's really intensive instruction, the ESL teacher should be going to fourth grade, a special ed teacher should be going to nine, you know, the ninth grade algebra...and supporting kids in that setting. (personal communication, February 1, 2002)

Although the shift from thinking of special education or ESOL as a place to a service is an important one, it is also important to think about the ways in which the least restrictive environment can become one that embraces the many kinds of differences, and not just learning differences, found in the classroom.

Recent work in the area of special education for English language learners has begun to address the "cultural characteristics" of students as an essential part of the work of teaching and learning in the classroom.

Cloud's (in press) work is particularly useful in that it both makes the case that culturally responsive pedagogy is essential for linguistically diverse students with disabilities, but also underscores multiple times that "teachers can expect to find variations both between and within groups" (p. 11) and that "culture is a dynamic and complex phenomenon" (p. 12). In addition, she addresses the central importance of the relationship between home and school for bilingual students and the ways in which norms for interaction within classrooms and between parents and teachers vary considerably across and within cultural groups.

In Cloud's (in press) discussion of culture, community, and relationships, the emphasis is quite productively directed toward the ways in which teachers need to learn about the beliefs, preferences, and practices of their culturally and linguistically diverse students who have disabilities and to incorporate this knowledge into their curriculum and classroom practices. However, what is missing from this discussion are the essential ways that classrooms create communities within the school context that are also crucially connected to the learning of students. As Cummins (2000) suggests, "The starting point for understanding why students choose to engage academically or withdraw from academic effort is to acknowledge that *human relationships are at the heart of schooling*" (p. 40).

In a similar vein, the Civil Rights Project at Harvard University recently released findings of a study on the connections between racial and ethnic diversity and academic success for students at Cambridge's public high school. The report shows "overwhelmingly positive effects" of diversity that are often ignored in current discussions on education policy: "Most discussion on education is on math and reading scores. We didn't create public schools for math and reading scores.... Our study goes beyond math and reading scores. It is about life, about community, and about experiences" (Orfield, n.d.). One of the students surveyed wrote: "Living and learning among different people has made me a strong, mature individual and student. I'm thankful that I have been able to internalize what diversity is and its importance in a school, community, and the world" (Skier, n.d.).

One important issue not typically addressed in thinking about the impact of culture in meeting the needs of this student population is the way that the notion of "disability" itself is socially and culturally constructed. Family and school assessments of what counts as a disability may be in conflict with each other. As Meyen and Skrtic (1995) suggest, "Disability is a particular frame of mind by which to organize the world.... It also has symbolic meaning in terms of what society values and what it degrades" (as cited in Gallegos & McCarty, 2000, p. 266). Our definitions of disability are not facts, but rather socially and culturally constructed values. This is a crucial aspect of disability to address, particularly in meeting the needs of linguistically diverse students with disabilities.

The teachers we interviewed talked about culture in multiple ways that had to do both with students' countries of origin and with the multilingual and multicultural interaction of the classroom. One ESOL teacher said,

> Of course, the other piece is that we also have to have cultural sensitivity about how middle level students interact with each other. If we think in terms of learning styles...some students need to get up and interact and move around and other students prefer to be lectured to. It's very important to be sensitive to learning styles from different cultures and even their own individual learning styles to be able to integrate content knowledge. I have to be extremely flexible.... I think it's really important for teachers to learn as much as they can about the cultures of the students they work with.... It helps in interacting with the parents ...so you're not in the dark. (Lori, personal communication, February 20, 2002)

In this quote, the teacher shows that the importance of culture does not have to do with what Cary (2000) has called the "concrete culture trap." Instead, it has to do with looking at individual student differences and finding ways to include all students in the rhythm of the classroom.

One of the ESOL teachers we interviewed talked about the optimal conditions for meeting the needs of culturally and linguistically diverse students with disabilities. She also discusses the flexibility and responsiveness to student interests needed to create a stimulating classroom community for all. She said:

> In the best of all possible worlds, with the greatest of resources, more constructivist schools would have the personalism and flexibility that could be deeply attractive to all learners, across cultural lines. IEPs are individualized in terms of the rate at which special students are expected to achieve certain skills and knowledge, but there's nothing very individualized about the process. When I visit private schools on occasion and see students deeply engrossed in their own projects, free to move around and do their own productive thing with encouragement, guidance, and occasional corrections from caring adults, I am deeply angered that the children who need those settings the most are the ones who are least likely ever to have them. "What do you want to learn about?" What kid, special needs or not, is not turned on by that invitation? (Pamela, personal communication, February 18, 2002)

Our goals as educators are not just about addressing the instrumental needs of students, but rather the whole student. In terms of LRE, this means not just access to general education curriculum but full inclusion in the classroom and school community, which includes the cultural and affective dimensions. Teaching these students isn't just about language and special education, but making education culturally relevant in relation to home–school relationships, expectations about classroom participation, and content (Cloud, in press). It is also about creating classroom and school communities that respect the strengths and abilities of all students. This is a central dimension of an integrated system; education is not only about academics.

A MODEL FOR PROFESSIONAL DEVELOPMENT: TEACHER COLLABORATION, CROSS-FERTILIZATION, AND INQUIRY

Freeman (1996) has discussed three conceptions of teacher education. The first is the behavioral view, which sees "teaching as doing." This perspective has supported a process–product view of teaching and learning. That is, if teachers use the right techniques (regardless of context), they will be good teachers. The second is the cognitive view, which sees "teaching as thinking and doing." This view has lead to thinking about the decision making teachers are involved in as they teach. The final view is the interpretive view, which sees "teaching as knowing what to do." Within this perspective, teachers are professionals who continually assess their teaching context and try new things to meet the needs of their students.

Our vision of meeting the needs of linguistically diverse students requires an interpretive view. Within this conceptualization of teaching, Johnson (2000) has called for rethinking the knowledge base of teacher education so that it focuses on the activity of teaching itself. She discusses the importance of focusing on the teacher his/her self, as well as on what teachers do, where they do it, how they do it, when they do it, and why they do it. Our research takes as its premise that understanding the details of the "activity of teaching" of those who are successfully meeting the needs of linguistically diverse students with disabilities is an essential part of improving both teacher education and instructional services. Central to this model is a vision of teachers as active creators of knowledge through their practice and not merely implementers of mandated policies and procedures.

The model we are proposing includes three dimensions: collaboration, cross-fertilization, and teacher inquiry. These dimensions include all teachers and not only those who are seen as specialists in a particular area. Although we believe that there is a need for those with specialized knowledge and abilities, we also believe that *every* teacher has some responsibility for the learning of *every* student. This is a call for a shift in the way we think about the domains of responsibility of teachers and the possibilities of differentiated learning. The notion of differentiated learning has strong support in the middle school reform literature (Jackson & Davis, 2000), the special education literature on inclusion (Flavely, 1995: Gianreco, 1997;

Villa & Thousand, 2000), and the TESOL literature's discussion of working with multilevel groups (Richards, 1998; Wrigley & Guth, 1992).

Teacher Collaboration

Ortiz (2001) makes several important suggestions about creating positive school environments where all students can find success. These include (a) emphasizing the need for preventive practices within the general education classroom; (b) stressing the importance of utilizing multiple approaches before formally referring a student to receive special education services; and (c) highlighting the importance of "shared decision-making among ESOL teachers, general education teachers, administrators, and parents" (p. 2). All three of these suggestions underscore the importance of collaboration among practitioners in schools in order to meet the needs of linguistically diverse students with disabilities.

Collaboration is more than having two or more teachers responsible for a group of students. As teacher educators from K–12, educational linguistics, and special education backgrounds, we have much work to do in figuring out how to help all teachers see the linguistic, learning, and subject-matter needs of each student as part of their responsibilities and not as someone else's (Lee & Fradd, 1998). Perhaps even more critically, we need to make collaboration among teachers more possible, both in the ways that we educate teachers and in the ways we structure the school day so that there is time for teachers to think together about instructional plans for the children. As DiPardo (1999, p. 153) suggests, "For all our talk about collaboration, we prepare new teachers in the same old individualistic ways, eventually certifying their capacity to function separately, lone adults in rooms full of kids. Perhaps what is most remarkable is not the relative absence of collaboration among teachers, but the fact that it ever takes place at all."

Collaboration is discussed by all of the teachers we interviewed. All see it as important and many struggle to find ways to make it work. As one bilingual teacher said, "We have the inclusion model. There is not nearly enough collaboration between teachers. Provisions are not made for teachers to collaborate" (Naomi, personal communication, January 28, 2002).

An ESOL teacher talks about it in relation to desperation. She said:

> I have a desperate need to collaborate with the regular classroom teachers of my fourth/fifth grade.... There is no support for collaboration, no time to plan. Teachers seem loath to plan after-school meetings for things like this, but I don't see how else it is going to happen.... The teachers as a group

seem stressed and preoccupied; hard to connect. (Pamela, personal communication, January 28, 2002)

Their comments make it clear that what is needed is not just support for how to collaborate effectively, but structural changes to the school day that would allow this to be possible.

Some steps have been made to shift structures so that this kind of collaboration can take place. As the cofacilitator of the English Language Learners/Special Education Steering and Planning Committees said:

> What we were trying to do is have team teaching in the classrooms between ESL teachers and grade teachers and it was hard to convince the first cohort of folks to try it out because they liked their little niche and they liked having their room.... But in any case, what we tried to do was also set the conditions so that kind of teamwork would be successful. So we insisted on having common planning time ... and then making sure that the teachers have a common philosophy of education and a common philosophy of discipline. In other words, they had the basis for a marriage, and it wasn't going to be this horrific partnership. (personal communication, February 1, 2002)

In addition to the need to create time for collaboration within the school day, this administrator acknowledges the need for common philosophies of education and discipline to make it work.

Findings from an earlier study investigating co-teaching among content and ESOL teachers (Skilton-Sylvester, Jimenez, & Laramee, 1998) suggest that meaningful collaboration among teachers of bilingual special education students requires at least the following: (1) teacher commitment to inclusive education; (2) teacher decision-making power, support from the principal, and flexibility with the school about how implementation of services happens; (3) teacher confidence in their own abilities as teachers; (4) trust in other members of the team; and (5) time for collaborative thinking, planning, and assessing.

Teacher Cross-Fertilization

In addition to needing experts about language, content, disabilities, and learning differences who can collaborate, our schools need teachers who have some general knowledge of all these areas, an ability to teach within heterogeneous groups, and a willingness to learn in the process of collaboration. Professional development across traditional disciplinary boundaries is also necessary as well as time within professional development sessions to share ideas and challenges with others doing similar work. It is not, however, enough to have experts learn information from other experts in looking at the intersections of their knowledge; it requires an integration of knowledge across boundaries. The integration of services for these students corresponds to a reintegration of many kinds of services in the work world and in education (Skilton-Sylvester, 1998) as our economy moves away from the assembly lines of yesterday and toward the future. In classrooms that work to provide engaging, stimulating, and successful learning experiences for bilingual, special education students, this reintegration of services is essential and one that involves both new ways of teaching children and new ways of preparing teachers.

Some of the teachers we met talked about the value of learning from those who have other specializations. One ESOL teacher said: "I think having coworkers who are special ed teachers [helps]. They help you to understand ways in which you can help these students. They support you and give you a better insight on the children you teach" (Jennifer, personal communication, January 20, 2002). Another teacher explained,

> If the special education teacher doesn't know about ESL, that can weaken the team just as much as if the ESOL teacher doesn't know about special education. It does help if there's some knowledge of the other field. There are some special education people at my school who are really interested in learning about languages issues, but there are others that don't feel like they have time to listen. It has to do with administrative support.... (Lori, personal communication, February 20, 2002)

This is one of the goals of the English Language Learner/Special Education Steering Committee in Philadelphia. As one of the cofacilitators said,

> One of the things that we say we try to do with our project is to have some cross-training between ESL and special ed teachers, so I think we still have to work on that part, but it's something that we aim to do. (personal communication, February 1, 2002)

In particular, teachers and administrators alike talk about the need for more explicit reading pedagogies addressing phonemic awareness for English language learners with disabilities. One administrator explained:

> I would say that for us, teaching reading is an important thing...teaching, you know, emergent literacy at all levels, because we have kids coming in at the middle school and high school level who've had no schooling or a severely interrupted form of schooling. So, teachers need to know about how to teach reading and it may be a little bit different with special ed.... They need to know the different kinds of approaches that second language learners need, you know, including phonemic awareness training, things like that, for regular people who cross over from the regular population, because...you can take that for granted, but you can't take that for granted

because the kid's learning a second language. (personal communication, February 1, 2002)

Some attention has been given to the idea of creating a cadre of "super-specialists" through cross-training who are experts on special, ESL, or bilingual education (Cloud, 2002; Gallegos & McCarty, 2000). Although we believe this is a positive step and might productively include those who specialize in middle level education for linguistically diverse students with disabilities, we argue that this is necessary but not sufficient. First, it conveys the notion that those specialists have total responsibility for the learning of linguistically diverse students with disabilities. Second, it delays the need for a timely response to support teachers in addressing the needs of English language learners with disabilities. Third, it creates logistical problems concerning where these specialists will be and who will have access to them. And finally, it supports the development of specialist-dependent structures, policies, and practices, while undermining the knowledge of other education professionals.

Cross-fertilization is a bit different from "cross-training" in that it involves not only adding new knowledge to the expertise of ESOL, bilingual, and special education teachers, but also includes content-area teachers in the dynamic construction of shared knowledge that transcends each individual specialization. In this way, not unlike recent models of the way that the bilingual brain works, the "whole" that is constructed is larger than the "sum of the parts" and what is created is not dual competence but multicompetence. The ability of each individual member not only to play a part in the system as a whole but also to be able to think about how the parts fit together and what that means for each teacher's own practice moves us toward improving the education of whole students throughout the school day.

Teacher Inquiry

There is a long tradition of researchers informing teachers about what they need to do in the classroom. Although university researchers' studies of classrooms are an important part of the knowledge base of teaching, knowledge generated by teachers themselves is crucial to our contextualized understanding of teaching and learning processes. This requires a shift in thinking about where expertise comes from, and repositioning teachers as knowledge-generators rather than primarily knowledge consumers. As Cochran and Lytle (1993) state in outlining their vision of the contribution of teacher research,

Teachers would be among those who have the authority to know—that is, to construct Knowledge (with a capital K) about teaching, learning and schooling. And what is worth knowing about teaching would include teachers' "ways of knowing" (Belenky, Clinchy, Goldberger, & Tarule, 1986) or what teachers who are researchers in their own classrooms, can know through systematic subjectivity. (p. 43)

In particular, in looking at our understanding of the education of linguistically diverse middle level students with disabilities, much of the potential for understanding the complexity of the process needs to begin from the ground up. What is happening in particular classrooms? What is working for particular students? How is collaboration working in assessment and instruction?

In our interviews with teachers, many talk about the ways that their professional training has assisted them in meeting the needs of this population. Nearly all, however, talk about the value of what they've learned from what they call "trial and error." Many times, this has to do with not having received formal training that integrated these approaches. As one bilingual teacher explained, "[I've had] no training. I learned mostly on the job, making mistakes and observing as I went along. This occurred because I did not start out expecting to work with students with disabilities" (Naomi, personal communication, January 28, 2002). Learning and observing "as I went along" was also echoed by the bilingual special education teacher who had the most cross-training. She said:

I was trained at [the university] through a particular program that combined the areas of special education and bilingual education. I believe that gave me a good base but the reality is that formal preparation is not the key to successful teaching of this special population. (Valeria, personal communication, February 10, 2002)

An ESOL teacher also reinforced the idea that it was through actual experiences with students that she became more confident in meeting the needs of these students. She said,

I…think that your experience with the students help and teach you to learn as you go. You begin to realize which methods or strategies work through trial and error. (Jennifer, personal communication, January 20, 2002)

Creating new knowledge and supporting the professional development of teachers who work with this population can be greatly supported by helping teachers learn how to do research on their own practices, successes, and challenges to turn this process of "trial and error" into systematic inquiry about their practices. Improving middle level education for linguistically diverse students with disabilities will not come primarily telling teachers what to do, but in asking teachers what they do and, as Johnson (2000) suggests, "where they do it, how they do it, when they do it and why they do it."

CONCLUSION

Prior to writing this chapter, we thought our disciplines could intersect at several points. Now, we know that not only can they be intersected and their boundaries crossed, but also they can be integrated into a whole that is greater than a sum of its parts. In the process of doing this research, we concluded that we have used the very processes that we are advocating here. We have *collaborated* by bringing our professional knowledge and expertise in our own fields to the process and respecting each other's, taking on both shared and individual roles in the research and writing process, and supporting each other in being able to manage multiple professional responsibilities during the process. This collaboration made *cross-fertilization* possible in several ways: (a) by providing opportunities to bounce ideas back and forth and come up with ways to integrate and synthesize these ideas, (b) by critically thinking about our own fields and biases while extending into new territory, and (c) by constructing the majority of the chapter collaboratively in front of the same computer screen. As teacher educators, we have also been engaged in *teacher inquiry* into our own practices as we prepare future teachers, advocate for students and families, and build a research agenda in this area, using an integrated, holistic, and dynamic model for meeting the needs of linguistically diverse students with disabilities and their teachers.

ACKNOWLEDGMENTS

The authors would like to thank the numerous teachers and administrators who contributed to this chapter who remain anonymous for reasons of confidentiality. We also thank Leslie Kirshner-Morris.

NOTES

1.   Although it is critical to look holistically at the needs of these students, it is also critical to acknowledge that speaking English as a second language is not a disability. In fact, we see multilingualism as a resource.

2.   Government documents refer to speakers of languages other than English as "limited English proficient" (LEP). Because this term focuses on the limitations of students, many prefer to use the term "culturally and linguistically

diverse" (CLD) or English language learner (ELL). The most common descriptor used in Philadelphia schools is English language learner, which is the term that we typically use throughout this document.

3. For more specifics on teacher staffing and the middle school reform effort in Philadelphia, see Useem (2001).

4. All names are pseudonyms.

5. According to Crawford (1996), "Between 1981 and 1986, school districts were nine times less likely to be the subject of Lau compliance reviews or monitoring visits than between 1975 and 1980, according to an *Education Week* analysis of OCR statistics. The declining trend continued until the early 1990s. Beginning in 1993, the Clinton administration substantially increased Lau enforcement, but has retained the 'case-by-case' policy on appropriate instruction."

REFERENCES

August, D., & Garcia, E. (1988). Litigation policy. In D. August & E. Garcia (Eds.), *Language minority education in the United States: Research, policy and practice* (pp. 57–71). Springfield, IL: Charles C. Thomas.

Baca, L. M., & Cervantes, H. T. (1998). *The bilingual special education interface* (3rd ed.). Upper Saddle River, NJ: Prentice Hall.

Cary, S. (2000). *Working with second language learners: Answers to teachers top ten questions.* Portsmouth, NH: Heinemann.

Cenoz, J., & Genesee, F. (1998). Psycholinguistic perspectives on multilingualism and multilingual education. In J. Cenoz & F. Genesee (Eds.), *Beyond bilingualism: Multilingualism and multilingual education* (pp. 16–32). Clevedon, UK: Multilingual Matters.

Cloud, N. (in press). Culturally and linguistically responsive instructional planning for English language learners with disabilities. In A. J. Artiles & A. A. Ortiz (Eds.), *English language learners with special education needs: Identification, placement, and instruction.* McHenry, IL, & Washington, DC: Delta Systems & Center for Applied Linguistics.

Cloud, N. (2002, February). *Linguistically diverse students with disabilities.* Presentation at CAPA High School, School District of Philadelphia.

Cochran, M., & Lytle, S. L. (1993). *Inside outside: Teacher research and knowledge.* New York: Teachers College Press.

Cohen, E., & Lotan, R. (1997). *Working for equity in heterogeneous classrooms.* New York: Teachers College Press.

Cook, V. (1992). Evidence for multi-competence. *Language Learning, 42,* 557–591.

Cook, V. (1993). *Linguistics and second language acquisition.* London: Macmillan.

Cook, V. (1995). Multi-competence and the learning of many languages. *Language, Culture and Curriculum 8,* 93–98.

Crawford, J. (1996). *Revisiting the Lau decision 20 years after: Proceedings of a national commemorative symposium.* Oakland, CA: ARC Associates.

Cummins, J. (2000). *Language, power and pedagogy: Bilingual children in the crossfire.* Clevedon, UK: Multilingual Matters.

DiPardo, A. (1999). *Teaching in common: Challenges to joint work in classrooms and schools.* New York: Teachers College Press.

Fine, L. (2002, January). Paige tells commission on special education to issue report by July. *Education Week, 21*(19), 22–23.

Flavely, M. (1995). *Inclusive and heterogeneous schooling: Assessment, curriculum and instruction.* Baltimore: Paul Brookes.

Freeman, D. (1996). Redefining the relationship between research and what teachers know. In K. Bailey & D. Nunan (Eds.), *Voices from the language classroom* (pp. 88–115). Cambridge: Cambridge University Press.

Gallegos, A., & McCarty, L. L. (2000). Bilingual multicultural special education: An integrated personnel preparation program. *Teacher Education and Special Education, 23*(4), 264–270.

Gianreco, M. (1997). *Quick-guide to inclusion: Ideas for educating students with disabilities.* Baltimore: Paul Brookes.

Grosjean, F. (1989). Neurolinguists, beware! The bilingual is not two monolinguals in one person. *Brain and Language, 36,* 3–15.

Grosjean, F. (1992). Another view of bilingualism. In R. J. Harris (Ed.), *Cognitive processing in bilinguals* (pp. 51–62). Amsterdam: North-Holland.

Individuals with Disabilities Education Act (IDEA) of 1997 [Online]. Available: www.edgov/offices/OSERS/policy/IDEA/regs.html [2002, February 1].

Jackson, A. W., & Davis, G. A. (2000). *Turning points 2000: Educating adolescents in the 21st century.* New York: Teachers College Press.

Johnson, K. E. (2000). (Ed.). *Teacher education.* Alexandria, VA: Teachers of English to Speakers of Other Languages.

Knowles, T., & Brown, D. F. (2000). *What every middle school teacher should know.* Portsmouth, NH: Heinemann.

Lara, J. (1995). *Second-language learners and middle school reform: A case study of a school in transition.* Washington, DC: Council of Chief State School Officers.

LeCompte, M. D., & Schensul, J. J. (1999). *Analyzing and interpreting ethnographic data.* Walnut Creek: Altamira Press.

Lee, O., & Fradd, S. (1998). Science for all, including students from non-English language backgrounds. *Educational Researcher, 27*(4), 12–21.

Lyons, J. (1990). The past and future directions of federal bilingual-education policy. In C. Cazden & C. Snow (Eds.), *The annals of the American academy of political and social science: English plus: Issues in bilingual education* (pp. 66–80). Philadelphia: Sage.

Malakoff, M. L., & Hakuta, K. (1990). History of language minority education in the United States. In A. M. Padilla, H. H. Fairchild, & C. Valadez (Eds.), *Bilingual education: Issues and strategies* (pp. 27–44). Newbury Park, CA: Sage.

Meyen, E. L., & Skrtic, T. M. (1995). *Special education and student disability: An introduction* (4th ed.). Denver, CO: Love.

New London Group. (1996). A pedagogy of multiliteracies: Designing social futures. *Harvard Educational Review, 66* (1), 60–92.

Orfield, G. A. (n.d.). *The impact of racial and ethnic diversity on educational outcomes: Cambridge, MA School District* [Online]. Available: http://www.law.harvard.edu/groups/civilrights/publications/cambridgediversity/synopsis.html [2002, February 10].

Ortiz, A. (2001). *English language learners with special needs: Effective instructional practices* (EDO-FL-01–08). Washington, DC: ERIC Clearinghouse on Language and Linguistics.

Ortiz, A. A., & Yates, J. R. (2001). A framework for serving English language learners with disabilities. *Journal of Special Education Leadership, 14*(2), 72–80.

Pennsylvania Department of Education. (2002). *English as a second language/bilingual education* [Online]. Available: http://www.pde.psu.edu/k-3,8.html [2002, February 10].

Richards, J. (1998). (Ed.). *Teaching in action: Case studies from second language classrooms.* Alexandria, VA: TESOL.

School District of Philadelphia. (2002). Mission Statement of the English Language Learners/Special Education Steering Committee, Philadelphia.

Skier, S.M. (n.d.) *Students say: Diversity improves education* [Online]. Available: http://www.thecrimson.com/ article.aspx?ref=161384 [2002, February 15].

Skilton-Sylvester, E. (in press). Legislation, litigation, teacher policymaking and the multilingual classroom: Constraining and supporting Khmer/English biliteracy in the United States. *International Journal of Bilingual Education and Bilingualism.*

Skilton-Sylvester, E., Jimenez, O., & Laramee, P. (1999, March). *Preparing ESL teachers for leadership and change.* Paper presented at the Teachers of English to Speakers of Other Languages Conference, New York.

Skilton-Sylvester, P. (1998). *Putting school/work back together?: A comparison of organizational change in an inner city school and a Fortune 500 company.* Unpublished doctoral dissertation, University of Pennsylvania, Philadelphia.

Thurlow, M. L., & Liu, K. K. (2001). Can "all" really mean students with disabilities who have limited English proficiency?: Rethinking culture in school reform. *Journal of Special Education Leadership, 14*(2), 63–71.

Useem, E. (2001). New teacher staffing and comprehensive middle school reform: Philadelphia's experience. In V. Anfara (Ed.), *Handbook of research in middle level education* (pp. 143–160). Greenwich, CT: Information Age Publishing.

Valles, E. (1998). The disproportionate representation of minority students in special education: Responding to the problem. *Journal of Special Education, 32*(1), 52–54.

Villa, R. A., & Thousand, J. S. (2000). *Restructuring for caring and effective education: Piecing the puzzle together* (2nd ed.). Baltimore: Paul Brookes.

Wrigley, H., & Guth, G. (1992). *Bringing literacy to life: Issues and options in adult ESL literacy.* San Diego, CA: Dominie Press.

CHAPTER 6

AUTHENTIC CURRICULUM

Strengthening Middle Level Education

Micki M. Caskey
Portland State University

ABSTRACT

The quest for a preferred middle level curriculum continues. The author proposes authentic curriculum as a viable choice for middle level education. Authentic middle level curriculum merges the attributes of integrative, coherent, and democratic curriculum to attend to the learning needs of young adolescents. After detailing a theoretical background, the focus shifts to how to design authentic curriculum that will engage students as knowledge workers. Design components include purposeful objectives, educative experiences, and assessments that promote learner engagement and foster understanding. Subsequently, exemplars of authenticity such as integrative curriculum, standards of authentic instruction, and types of authentic learning experiences are shared to underscore facets of authentic work.

Middle School Curriculum, Instruction, and Assessment, pages 103–118
Copyright © 2002 by Information Age Publishing
All rights of reproduction in any form reserved.

INTRODUCTION

Middle school curriculum continues to be the focal point of substantive research, thoughtful inquiry, heated debates, and countless conversations about middle level education. At the core of these processes is the critical question of middle level education: what should comprise the curriculum of the middle school? Addressing the curriculum question calls for diligence, dedication, and undoubtedly, more discussion. Attending to the question is essential since curriculum remains the cornerstone of every middle school program. To that end, authentic curriculum is a way to strengthen and renew middle level education.

Middle-level education needs an authentic middle level curriculum—a curriculum that engages students actively in learning or knowledge work: critical thinking; rigorous inquiry; thoughtful reflection; purposeful discourse; collaborative exchange; and systematic application, analysis, synthesis, and evaluation of information. Most middle level curricula target meaningful content and worthwhile experiences for young adolescents, but authentic curriculum ensures real-world learning, content connections, and coherence, and brings forward the student voice. An authentic middle level curriculum focuses on the highest levels of student academic achievement while attending to young adolescents' social, emotional, and physiological needs (Caskey, 1996). The authentic curriculum enhances middle level student's knowledge and skills, just as it promotes health, wellness, and human dignity. Without question, every middle school deserves an authentic curriculum because it provides a pathway to authentic learning.

This chapter presents dimensions of authentic curriculum. First, theoretical background is discussed in building a case for authentic curriculum. Then, curriculum planning is explored in creating authentic curriculum. Finally, exemplars of authentic work and some concluding thoughts are presented.

BUILDING A CASE FOR AUTHENTIC CURRICULUM

Curriculum is defined as "a plan to engage students in learning" (Hawkins & Graham, 1994, p. 43). To be comprehensive, the plan needs to describe the goals or outcomes for learning, assessment techniques, instructional processes, and learning experiences. Additionally, curriculum must be thought of broadly, since "curriculum encompasses every aspect of a school or team's program" (Smith, 1999). Consequently, teachers and students, as well as other stakeholders, are involved in developing the curriculum—curriculum that encompasses more than a set of skills, sequential list of concepts, or content frameworks. To be truly authentic, curriculum is a fluid, dynamic, and ever-changing script for learning (Caskey, 1996).

Organization of this ever-changing script for learning or curriculum has been of primary importance at the middle level. Middle level researchers and advocates (Beane, 1993; Drake, 1998; Lipka et al., 1998; Powell & Van Zandt Allen, 2001; Toepfer, 1997) have analyzed and synthesized the curriculum's rich history. A brief overview of middle level curriculum may help to provide a context for establishing the timeliness of authentic curriculum.

Secondary education curriculum has a long tradition of being organized around content-specific disciplines. In the early 1900s, the separate subject-centered approach of the university was deemed appropriate for secondary levels including the junior high, the predecessor of middle schools. Interestingly, a movement away from the separate-subject curriculum toward a more unified one also emerged. Dewey (1938) and other educators criticized the narrowness of a separate discipline approach and proposed an experiential curriculum that centered on children's real-world experiences. Researchers in the progressive era examined different curricular and instructional approaches in the Eight Year Study, "the most comprehensive long-range experimental educational research study ever conducted in school settings" (Lipka et al., 1998, p. 1). Results from this renowned study indicated that students engaged in experimental interdisciplinary curricula that was problem-based, socially constructed, and centered on learners' needs and interests out-scored those students who participated in the conventional separate-subject curricula. The findings exposed numerous shortcomings of secondary education and revealed that "the more experimental the school, the greater degree of success in college" (Powell & Van Zandt Allen, 2001, p. 111). Despite Dewey's study of experiential curricula or the conclusions of the Eight Year Study's researchers, the majority of secondary schools remained deeply rooted in subject-centered curricula.

The emergence of the middle school model gave way to new curriculum trends in the 1960s and 1970s. Institutional changes such as interdisciplinary teaching teams and advisory programs facilitated more learner-centered curricula. Curriculum models focused on the developmental characteristics of young adolescents. Eichorn's model focused on the physical, cognitive, social, and cultural characteristics of students, while Alexander's model targeted young adolescent's personal development and interests as well as skills for continued learning and organized knowledge centers (Toepfer, 1997). Lounsbury and Vars (1978) recommended a "core" curriculum to address personal characteristics and social concerns, and Toepfer (1997) proposed curricula that were designed locally to support the identified characteristics and needs of young adolescents. These curriculum models responded to developmental characteristics of middle level learners.

The case for integrated curriculum is strong. Curriculum for young adolescents needs to be integrative for students to make sense out of their life experiences and to connect school experiences to their daily lives outside of school (National Middle School Association, 1995). Genuinely integrated curriculum empowers teachers and their students to make connections between their school learning experiences and real life (Caskey, 1996), while the separate-subject approach often leaves students with a disconnected view of knowledge that "fails to reflect the way that real people attack problems in the real world" (Daniels & Bizar, 1998, p. 20). Relevance is a notable strength for integrated curriculum.

Middle level researchers and curriculum designers advance the integrated approach to curriculum. Jacobs (1989) offers a continuum of curricular approaches from discipline based to fully integrated experiences. Her interdisciplinary concept model describes systematic approaches to connecting discipline perspectives for an investigation of a target theme, problem, or issue. She cautions against forced, superfluous, or artificially constructed connections among the disciplines and recommended instructional experiences planned to engage students. Beane (1993) proposes a model that departs from the separate-subject approach toward a truly student-centered integrated curriculum in which central themes are derived from the intersection of young adolescent's personal concerns and issues of society. He stresses the importance of providing students with opportunities to integrate their knowledge into "schemes of meaning" situated in unforgettable learning experiences (Beane, 1993). Furthermore, other scholars and practitioners (Bergstrom, 1998; Daniels & Bizar, 1998; Five & Dionisio, 1996; Pate, 2001; Stevenson & Carr, 1993; Zemelman, Daniels, & Hyde, 1998) detail exemplars of and experiences with integrated curriculum. A substantial theoretical foundation and research establishes the importance of integrated curriculum.

Similarly robust is the case for a coherent curriculum. Curriculum that is coherent helps students to connect school experiences to their daily lives outside of school and encourages them to reflect on the totality of their experiences (National Middle School Association, 1995). Overarching features of a coherent curriculum are logical connections and cohesiveness.

Beane (1995) asserts curricular coherence entails creating and maintaining visible connections between purposes and everyday learning experiences. Teachers and students must share a common understanding of the larger purposes of the curriculum and how the students' learning experiences will help them to achieve those purposes. Learning experiences must be arranged to occur in relevant, meaningful contexts. "The repositioning of learning experiences into meaningful contexts is the point of much of the current work on curriculum organization" (Beane, 1995, p. 8). Integrated curriculum that emphasizes young adolescents' personal concerns and real world issues provides just such a curricular structure. Confounding many efforts towards coherence are schools that chop the student day into seven or eight disconnected segments (Zemelman et al., 1998). Nevertheless, middle schools must continue to seek coherence in the curriculum. Coherence can be advanced through organizational structures like block scheduling or creative, flexible use of time; however, it can also be realized in every middle school classroom. Wiggins (1995) describes curricular coherence as a visible connection between assessment design and curriculum design. He notes that coherence must be planned from the learner's perspective. Indisputably, coherent curriculum requires that the plans, teaching, and assessments fit together. Teachers and students are capable of codeveloping coherent curricula that deliberately connect purposes, learning experiences, and assessments.

The rationale for a democratic curriculum is equally sound. Democratic curriculum underscores society's democratic principles and processes. Students need opportunities to learn what it means to live and participate in a democratic way of life (Dewey, 1916). A democratic curriculum creates a space for multiple viewpoints, encourages underrepresented voices, and promotes the open exchange of ideas. These democratic practices require active participation of teachers and students alike. Students and teachers collaborate and make decisions about content and instructional experiences that are to engage the learner. Both pose questions to guide learning and deepen understandings of the content. Apple and Beane (1995) note that "a democratic curriculum induces young people to shed the passive role of knowledge consumers and assume the active role of 'meaning makers'" (p. 16). Such active participation in curriculum development allows students to experience the social processes of democracy. This curriculum "treats students with dignity, as real people, who live in the real world and care about its condition and fate" (Beane, 1998, p. 10). Students and their teachers share teaching and learning experiences in the context of a democratic curriculum.

Authentic middle level curriculum encompasses the key concepts of integrated, coherent, and democratic curricula. An authentic curriculum stems from the intersection of young adolescents' personal interests and issues of society. It is codeveloped by teachers and students; it is a collaborative effort, a negotiated plan for learning. An authentic curriculum creates and connects learning experiences in the school context to be more like learning and life outside school. It requires the learner to construct knowledge, conduct inquiry, and perform tasks that have a purpose beyond simply satisfying the assignment (Caskey, 1996). Authentic curriculum systematically arranges for young adolescents to be engaged in rigorous and meaningful knowledge work. Functioning as coconspirators, teachers and students make informed decisions about curricular purposes, content, and learning experiences. Multiple perspectives are sought and embraced. In conclusion, authentic curriculum must be integrative, coherent, and democratic in nature.

CREATING AUTHENTIC CURRICULUM

The authentic curriculum requires clear intent before it is launched. Though many curriculum experts describe ways to design curricula, the principles forwarded by the father of curriculum reform, Ralph Tyler, remain vital to authentic curriculum planning. Tyler (1949) suggests a framework for deliberately designing and evaluating curriculum. The *Tyler rationale* is a set of four essential questions that serve as general guidelines for curriculum developers to consider when planning any curriculum:

1. What educational purposes should the school seek to attain?
2. What educational experiences can be provided that are likely to attain these purposes?
3. How can these educational experiences be effectively organized?
4. How can we determine whether these purposes are being attained? (Tyler, 1949, p. 1)

Authentic curriculum, like any effective curriculum, needs defined purposes or educational objectives. These objectives are the criteria for identifying curricular content, selecting instructional procedures and materials, and preparing assessments (Tyler, 1949). When determining the educational objectives, Tyler stresses the importance of considering learner needs and interests, since the most useful objectives designate learner behavior and the context in which the behavior is to be applied. Arrays of educational experiences are available for curriculum designers to achieve the objectives. To effectively organize experiences, Tyler calls for continuity, sequence, and integration of learning experiences (1949, p. 84). Not only does curriculum development require the selection of objectives and arrangement of learning experiences, but also an evaluation process to determine the extent to which the educational objectives are being realized. Certainly, Tyler's basic principles of curriculum remain germane and applicable for making authentic curricular decisions.

Another building block of authentic curriculum is collaboration. Collaboration at the middle level is crucial when "everyone has a right to participate in curriculum conversations about what should form the bases of the middle school curriculum" (Gatewood, 1998, p. 40). Moreover, a collaborative effort is required to address Tyler's four essential questions. To make wise and comprehensive curricular decisions requires the multiple perspectives and voices of scholars, parents and community members, students, and educators (Hass, 1979). Scholars advise which central concepts should be taught and ways to operationalize the curriculum while parental and community member support is indispensable for curriculum adoption. Students need to co-plan with their teachers the educational objectives and related learning experiences that maximize achievement. Educators coordinate the curricular planning process, and ultimately classroom teachers implement the curriculum. The teacher serves as the linchpin for curricular collaboration since, as Tyler states, "whatever the teacher does determines what the curriculum is" (Lipka et al., 1998, p. xi). Teachers should be trusted to make curricular decisions based upon their knowledge of individual learner needs (Monson & Monson, 1993) as well as in collaboration with scholars, parents, students, and other educators.

In addition, authentic curriculum needs to be developed locally—at the site of curricular implementation, reflection, and transformation. Considerable evidence exists to support the local, contextual approach to curriculum development (Five & Dionisio, 1996; Hargreaves, Earl, Moore, & Manning, 2001; Lipsitz, 1984; Pate, 2001; Pate, Homestead, & McGinnis, 1997; Stevenson & Carr, 1993). In other words, authentic curriculum development is best positioned at the building level. Curriculum development is the shared responsibility of the local middle level stakeholders: students, parents, teachers, administrators, and support staff (Caskey, 1996). "A curriculum developed apart from the teachers and young people who must live it is grossly undemocratic in the ways that it deprives them of their rights to have a say in their own lives and to learn and apply the skills and understandings associated with making important decisions" (Beane, 1993, p. 16). Authentic curriculum is codeveloped with students who help to make select relevant and meaningful curricular objectives, educative experiences, and assessments.

Accepting the requirements of collaboration and site specification, the next challenge is how middle schools create an authentic curriculum. Though there is no single methodology, one school-wide approach holds promise (Caskey, 1996). A first step would be to form a leadership team of middle level stakeholders of teachers, students, administrators, family, and community members to design an authentic curriculum. The team should be comprised of those dedicated to curriculum development and continuous improvement. Second, assemble significant data and ask critical questions to uncover the culture of the middle school and the community. Third, establish a set of guiding principles or core beliefs for the school. Revisit or create the goals, vision, and mission statement for the school to ensure alignment with the guiding principles, and then, publicly display the goals, vision, and mission statement. Fourth, establish a climate of academic achievement that invites all learners to engage in authentic work. Identify ways for the entire school community to support efforts toward academic success. Fifth, design an authentic curriculum collaboratively. Write a plan for learning that responds to the school's guiding principles and climate of academic achievement. The plan needs to identify educational objectives, arrange educative experiences to engage young adolescent learners, and prepare assessments to measure goal attainment. Finally, continue to seek improvement through review and revision of curricular script. At the middle level, creating authentic curriculum is a shared and purposeful venture.

Developing effective, authentic curriculum is also a focused endeavor. A suggested approach to focus planning efforts is the backward design. Though backward design is garnering considerable attention, it stems from a solid foundation. Tyler describes "the logic of backward design clearly and succinctly about 50 years ago" (Wiggins & McTighe, 1998, p. 8). He notes that educational objectives are criteria for ascertaining the curricular content, educative experiences, instructional practices and materials, and for preparing assessments (Tyler, 1949). Wiggins and McTighe's (1998) backward design process guides teachers to consider accepted standards or educational objectives, determine evidence of learner understanding, and plan educative experiences. When considering acceptable standards, curriculum developers must frame a set of enduring understandings and essential questions that will guide the preparation of assessments and learning experiences. Backward design affords curriculum developers an opportunity to plan for integration and coherence in the curriculum. "To direct teaching and learning toward understanding will require uncovering the absolutely essential concepts and ideas embedded in lengthy standards and developing curriculum that reflects these essential concepts, both subject specific and generic, thus revealing connections within and across content areas" (Jackson & Davis, 2000, p. 39). In addition, collaboration among teachers and students during the curriculum design process fosters democratic practice and facilitates the advancement of authentic curriculum.

Planning an authentic curriculum is difficult work, especially with the recent emphasis on accountability. Researcher opinion about standards-based reform and its effect on curriculum development varies considerably. Pate (2001) recounts exemplars of how teachers are making sense of the standards and dealing with the standards in a responsive and relevant manner. Jacobs (1989) details how state and district level content area frameworks can be incorporated while developing integrative units of study. In contrast, Hargreaves and colleagues (2001) warn that standards-based reform may lead to a curriculum that is over standardized, underresourced, deprofessionalized, and narrow. Vars and Beane (2000) promote the use of "common learnings" compiled by educational "think tanks" when developing curriculum. Researchers express concern for middle level teachers who must cope with societal pressures for standards-based reform and state tests while attending to the needs, interests, and issues of young adolescents (Vars, 2001; Vars & Beane, 2000). Tension created by the high-stakes testing and other facets of standards-based reform may impede efforts to create relevant, integrated curriculum for young adolescents (Caskey, 2001). Although teachers are held accountable for planning curriculum, authentic or otherwise, they are also held responsible for meeting the standards of their state's mandates.

However, the National Middle School Association (1995) and other advocates for young adolescents (Beane, 1993; Vars, 2001) assert that curriculum in the middle school should address the needs of learners. An authentic middle level curriculum responds to learners' needs and interests. Just as genuine curriculum integration springs from students' interests and concerns (Beane, 1993), authentic curriculum emerges from students' interests and concerns. To meet the needs of middle level learners, the curriculum should be relevant, engaging, and rigorous (Beane, 1998). Students are motivated to learn when content and experiences address and satisfy their own needs and interests (Glasser, 1992). Students' success in schools is furthered by warm, supportive human relationships and real choice (Glasser, 1997). Authentic curriculum seeks student voice and offers students choice; it empowers young adolescents. When students have a voice in developing the curriculum, subsequent instruction is more effective (Davies, 1992). Young adolescents prefer active and contextual learning experiences as well as those that include peer interaction (Pate, 2001). The responsibility for learning moves from the teacher domain exclusively to encompass both the student and teacher (Caskey, 1996). Interestingly, an authentic middle level curriculum has the potential to expand the concept of inclusion to extend to all learners. When authentic curriculum is co-constructed carefully, it works to anticipate, address, and accommodate learner differences. It is amenable to the varied needs of young adolescents and can truly support the needs of every student. Because students will work hard when they believe in the quality of the education experience (Glasser, 1992), codeveloping authentic curriculum with students is most logical.

Creating authentic curriculum that is integrative, coherent, and democratic is thought-provoking and time-intensive work. Designing curriculum in this manner cannot be accomplished in a single professional development workshop or one after-school inservice. Planning to this extent takes significant effort and commitment as well as continual local support. Initially, teachers may find the process of developing authentic curriculum difficult because exemplars are not widely available for teachers' scrutiny. Some teachers may have limited experience in coplanning curriculum. Others may not been given opportunities to exchange ideas or share their own experiences creating and implementing an authentic curriculum. Nevertheless, investing in authentic curriculum leads to what matters most—authentic learning.

EXEMPLARS OF AUTHENTIC WORK

At the heart of authentic curriculum is student learning. The purpose of authentic curriculum is to arrange challenging and relevant learning experiences that engage students in real work. As knowledge workers, students construct knowledge, conduct inquiry, and perform tasks. Creating these authentic learning experiences increases the quality of student engagement, which leads to understanding. Ideally, authentic curriculum provides a context in which students are motivated to learn and to sustain engagement in educative experiences by their desire for understanding. Cooperative and collaborative interactions among young adolescents, teachers, and others support students' quest for understanding. Student understanding is evidenced by the application of knowledge through performance assessments (Wiggins & McTighe, 1998). Just as with developing the plan or script for learning, authenticity is paramount throughout instruction and assessment processes.

Learner understanding is substantiated by learner performance; so performance assessment becomes an integral component of authentically constructed curriculum (Caskey, 1996). Performance assessment requires learners to exhibit their understandings, abilities, and strategies by generating a response or product. Moving beyond simple recall of isolated pieces of information measured by many teacher and standardized tests, performance assessment involves complex displays of student ability to communicate, process, apply, and construct knowledge. Students and teachers collaborate to design assessments that not only match the complexity of task, but also define the objectives and establish the criteria for learning (Caskey, 1996). Teachers use results of performance assessments to make curricular and instructional decisions about content and practices while students learn to self-evaluate and reflect upon their own academic competence. As knowledge workers, students produce and use information to solve problems or do genuine work. In essence, an authentic curriculum endorses young adolescents as active practitioners and evaluators of their own performances.

An inspection of a few exemplars may help educators examine authentic instruction, learning, and the overall authentic nature of their middle school curriculum. Among these illustrative exemplars are models of integrative curricula, essential features of authentic curricula, standards of authentic instruction, and educative experiences that engage learners as knowledge workers.

Integrative curriculum lays the groundwork for authentic curriculum. Perkins (1989) suggests that integrated themes serve as a valuable lens for student thinking and understanding. He asserts that worthwhile themes must apply broadly and pervasively, disclose fundamental patterns, reveal similarities and contrasts, and fascinate the learner. Ackerman and Perkins (1989) envision an integration of content curriculum and the metacurriculum composed of the skills and strategies that help students acquire the content. In this approach, students "become more autonomous and proactive" and "are more likely to make connections between contexts" (p. 94). Jacobs (1989) details an interdisciplinary concept model for systematically developing integrated units of study. Guiding questions direct students' investigations and the selection and design of educational experiences and assessments. Beane (1993) advances an integrative, learner-centered curriculum where themes surface from the intersection of learners' personal concerns and society's issues. The goals of these integrative curriculum approaches are aligned with those of an authentic curriculum.

Essential features are another schema for examining the authenticity of curriculum. Caskey (1996) advises that authentic curriculum must be flexible, bold, and demanding. Middle level curriculum must be flexible and allow for ongoing adjustments. It needs to evaluate students' prior knowledge routinely and build upon students' previous experiences as well as offer expanded opportunities for uncovering and learning key concepts. Work with "young adolescents calls for great flexibility in the curriculum so that it engages young adolescents, has meaning for them, connects with their lives, and is grounded in relationships between teachers and students in which each knows the other well" (Hargreaves et al., 2001, p. xiii). Middle level curriculum must also be bold, which entails widening the learning space to include places outside the classroom and advocating the flexible use of time. Finally, the authentic middle level curriculum is demanding. Demanding curriculum requires students to set goals and assess their own progress throughout the learning process. When it's done well, an authentic curriculum stretches young adolescents to reach their own highest levels of academic achievement.

When designing authentic curriculum, teachers need to plan for authentic instruction. Newmann and Wehlage (1993) formulated a set of standards for examining authentic instruction: higher-order thinking, depth of knowledge, connectedness to the world beyond the classroom, substantive conversation, and social support for student achievement, which may inform instructional practice. Higher-order thinking compels learners "to manipulate information and ideas in ways that transform their meaning and implications, such as when students combine facts and ideas in order to synthesize, generalize, explain, hypothesize, or arrive at some conclusion or interpretation" (Newmann & Wehlage, 1993, p. 9). Depth of knowledge is also a consideration. Knowledge is deepened when students focus on significant concepts and develop complex understandings, which may necessitate limiting the number of concepts to be understood. Connectedness to the world beyond the classroom targets links to the larger community in which the students function. This is a real-world dimension that uses learners' personal experiences as the context for applying their understandings. Another facet of authentic instruction is substantive conversation or student discourse. Extensive interactions, idea sharing, and coherent dialogue that furthers learner understanding characterize substantive conversations. Additionally, social support for student achievement needs to be orchestrated. Strong social support means high expectations for all students and depends on a climate of mutual respect. Teachers and students alike evidence positive attitudes toward learning and hard work. In general, authentic instruction promotes significance and meaningfulness across the learning experience.

Thoughtfully designed learning experiences also exemplify authentic curriculum. Many powerful experiences are organized around questions and problems (Beane, 1993; Jacobs, 1989; Stepien & Gallagher, 1993; Wiggins & McTighe, 1998). In fact, Stepien and Gallagher (1993) assert, "problem-based learning is as authentic as it gets" (p. 25). Problem-based learning places students in the active role of problem solvers confronted with an ill-structured problem. This approach requires students to delve deeply, formulate questions, and grapple with the problem's complexity in order to arrive at a solution. Throughout the process, teachers are cognitive coaches who help to organize learners' thinking. Authentic learning experiences often situate students as knowledge workers who adopt the role and work of authors, historians, mathematicians, scientists, artists, and other practitioners. For instance, students work as historians when they view, interpret, and analyze primary source documents or artifacts.

Online resources allow students to explore primary source and archival material relating to culture and history. Specific examples include the Library of Congress' American Memory (2002) and the National Archives (2002). Similarly, students work with print and online resources to locate, build, and use information that is relevant and necessary for understanding. Other examples of authentic work include drafting letters to political representatives about community issues as concerned citizens, collecting data as scientists in local environments, and conducting genuine, contextually based studies as researchers. The authenticity of learning experiences is a component of the authentic curriculum design.

CONCLUSION

Authentic middle level curriculum that is integrative, coherent, and democratic remains elusive. The integrative aspects depart from the conventional and deeply entrenched attitudes that support subject-centered approaches to curriculum. National organizations, schools, universities, state departments of education, commercial textbooks, and standardized tests are built on traditional subject separations. Coherent curriculum demands that teachers and students invest time and energy. Teachers need time to plan, instruct, assess, and reflect, while learners require expanded occasions to make the connections between school and life experiences as well as to reflect upon these experiences. For both the teacher and learner, the demand for content coverage impedes efforts for coherence. Furthermore, educators do not universally embrace democratic curriculum principles. Nevertheless, the costs of failing to provide young adolescents with authentic curriculum are high. Among the consequences may be further decline in student learning, poor academic achievement, and a loss of public confidence in the middle level school as an academic institution. Despite the mounting evidence for shifting to authentic curriculum, it will take sustained effort, hard work, and additional study.

Every middle school is worthy of an authentic curriculum. Authentic curriculum brings real purposes, genuine learning experiences, and performance assessments under one umbrella. Definitely, authentic curriculum provides an avenue to authentic learning. However, specific and extensive evidence of how, when, and where authentic curriculum is flourishing at the middle level needs to be exchanged. Through inquiry, middle level researchers and practitioners can attend to these questions and provide additional insights into authentic curriculum.

REFERENCES

Ackerman, D., & Perkins, D. N. (1989). Integrating thinking and learning skills across the curriculum. In H. H. Jacobs (Ed.), *Interdisciplinary curriculum: Design and implementation* (pp. 77–95). Alexandria, VA: Association for Supervision and Curriculum Development.

Apple, M. W., & Beane, J. A. (1995). The case for democratic schools. In M. W. Apple & J. A. Beane (Eds.), *Democratic schools* (pp. 1–25). Alexandria, VA: Association for Supervision and Curriculum Development.

Beane, J. A. (1993). *The middle school curriculum: From rhetoric to reality* (2nd ed.). Columbus, OH: National Middle School Association.

Beane, J. A. (1995). Introduction: What is a coherent curriculum? In J. A. Beane (Ed.), *Toward a coherent curriculum* (pp. 1–14). Alexandria, VA: Association for Supervision and Curriculum Development.

Beane, J. A. (1998). Reclaiming a democratic purpose for education. *Educational Leadership, 56*(2), 8–11.

Bergstrom, K. L. (1998). Are we missing the point about curriculum integration? *Middle School Journal 29*(4), 28–37.

Caskey, M. M., with Johnston, J. H. (1996). Hard work ahead: Authentic curriculum under construction. *Schools in the Middle, 6*(2), 11–18.

Caskey, M. M. (2001). A lingering question for middle school: What is the fate of integrated curriculum. *Childhood Education, 78*(2), 97–99.

Daniels, H., & Bizar, M. (1998). *Methods that matter: Six structures for best practice classrooms.* Portland, ME: Stenhouse.

Davies, M. A. (1992). Are interdisciplinary units worthwhile? Ask students. In J. Lounsbury (Ed.), *Connecting the curriculum through interdisciplinary instruction* (pp. 37–41). Columbus, OH: National Middle School Association.

Dewey, J. (1916). *Democracy in education.* New York: Macmillan

Dewey, J. (1938). *Experience and education.* Bloomington, IN: Kappa Delta Pi.

Drake, S. M. (1998). *Creating integrated curriculum: Proven ways to increase student learning.* Thousand Oaks, CA: Corwin Press.

Five, C. L., & Dionisio, M. (1996). *Bridging the gap: Integrating curriculum in upper elementary and middle schools.* Portsmouth, NH: Heinemann.

Gatewood, T. (1998). How valid is integrated curriculum in today's middle schools? *Middle School Journal, 29*(4), 38–41.

Glasser, W. (1992). *The quality school: Managing students without coercion.* New York: Harper & Row.

Glasser, W. (1997). A new look at school failure and school success. *Phi Delta Kappan, 78*(8), 596–602.

Hargreaves, A., Earl, L., Moore, S., & Manning, S. (2001). *Learning to change: Teaching beyond subjects and standards.* San Francisco: Jossey-Bass.

Hass, G. (1979). Who should plan the curriculum? In F. W. Parkay & G. Hass (Eds.), *Curriculum planning: A contemporary approach* (pp. 301–305). Boston: Allyn & Bacon.

Hawkins, M., & Graham, M. (1994). *Curriculum architecture:Creating a place of our own.* Columbus, OH: National Middle School Association.

Jackson, A. W., & Davis, G. A. (2000). *Turning points 2000: Educating adolescents in the 21st century.* New York: Teachers College Press.

Jacobs, H. H. (1989). The interdisciplinary concept model: A step-by-step approach for developing integrated units of study. In H. H. Jacobs (Ed.), *Interdisciplinary curriculum: Design and implementation* (pp. 53–65). Alexandria, VA: Association for Supervision and Curriculum Development.

Library of Congress American Memory Home Page. (2002). *American memory* [Online]. Available: http://memory.loc.gov/ [2002, January 10].

Lipka, R. P., Lounsbury, J. H., Toepfer, C. F., Vars, G. F., Alessi, S. P., & Kridel, C. (1998). *The eight-year study revisited: Lessons from the past for the present.* Columbus, OH: National Middle School Association.

Lipsitz, J. (1984). *Successful schools for young adolescents.* New Brunswick, NJ: Transaction.

Lounsbury, J. H., & Vars, G. F. (1978). *A curriculum for the middle school years.* New York: Harper & Row.

Monson, M. P., & Monson, R. M. (1993). Who creates curriculum? New roles for teachers. *Educational Leadership, 51*(2), 19–21.

National Archives and Records Administration Home Page. (2002). *National archives* [Online]. Available: http://www.nara.gov [2002, January 10].

National Middle School Association. (1995). *This we believe: Developmentally responsive middle level schools.* Columbus, OH: Author.

Newmann, F. M., & Wehlage, G. G. (1993). Five standards for authentic instruction. *Educational Leadership, 50*(7), 8–12.

Pate, P. E. (2001). Standards, students, and exploration: Creating a curriculum intersection of excellence. In T.S. Dickinson (Ed.), *Reinventing the middle school* (pp. 79–95). New York: RoutledgeFalmer.

Pate, P. E., Homestead, E. R., & McGinnis, K. L. (1997). *Making integrated curriculum work: Teachers, students, and the quest for coherent curriculum.* New York: Teachers College Press.

Perkins, D. (1989). Selecting fertile themes for integrated learning. In H. H. Jacobs (Ed.), *Interdisciplinary curriculum: Design and implementation* (pp. 67–76). Alexandria, VA: Association for Supervision and Curriculum Development.

Powell, R., & Van Zandt Allen, L. (2001). Middle school curriculum. In V. A. Anfara (Ed.), *The handbook of research in middle level education* (pp.107–124). Greenwich, CT: Information Age Publishing.

Smith, C. (1999). Middle level curriculum that is challenging, integrative, and exploratory. [Online]. *VAMLEGram, 13*(2), 4–5. Available: http://www.vamle.org/home/learning/publications/focus/smith_6_99.htm [2002, January 3].

Stepien, W., & Gallagher, S. (1993). Problem-based learning: As authentic as it gets. *Educational Leadership, 50*(7), 25–28.

Stevenson, C., & Carr, J. F. (1993). *Integrated studies in the middle grades: Dancing through walls.* New York: Teachers College Press.

Toepfer, C. (1997). Middle level curriculum's serendipitous history. In J.E. Irvin (Ed.), *What current research says to the middle level practitioner* (pp. 163–177). Columbus, OH: National Middle School Association.

Tyler, R. (1949). *Basic principles of curriculum and instruction.* Chicago: University of Chicago Press.

Vars, G. F. (2001). Can curriculum integration survive in an era of high-stakes testing? *Middle School Journal, 33*(2), 7–17.

Vars, G. F. (1997). Effects of integrative curriculum and instruction. In J.E. Irvin (Ed.), *What current research says to the middle level practitioner* (pp. 179–186). Columbus, OH: National Middle School Association.

Vars, G. F., & Beane. J. A. (2000). Integrative curriculum in a standards-based world. *ERIC Digest* [Online]. Available: http://www.ed.gov/databases/ERIC_Digests/ed441618.html [2001, September 13].

Wiggins, G. (1995). Curricular coherence and assessment: Making sure that the effect matches the intent. In J. A. Beane (Ed.), *Toward a coherent curriculum* (pp. 101–119). Alexandria, VA: Association for Supervision and Curriculum Development.

Wiggins, G., & McTighe, J. (1998). *Understanding by design.* Alexandria, VA: Association for Supervision and Curriculum Development.

Zemelman, S., Daniels, H., & Hyde, A. (1998). *Best practice: New standards for teaching and learning in America's schools* (2nd ed.). Portsmouth, NH: Heinemann.

CHAPTER 7

THE RELATIONSHIP BETWEEN MIDDLE-GRADES TEACHER CERTIFICATION AND TEACHING PRACTICES

Steven B. Mertens, Nancy Flowers and Peter Mulhall
Center for Prevention Research and Development
University of Illinois, Urbana-Champaign

ABSTRACT

Middle school advocates argue that specialized certification for middle-grades teachers is a necessity if we are to appropriately address the educational and developmental needs of young adolescents. This study focuses on the relationship between types of teacher certification and the levels of interdisciplinary team and classroom practices. The participants are classroom teachers in Michigan middle-grades schools from which self-reported levels of practices were collected through a survey and are reported as scale measures representing 11 different types of team and classroom practices. Teachers with elementary or middle-grades certification were found to have higher levels of both team and classroom practices. Middle-grades certified teachers engaged in teaming with high levels of common planning time had the high-

Middle School Curriculum, Instruction, and Assessment, pages 119–138
Copyright © 2002 by Information Age Publishing
All rights of reproduction in any form reserved.
119

est levels of team and classroom practices. While it is not possible to directly link the effects of teacher certification to student achievement outcomes, this study provides evidence to support an indirect link through heightened levels of practices and school-level teaming implementation.

INTRODUCTION

Middle-level teacher certification has been a topic of discussion and debate for several decades. Advocates and proponents of middle level education argue that staffing middle-grades classrooms with teachers who have not been trained to work with young adolescents is a great social injustice to future generations. While some progress has been made over the years, middle level advocates, teachers, and administrators believe there is still much to accomplish. Many teachers currently serving in the middle grade levels have had little or no specialized middle level preparation.

Turning Points: Preparing American Youth for the 21st Century, the seminal work on reforming middle-grades education, recommended that middle-grade schools be staffed with teachers who are expert at teaching young adolescents (Carnegie Council on Adolescent Development, 1989). Over a decade later and based on a growing body of experience and research, *Turning Points 2000* (Jackson & Davis, 2000) presented a revised set of recommendations for middle-grades schools. *Turning Points 2000* still recommends that we "staff middle grades schools with teachers who are expert at teaching young adolescents, and engage teachers in ongoing, targeted professional development opportunities" (Jackson & Davis, 2000, p. 23).

Specialized middle-grades teacher preparation programs have been promoted and supported by several professional organizations, including the National Middle School Association (1991) and the National Association of Secondary School Principals. Promotion, advocacy, and support have also come from organizations such as the National Forum to Accelerate Middle Grades Reform and the Southern Regional Education Board through policy position papers and recommendations (Cooney, 2000; National Forum to Accelerate Middle Grades Reform, 2002).

Unfortunately, most middle-grades teachers do not receive the type of specialized preparation necessary for them to fully address the developmental and learning needs of young adolescents. Numerous studies have demonstrated the relatively low percentage of middle-grades teachers who received any preservice specialized preparation (McEwin, Dickinson, & Jenkins, 1996; Scales, 1992; Scales & McEwin, 1994). In a 1980 survey, 41% of nearly 1,500 middle level principals found that teachers in their schools had no specific middle-level preparation (Valentine, Clark, Nickerson, & Keefe, 1981). Similar results were found in a 1988 study of 670 middle-grade schools where nearly 50% of principals indicated that less than 25% of their teachers had any specific preparation for teaching at the middle level (Alexander & McEwin, 1989).

A number of studies have also shown that middle-grades teachers and principals strongly support specialized teacher preparation for the middle grades (McEwin, Dickinson, & Hamilton, 2000; Scales & McEwin, 1996). Additional research has addressed teacher perceptions about the quality of their preparation programs. A national study of middle school teachers who received specialized middle-grades preservice preparation found that teachers generally rated their programs very high (Scales & McEwin, 1994).

In the past, very few states (some notable exceptions being Georgia, Missouri, and North Carolina) have made the commitment to implement and sustain specialized middle-grades certification. Even as more states begin to adopt these specialized teacher preparation programs, the quantity and availability of these programs is still well short of the current demand for them. Additional research has even proposed specific recommendations and strategies to improve and strengthen current or developing programs (McEwin & Dickinson, 1995; Scales & McEwin, 1994).

The current research literature clearly addresses the need for more specialized middle-grades teacher preparation programs, specific licensure for teachers in the middle-grade levels, and improved quality of existing programs. To further strengthen the argument for specialized middle-grades teacher preparation, additional research is needed to effectively demonstrate the impact and effects of specialized teacher preparation on outcomes such as improved teaching and learning practices and eventually student performance.

This study examines the effects of teacher certification types (elementary, secondary, and middle grades) on interdisciplinary team and classroom practices, as assessed by teacher survey data. To control for any biases of younger versus more mature teachers, these data are examined by the length of time teachers have worked in the field of education. Finally, we examine teacher-level practices by certification type for groups of schools with varying levels of implementation of interdisciplinary teaming and common planning time.

DATA AND METHODS

Data Collection

The data for this study were collected through the School Improvement Self-Study, developed and conducted by the Center for Prevention Research and Development (CPRD) at the University of Illinois. The Self-

Study is a data collection system consisting of a set of survey measures, including teacher, student, administrator (school principal), and parent surveys. The Self-Study examines several different areas of school improvement including attitudes toward middle-grades' educational practices, parent contact and involvement, classroom and interdisciplinary team practices, school and classroom climate, and professional development activities and needs. Although the teacher survey is anonymous, teachers are asked to supply basic descriptive information (e.g., subject areas and grade levels taught, type of teacher certification, types and length of teaching experience).

Its intended design and purpose are twofold. First, the Self-Study provides schools with quantitative data to document and track the changes in their schools as part of existing school improvement plans. It also provides schools with a way of establishing dialogue about school improvement, setting priorities, determining goals, and, most importantly, assessing and measuring the outcomes of new programs and practices. Second, it can provide data at an aggregate level (e.g., district, region, state) that enables both cross-sectional and longitudinal analyses of multiple schools. At an aggregate level, the Self-Study is particularly beneficial in strategic planning: identifying areas of focused improvement, providing overall needs assessment, and informing the development of district- or state-level educational policy with the outcome of improved teaching and learning for young adolescents.

Study Sample

Beginning in 1994, the Michigan Middle Start initiative, funded by the W. K. Kellogg Foundation, was designed to promote and improve middle-grades education for all Michigan's young adolescents and sustain increased achievement and developmental responsiveness over time (Lewis, 2000). The initiative, currently in its eighth year, has provided numerous opportunities for schools including grant making, professional development, and networking. Because of the importance placed on data-based decision making at both the individual school-level and the initiative level, Middle Start schools were required to participate in the CPRD Self-Study on a biennial basis beginning in 1994/95. Thus far, the Self-Study has been conducted four times as part of the Michigan Middle Start initiative.

The data for this study are derived from a sample of middle-grade schools that participated in the Self-Study as part of the Michigan Middle Start initiative during the 2000/01 school year. During that year, over 3,700 teachers from 134 middle-grade schools participated in the Self-Study. To ensure the most appropriate sample for the intended analysis, a subset of

2,001 teachers was selected based on the following criteria. First, only teachers indicating that they taught a core, academic subject area (e.g., language arts, math, science, social studies) were selected. Since the purpose of the study is to study the relationship between types of teacher certification and the levels of interdisciplinary team and classroom practices in middle-grade schools, the teachers included in the analysis were required to be academic subject-area teachers and not exploratory and/or elective teachers. CPRD has observed that the level of classroom or team practices engaged in by academic, content area teachers are generally different from exploratory or elective subject teachers (e.g., art, music, physical education teachers). Exploratory and/or elective teachers are more likely to engage in certain types of practices, such as small group instruction or authentic instruction/assessment practices, at higher levels.

Second, teachers needed to indicate that they considered their primary role in the school to be a classroom teacher, although not a special education teacher in a self-contained classroom. Although the content of the teacher Self-Study survey focuses primarily on teacher interactions with students, schools may encourage as many staff as possible to participate since its purpose is to gather data for school improvement. In some cases schools have included counselors, library/media center staff, onsite health practitioners, and social workers in the Self-Study process.

Third, since the focus of this study is on teacher practices in middle-grade schools, it was necessary to select out only those teachers that indicated they taught in the middle grades: fifth, sixth, seventh, or eighth grade. Middle-grade levels can be found in schools with a variety of grade configurations. There are schools in the Michigan sample with primarily elementary configurations (K–6, K–8), middle level or traditional junior high configurations (5–8, 6–8, 7–8, 7–9), and middle-high school configurations (7–12, 8–12).

MEASURES FOR ASSESSING PRACTICES

Two of the most important and predictive types of data derived from the Self-Study are teacher reports of their levels of engagement in specific interdisciplinary team and classroom practices. The interdisciplinary team and classroom practices measured by CPRD's Self-Study were identified by practitioners and researchers as effective strategies for impacting student success. The practices are defined quantitatively as scales or dimensions with each scale consisting of a series of questions on the teacher survey regarding how often specific team or classroom instructional activities occur.

The Self-Study contains four scales to assess levels of interdisciplinary team practices, including the areas of curriculum coordination and integration practices, coordination of student assignments and assessments, parent contact and involvement, and contact with other building resource staff. The seven classroom practices' scales included in this study are small group, active instruction; integration and interdisciplinary practices; authentic instruction and assessment; critical thinking practices; mathematical skill practices; reading skill practices; and writing skill practices. The frequency metric for both the team and classroom practices' scales ranged from 1 (*never*) to 7 (*daily*); the scales, however, are not exactly identical (see note in Table 7.3). When these types of data are reported back to a school, only the responses of core academic teachers (e.g., language arts, math, science, social studies) are included and the data are aggregated at the school level.

Internal consistency (Cronbach's alpha) measures were calculated for each scale (see Table 7.1). The reliability analysis sample was comprised of approximately 2000 Michigan middle-grades teachers who indicated they taught a core, academic subject area. The alpha coefficients for the eleven scales ranged from .66 to .97.

Table 7.1.   Reliability Coefficients for Scales on Interdisciplinary Team and Classroom Practices

Scale	No. of items	Sample size	Alpha[a]	Example item
Interdisciplinary team practices				
Curriculum coordination and integration practices	9	1,937	.85	Set goals and objectives relating to student learning.
Coordination of student assignments and assesments	9	1,954	.85	Monitor and coordinate student tests across subjects.
Parent contact and involvement	4	2,067	.76	Plan and implement strategies to increase parent involvement
Contact with other building resource staff	5	1,976	.68	Coordinate efforts with special education, Title I, bilingual education, music, etc.
Classroom practices				
Small group active instruction	5	2,020	.83	Students engage in group problem solving, negotiation, and consensus development.
Integration and interdisciplinary practices	5	2,070	.83	Teachers from other subject areas help plan and carry out instructional units.

Table 7.1.   Reliability Coefficients for Scales on Interdisciplinary Team and Classroom Practices (Cont.)

Scale	No. of items	Sample size	Alpha[a]	Example item
Authentic instruction and assessment	7	2,000	.79	Exhibitions of students' work are used as part of instruction and assessment.
Critical thinking enhancement practices	5	2,076	.69	Students revise their reports and papers
Mathematical skill enhancement practices	4	2,040	.97	Mathematical concepts are taught using real-world examples.
Reading skill enhancement practices	5	2,061	.70	Students read and discuss newspaper articles
Writing skill enhancement practices	4	2,059	.66	Students write and keep journals.

a. Measure of internal consistency is Cronbach's alpha

ANALYSIS AND RESULTS

Teacher Certification Findings

The 2,001 teachers comprising the study sample possess several different types of teacher certifications or even multiple types of certifications (Table 7.2). The three types of certification primarily examined in the analysis were elementary, secondary, and middle-grades certification; thus, 95% (n = 1898) of the teachers have at least one of these certifications. An additional 14% (n = 272) indicate having two of these types; a very small percentage, 0.6% (n = 13), indicate having all three types; and 5% (n = 103) do not have elementary, secondary, or middle-grades certifications. The teachers comprising this last group report certifications in other areas such as administration, special education, provisional, or other. Only 10 teachers out of the entire sample indicated they possessed no teaching certification.

Table 7.2.   Frequency of Teacher Certificates

	Teachers	
Certificates	N	%[a]
Elementary	1,152	58
Secondary	916	46
Middle-grades	128	6
Middle-grades endorsement	238	12

Table 7.2.   Frequency of Teacher Certificates (Cont.)

Certificates	Teachers	
	N	%[a]
Adminstrative	139	7
Special education	188	9
Uncertain	10	1
Provisional	335	17
Other	165	8

a. Percentages do not total to 100% because teachers are permitted to select more than one type of certification.

A closer examination of the teachers reporting an elementary, secondary, or middle-grades certification revealed the following information. The majority of teachers (58%, n = 1152) have elementary certification, 46% (n = 916) have a secondary certification, and only 6% (n = 128) have a middle-grades certification. Of the 128 teachers with middle-grades certification, 80% (n = 103) also have elementary certification, 23% (n=29) have secondary certification, and an additional 22% (n = 28) also indicate that they have a middle-grades endorsement. Middle-grades endorsement is typically defined as an add-on to either an elementary or secondary certification and consists of additional coursework (i.e., 2 to 4 courses).

While it is important to be attuned to the educational needs of future generations of teachers in preservice programs, there are currently middle-grades teachers in the classroom that desire additional professional development or an advanced certification specific to middle-grades education. We know from our data that these middle-grades practitioners choose to remain in the middle grades because an overwhelming majority (87%) indicate a preference for teaching in the middle grades, as opposed to elementary or high school grade levels. The ongoing professional development needs of these teachers should be considered just as important and valid an issue as preservice teacher preparation.

Teachers participating in the Self-Study are also asked to indicate the length of time they have worked in education and how long they have worked with students in the middle grades. These are categorical variables with the response metric indicating the number of years (less than one year, 1–3 years, 4–5 years, 6–10 years, 11–15 years, and more than 15 years). A majority of teachers report that they have worked in the field of education for 15 or more years: 45% (n = 509) for elementary-certified teachers; 50% (n = 442) for secondary-certified teachers; and 40% (n = 49) for middle-grades-certified teachers. Over 60% of elementary- and secondary-certified teachers have 11 years or more experience in the field of education. In examining only those teachers with middle-grades certification, 40% (n = 49) report having worked in the field of education for more than 15 years, 26% (n = 33) for 5 years or less, and the remaining 34% (n = 42) with between 6 to 15 years' experience.

When we examine only those teachers who have worked in education for 5 years or less, there are slightly higher percentages of teachers with middle-grade certification (26%), as compared to elementary (21%) or secondary certification (23%). This indicates, at least in Michigan, that a slightly higher percentage of the new generation of teachers (i.e., those with 5 years or less experience) currently working in middle-grades schools have had specialized middle-level teacher preparation.

In addition to examining the length of time in the field of education, we also looked at how long teachers have worked with students in the middle-grade levels. When we select out teachers with 5 years or less experience, we find that over half, 52% (n = 67), are middle-grades certified, compared to 45% (n = 512) for elementary certified, and 37% (n = 340) for secondary certified. In addition, over 25% (n = 34) of the middle-grades-certified teachers have worked with middle grade students for 11 years or more. Of those teachers with 15 years or more experience, 31% (n = 279) are secondary certified (the highest of any group); however, only 12% (n = 16) are middle-grades certified. This finding provides at least some indication that higher percentages of middle-grades-certified teachers actually find themselves teaching in middle-grade schools.

Before moving on to an examination of middle grades teaching practices, let us first highlight some of the findings regarding teachers with a middle-grade endorsement. In our Michigan Middle Start sample, 12% (n = 238) of teachers report having a middle-grades endorsement. Of those teachers with a middle-grades endorsement, 70% (n = 166) also hold an elementary certification, 32% (n = 75) have a secondary certification, and an additional 12% (n = 28) have a middle-grades certification. The largest percentage (38%) of teachers with a middle-grades endorsement report working in the field of education for more than 15 years, however, 46% (n = 109) of them have specifically worked with middle-grade students for 5 years or less.

To examine what affect the type of teacher certification has on the level of team and classroom practices, we conducted a means analysis of the team and classroom practices' scales. The means were calculated for elementary-, secondary-, and middle-grades-certified teachers, in addition to middle-grades-endorsed teachers. Teachers with two or more certification types contributed to each group for which they indicated they held a certification. For example, if teachers indicated that they had both an elementary and a middle-grades certification, then their reported levels of practices contributed to the mean for both the elementary and the middle-grades groups.

The most important finding was that the middle-grades-certified teachers reported similar levels of team and classroom practices as compared to elementary certified teachers (Table 7.3). Middle-grades-certified teachers actually reported higher levels of practices on one of the team practices' scale (contact with other building resource staff) and three of the seven classroom practices' scales (small group instruction, authentic instruction, and reading skill practices). There was only one practice (integration and interdisciplinary practices) where elementary-certified teachers were higher than middle-grades-certified teachers. Finally, and without exception, teachers with secondary certification had the lowest level of both team and classroom practices (Table 7.3).

Table 7.3.   Descriptive Statistics for Team and Classroom Practices' Scores by Certification Type

	Means, (standard deviations), and number of respondents		
Practices	Elementary certified	Middle-grades certified	Secondary certified
Team practices' scales			
Curriculum coordination and integration practices	3.12 (1.13) 1107	3.12 (1.11) 124	2.84 (1.15) 879
Coordination of student assignments and assessments	3.64 (1.28) 1108	3.65 (1.24) 126	3.27 (1.30) 878
Parent contact and involvement	4.30 (1.03) 1122	4.28 (1.02) 127	4.13 (1.09) 886
Contact with other building resource staff	3.59 (1.12) 1115	3.75 (1.08) 127	3.38 (1.14) 886
Classroom practices' scales			
Small group, active instruction	3.94 (1.26) 1132	4.15 (1.28) 126	3.67 (1.28) 898
Integration and interdisciplinary practices	2.57 (1.15) 1129	2.54 (1.13) 124	2.26 (1.08) 885
Authentic instruction and assessment	3.22 (1.09) 1133	3.33 (1.11) 125	2.98 (1.13) 887

**Table 7.3.   Descriptive Statistics for Team and Classroom Practices'
             Scores by Certification Type (Cont.)**

| | Means, (standard deviations), and number of respondents | | |
Practices	Elementary certified	Middle-grades certified	Secondary certified
Critical thinking practices	4.40 (1.08) 1143	4.46 (1.05) 126	4.11 (1.10) 901
Math skill practices	4.27 (2.27) 1121	4.18 (2.28) 124	3.64 (2.29) 879
Reading skill practices	3.61 (1.17) 1136	3.67 (1.19) 127	3.25 (1.19) 898
Writing skill practices	3.69 (1.26) 1140	3.67 (1.27) 127	3.37 (1.30) 899

Note. Team practices' scores range from 1 to 7 with (1) never, (2) once a year, (3) several times a year, (4) quarterly, (5) monthly, (6) weekly, and (7) daily. Classroom practices' scores range from 1 to 7 with (1) never, (2) several times a year, (3) monthly, (4) several times a month, (5) weekly, (6) several times a week, and (7) daily.

One aspect of this analysis that required further investigation was the effect of the length of time a teacher has worked in the field of education. It is feasible to suggest that teachers with more experience in the classroom, regardless of certification type, may engage more frequently in certain types of team and/or classroom practices. To address this question, two data subsets were created: (1) containing teachers with 5 years or less experience in the field of education (23% of teachers); and (2) containing only teachers with 15 years or more experience (45% of teachers).

An examination of the team and classroom practices of these two groups revealed similar results as that found with the overall group of teachers. In other words, it does not appear as though there is a bias in the sample for teachers with more or less teaching experience than the overall sample. There were, however, two notable exceptions. First, middle-grade-certified teachers with less than 5 years' experience in the field of education have slightly higher levels of most team practices than the overall sample, especially teachers with at least 15 years' experience. However, these same less-experienced teachers have slightly lower levels of classroom practices than the overall sample, especially teachers with at least 15 years' experience. This suggests that more experienced teachers engage in the identified classroom practices more frequently, yet use fewer team practices.

Importance of Interdisciplinary Teaming and Common Planning Time

Another approach to examining the effects of teacher certification on team and classroom practices is to consider the types of organizational structures present within the schools that enable teachers to better facilitate the implementation of middle-grades practices. A critical element to successful middle schools is the creation of small, personalized learning communities (i.e., interdisciplinary teaming). Interdisciplinary teaming is typically defined as a group of teachers from different subject areas who plan and work together and who share the same students for a significant portion of the school day. This type of organizational structure is intended to create a context that enables students and teachers to know one another better and allows teachers to better support and understand the educational needs of students. Teams generally focus on creating coordinated lesson plans; share and discuss student progress, problems, and issues; and integrate subjects around a central theme or issue (Epstein & Mac Iver, 1990; Erb, 2001; George & Alexander, 1993; Pate, 1997). The growing body of evidence supporting the positive impact of interdisciplinary teaming on middle-grades schools and students is difficult to refute. Students and teachers in schools that have implemented teaming and its associated practices with some degree of integrity consistently report more positive and productive learning environments (Arhar 1990, 1997; Dickinson & Erb, 1997; Lee & Smith, 1993; Steffes & Valentine, 1996). In addition, more large-scale and comprehensive studies have been conducted and successfully demonstrate the effects of teaming on student outcomes (Felner et al., 1997; Mertens, Flowers, & Mulhall, 1998; University of Illinois, 2001).

Research has demonstrated that in order for interdisciplinary teams to be effective, teachers on these teams need regular common planning time to work together as a group to integrate and coordinate curriculum, student assignments, and assessments, as well as to contact and involve parents (Erb & Doda, 1989; Flowers, Mertens, & Mulhall, 1999, 2000b; George & Alexander, 1993; Howe & Bell, 1998; Warren & Muth, 1995). Unlike individual planning time, common planning time enables teachers to meet together as a team to discuss the integration of interdisciplinary curricular, instructional, and assessment issues. Our prior research has demonstrated that when teachers in schools fully engaged in teaming are provided with high levels of common planning time (i.e., a minimum of four meetings per week at 30 or more minutes per meeting), student self-reported outcomes improve, including depression, behavior problems, self-esteem, and academic efficacy (Mertens et al., 1998). In addition, student achievement scores improved dramatically, particularly for those schools with high percentages (60% or more) of free/reduced-price lunch students.

School-Level Implementation Categories

In prior research, a subset of 75 of the schools in the existing sample had already been categorized, based on their level of interdisciplinary teaming and accompanying common planning time:

1. Schools that were engaged in teaming in all middle grade levels with accompanying high levels of common planning time (at least four meetings per week for a minimum of 30 minutes per meeting) (n = 26 schools),

2. Schools engaged in teaming in all middle grade levels with low levels of common planning time (n = 25 schools), or

3. Schools that have minimal components of teaming (e.g., teaming in some but not all of their middle grade levels) or they are not teaming at all (n = 24 schools).

The "level of teaming implementation" classification is based on an analysis of quantitative Self-Study survey data collected from teachers and principals and qualitative data gathered through telephone interviews (University of Illinois, 2001). References to common planning time are restricted to schools that have set aside separate and additional planning time for teachers working together as a team. Schools that use their individual planning time to meet as a team are not considered to have common planning time (Flowers et al., 1999, 2000b; Mertens et al., 1998).

Teacher Certification and School-Level Implementation Findings

When we examined the levels of team and classroom practices by both teacher certification type and the level of teaming implementation, several significant findings emerged. One of these findings is directly related to the impact of interdisciplinary teaming combined with common planning time. The other findings can be attributed to the combined effects of certification type and teaming implementation.

First, regardless of certification type, teachers in schools that are teaming with high levels of common planning time have higher levels of both team and classroom practices (Table 7.4). It is not surprising that teachers in schools engaged in teaming are reporting higher levels of team practices. However, interestingly, even the secondary teachers, who generally report lower levels of these types of practices, report higher levels of team practices if they are engaged in teaming.

Table 7.4. Descriptive Statistics for Team and Classroom Practices Scores by Certification Type and Level of Teaming Implementation

Means, (standard deviations), and number of respondents

Scales	Elementary certified			Middle-grades certified			Secondary certified		
	Teaming high CPT	Teaming low CPT	Other/not teaming	Teaming high CPT	Teaming low CPT	Other/not teaming	Teaming high CPT	Teaming low CPT	Other/not teaming
Team practices' scales									
Curriculum coordination and integration practices	3.46[a] (1.06) 251	3.24[b] (1.12) 193	2.91[ab] (1.24) 147	3.47[a] (0.95) 31	3.13[b] (1.05) 21	2.34[ab] (1.08) 25	3.22[a] (1.22) 200	3.09[b] (1.19) 144	2.35[ab] (1.04) 135
Coordination of student assignments and assessments	4.05[ab] (1.15) 250	3.58[a] (1.31) 195	3.41[b] (1.39) 146	4.23[a] (1.18) 32	3.49 (1.12) 23	2.95[a] (1.22) 24	3.81[a] (1.26) 199	3.39[a] (1.30) 144	2.76[a] (1.21) 134
Parent contact and involvement	3.97[ab] (1.03) 253	3.53[a] (1.11) 196	3.43[b] (1.25) 146	4.24 (0.94) 32	3.32 (0.94) 23	3.34 (1.06) 24	3.80[a] (1.07) 202	3.47[a] (1.20) 145	3.08[a] (1.17) 135
Contact with other building resource staff	4.65[ab] (0.95) 254	4.26[a] (1.00) 196	4.10[b] (1.08) 147	4.60[ab] (1.04) 32	4.17[a] (1.00) 23	3.91[b] (1.17) 24	4.64[a] (0.96) 203	4.11[a] (1.05) 146	3.68[a] (0.98) 134
Classroom practices' scales									
Small group, active instruction	4.11 (1.25) 253	3.94 (1.33) 196	4.07 (1.26) 163	4.63 (1.16) 32	3.99 (1.38) 23	4.00 (1.28) 24	3.70 (1.25) 202	3.76 (1.34) 145	3.79 (1.28) 146
Integration and interdisciplinary practices	2.74 (1.14) 249	2.77 (1.19) 197	2.60 (1.31) 157	2.83 (1.28) 32	2.43 (1.00) 22	2.31 (1.10) 23	2.55[ab] (1.20) 200	2.46[b] (1.24) 143	2.02[ab] (0.98) 142

Table 7.4. Descriptive Statistics for Team and Classroom Practices Scores by Certification Type and Level of Teaming Implementation (Cont.)

Means, (standard deviations), and number of respondents

Scales	Elementary certified			Middle-grades certified			Secondary certified		
	Teaming high CPT	Teaming low CPT	Other/not teaming	Teaming high CPT	Teaming low CPT	Other/not teaming	Teaming high CPT	Teaming low CPT	Other/not teaming
Authentic instruction and assessment	3.44 (1.10) 252	3.19 (1.05) 196	3.41 (1.12) 162	3.65 (1.01) 32	3.12 (0.97) 22	3.20 (0.05) 24	3.22 (1.12) 202	2.93 (1.08) 141	3.11 (1.19) 143
Critical thinking practices	4.53 (1.02) 254	4.45 (1.14) 197	4.47 (1.10) 165	4.70 (0.92) 31	4.36 (0.97) 23	4.24 (1.18) 24	4.21 (1.00) 203	4.13 (1.18) 145	4.16 (1.06) 145
Math skill practices	4.53 (2.24) 248	4.29 (2.28) 196	4.30 (2.23) 161	4.92 (2.03) 31	4.42 (2.21) 22	3.96 (2.21) 24	3.82 (2.33) 197	3.96 (2.30) 144	3.52 (2.25) 144
Reading skill practices	3.77 (1.14) 254	3.71 (1.24) 196	3.74 (1.10) 165	3.81 (1.23) 32	3.77 (1.11) 23	3.53 (1.03) 24	3.53 (1.09) 203	3.40 (1.28) 147	3.28 (1.15) 144
Writing skill practices	3.88 (1.20) 254	3.75 (1.34) 196	3.84 (1.25) 163	4.01 (0.98) 32	3.92 (1.48) 23	3.51 (1.11) 24	3.64 (1.23) 203	3.35 (1.42) 146	3.42 (1.19) 144

Note. CPT = Common Planning Time; team practices scores range from 1 to 7 with (1) never, (2) once a year, (3) several times a year, (4) quarterly, (5) monthly, (6) weekly, and (7) daily. Classroom practices scores range from 1 to 7 with (1) never, (2) several times a year, (3) monthly, (4) several times a month, (5) weekly, (6) several times a week, and (7) daily. a,b Means with a common letter differ from each other at p < .05 (Scheffe)

Prior research has indicated that when schools begin to move toward the middle school philosophy (i.e., interdisciplinary teaming, integrated curriculum and instruction, teacher-led advisory), that over time, they are able to demonstrate gains in teaming practices more readily than for classroom practices (Flowers, Mertens, & Mulhall, 2000a; Mertens et al., 1998). We have observed that gains in classroom practices often require a longer period of time and occur after teaming practices are established and have become a regular part of the curriculum and instruction.

A corollary of the above finding was that teachers in schools classified as teaming with low levels of common planning time have consistently higher levels of team practices than schools classified as not teaming/other. The effects of teaming are unquestionable. The more engaged a school is in interdisciplinary teaming, the higher the levels of both team and classroom practices.

An analysis of variance (ANOVA) was conducted to assess the effects of the teaming implementation variable. Within the three certification types, the mean differences by implementation groups for nearly all of the team practices' scales were statistically significant at the $p < .05$ level. The only exception was the implementation group means for middle-grades-certified teachers for the parent contact and involvement scale (see Table 7.4).

A second finding is that middle-grades-certified teachers in schools that are teaming with high levels of common planning time reported the absolute highest levels of both team and classroom practices, a pattern that is consistent across all 11 of the scales. This finding supports and reaffirms the belief that when teachers are both prepared to teach in the middle grades and are provided with a supportive environment (teaming) and resources (common planning time), they are able to implement with reasonable levels of fidelity the types of team and classroom practices recognized as being "best practices."

We do not advocate or support the recommendation for schools to adopt teaming in the absence of common planning time. However, results from this study have found that middle-grades-certified teachers, as compared to elementary or secondary certified, working in schools classified as teaming with low levels of common planning time, had higher levels of practices on nearly all of the classroom practices' scales. So, even though these middle-grades-certified teachers were not provided with all of the necessary components or resources, they were still able to demonstrate higher levels of team and classroom practices. This clearly suggests that the preparation programs these teachers experienced, together with some level of structural resources in their schools, enabled them to engage in higher levels of effective practices. This, however, is not to say that if we simply provide teachers with some, but not all, of the required preparation and resources they will still be able to impact student learning effectively.

DISCUSSION

In reviewing the results of this study, we observed three major findings. First, teachers possessing an elementary or middle-grades certification participated more frequently in the types of team and classroom practices that are known to be effective in teaching and learning with young adolescents. Scale scores for these two certification types were comparable; middle-grades-certified teachers actually reported slightly higher scores on four scales. Without exception, secondary-certified teachers reported the lowest levels for all practices.

Second, regardless of certification type, in schools where teaming has been implemented in all middle-grade levels combined with high levels of common planning time, teachers report higher levels of both team and classroom practices. The effects of teaming, especially when combined with common planning time, have been demonstrated, so the higher levels of team practices observed in schools actively engaged in teaming are not unexpected. The more interesting finding is the impact teaming has had on the team and classroom practices of secondary-certified teachers.

Third, middle-grade-certified teachers working in schools engaged in teaming with high levels of common planning time have the highest levels of practices on all team and classroom practices' scales. This finding is very significant and unequivocally demonstrates the effect on team and classroom practices when middle-grades-certified teachers are placed in highly implemented schools. Michigan teachers in this study who met these two criteria reported engaging in both team and classroom practices at a higher rate than any other combination of teacher certification and school-level implementation categories. Even middle-grades-certified teachers in less fully implemented schools reported higher levels of practices for the majority of classroom practices' scales.

The Self-Study teacher survey data are collected in an anonymous manner; therefore, directly linking student outcome data (i.e., achievement data) to school-level teacher certification data is impossible. However, this study now enables us to make the connection between teacher certification and student achievement outcomes through an alternative approach.

This study has established that teacher certification and teaming implementation have a combined and positive effect on the levels of team and classroom practices. Our prior research with middle-grades schools as part of the Michigan Middle Start Initiative has demonstrated a relationship between team and classroom practices and student achievement scores. Middle Start schools identified as teaming in all middle-grade levels with high levels of common planning time had the largest gain over time in their standardized student achievement scores (see Flowers et al., 1999; Mertens et al., 1988). Schools identified as not teaming had the lowest gains.

When the findings are combined, we get a clearer picture of the effect of teacher certification on student achievement outcomes. Teachers with middle-grades certification (i.e., specialized preservice education), in schools that are teaming with high levels of common planning time, have higher levels of team and classroom practices and subsequently have the potential for greater gains in student learning, as evidenced by the student achievement results.

CONCLUSION

The results of this study are very promising and serve to further strengthen the argument for specialized middle-grades teacher preparation programs. The data presented here clearly establish a link between teacher certification and the levels of research-based "best practices" occurring in middle-grade schools. Compared to secondary-certified teachers, teachers with elementary or middle-grades certification had higher levels of both team and classroom practices. The positive effects of middle-grades certification combined with the implementation of interdisciplinary teaming and high levels of common planning time observed in this study are unequivocal and demonstrate the nature of the interrelatedness of these middle school reform components. Proper preservice training and preparation of middle-grades teachers is critically important, but if the organizational structures within schools are not developed and sustained, teachers will fail to reach the full potential of their training.

Likewise, teaching and learning that are developmentally appropriate for young adolescents is essential, but successful implementation is dependent upon the level of teacher preparation and sustainable organizational structures. The creation of small, personalized learning environments is also important, but teaming and other organizational structures alone are not sufficient. To responsibly meet the needs of young adolescents during their middle school years, attention must be paid to all of the middle school reform elements, not simply those easiest to implement or achieve.

AUTHORS' NOTE

We would like to acknowledge the W. K. Kellogg Foundation for their ongoing support of our research and evaluation efforts as part of the Michigan Middle Start Initiative. We would also like to acknowledge the Association of Illinois Middle Level Schools and Robert Felner for their contributions to the development of the School Improvement Self-Study.

REFERENCES

Arhar, J. (1990). Interdisciplinary teaming as a school intervention to increase the social bonding of middle level students. In *Research in middle level education: Selected studies 1990.* Columbus, OH: National Middle School Association.

Arhar, J. (1997). The effects of interdisciplinary teaming on teachers and students. In J. Irvin (Ed.), *What current research says to the middle level practitioner* (pp. 49–55). Columbus, OH: National Middle School Association.

Alexander, W. M., & McEwin, C. K. (1989). *Schools in the middle: Status and progress.* Columbus, OH: National Middle School Association.

Carnegie Council on Adolescent Development. (1989). *Turning points: Preparing American youth for the 21st century.* New York: Carnegie Corporation of New York.

Cooney, S. (2000). *A middle grades message: A well-qualified teacher in every classroom matters.* Atlanta, GA: Southern Regional Education Board.

Dickinson, T. S., & Erb, T. O. (1997). *We gain more than we give: Teaming in middle schools.* Columbus, OH: National Middle School Association.

Epstein, J. L., & Mac Iver, D. J. (1990). *Education in the middle grades: National practices and trends.* Columbus, OH: National Middle School Association.

Erb, T. O. (2001). Transforming organizational structures for young adolescents and adult learning. In T. S. Dickinson (Ed.), *Reinventing the middle school* (pp. 176–200). New York: RoutledgeFalmer.

Erb, T. O., & Doda, N. M. (1989). *Team organization: Promise—practices and possibilities.* Washington, DC: National Education Association.

Felner, R. D., Jackson, A. W., Kasak, D., Mulhall, P., Brand, S., & Flowers, N. (1997). The impact of school reform for the middle years: Longitudinal study of a network engaged in Turning Points-based comprehensive school transformation. *Phi Delta Kappan, 78*(7), 528–532, 541–550.

Flowers, N., Mertens, S. B., & Mulhall, P. F. (1999). The impact of teaming: Five research-based outcomes of teaming. *Middle School Journal, 31*(2), 57–60.

Flowers, N., Mertens, S. B., & Mulhall, P. F. (2000a). How teaming influences classroom practices. *Middle School Journal, 32*(2), 52–59.

Flowers, N., Mertens, S. B., & Mulhall, P. F. (2000b). What makes interdisciplinary teams effective? *Middle School Journal, 31*(4), 53–56.

George, P. S., & Alexander, W. M. (1993). *The exemplary middle school* (2nd ed.). Fort Worth, TX: Harcourt Brace Jovanovich.

Howe, A. C., & Bell, J. (1998). Factors associated with successful implementation of interdisciplinary curriculum units. *Research in Middle Level Education Quarterly, 21*(2), 39–52.

Jackson, A. W., & Davis, G. A. (2000). *Turning points 2000: Educating adolescents in the 21st century.* New York: Teachers College Press.

Lee, V., & Smith, J. (1993). Effects of school restructuring on the achievement and engagement of middle-grades students. *Sociology of Education, 66*(3), 164–187.

Lewis, A. C. (2000). A tale of two reform strategies. *Phi Delta Kappan, 81*(10), K6–K18.

McEwin, C. K., & Dickinson, T. S. (1995). *The professional preparation of middle level teachers: Profiles of successful programs.* Columbus, OH: National Middle School Association.

McEwin, C. K., Dickinson, T. S., & Jenkins, D. M. (1996). *America's middle schools: Practices and progress—A 25 year perspective.* Columbus, OH: National Middle School Association.

McEwin, C. K., Dickinson, T. S., & Hamilton, H. (2000). National board certified teachers' views regarding specialized middle level teacher preparation. *The Clearing House, 73*(4), 211–213.

Mertens, S. B., Flowers, N., & Mulhall, P. F. (1998, August). *The Middle Start Initiative, Phase I: A longitudinal analysis of Michigan middle-level schools.* Unpublished manuscript, University of Illinois, Center for Prevention Research and Development.

National Forum to Accelerate Middle Grades Reform. (2002). *National Forum policy statement: Teacher preparation, licensure, and recruitment policy.* Newton, MA: Education Development Center.

National Middle School Association. (1991). *Professional certification and preparation for the middle level: A position paper of the National Middle School Association.* Columbus, OH: Author.

Pate, E. (1997). Teaming and decision making. In T. S. Dickinson & T. O. Erb (Eds.), *We gain more than we give: Teaming in middle schools* (pp. 425–442). Columbus, OH: National Middle School Association.

Scales, P. C. (1992). *Windows of opportunity: Improving middle grades teacher preparation.* Chapel Hill: University of North Carolina, Center for Early Adolescence.

Scales, P. C., & McEwin, C. K. (1994). *Growing pains: The making of America's middle school teachers.* Columbus, OH: National Middle School Association.

Scales, P. C., & McEwin, C. K. (1996). The effects of comprehensive middle level teacher preparation programs. *Research in Middle Level Education Quarterly, 19*(2), 1–21.

Steffes, B., & Valentine, J. (1996). The relationship between organizational characteristics and expected benefits in interdisciplinary teams. *Research in Middle Level Education Quarterly, 19*(4), 83–106.

University of Illinois, Center for Prevention Research and Development. (2001). *An evaluation of Michigan Middle Start Schools from 1994 to 2001.* Unpublished manuscript, University of Illinois, Urbana-Champaign.

Valentine, J., Clark, D., Nickerson, N., & Keefe, J. (1981). *The middle level principalship: A survey of middle level principals and programs* (Vol. 1). Reston, VA: National Association of Secondary School Principals.

Warren, L. L., & Muth, K. D. (1995). The impact of common planning time on middle grade students and teachers. *Research in Middle Level Education, 18*(3), 41–58.

CHAPTER 8

CHARACTER EDUCATION INFUSED INTO MIDDLE LEVEL EDUCATION

Thomas F. Mandeville and Rich Radcliffe
Southwest Texas State University

ABSTRACT

Columbine, vandalism, teen pregnancies, and suicides confront middle-level educators with the challenge of implementing character education. Although milestone studies, such as *Turning Points* and *Turning Points 2000,* call for character education, a wide variety of strategies exist including add-on, integration, and infusion models. Research findings for character education programs are scarce and often contain validity threats. Yet many character education experts advocate an infusion approach. Recent brain research findings suggest that early adolescence may be an opportune time for character education, and that this may be most effective when both cognitive and affective processes are engaged. In this chapter, therefore, we consider whether character education is effective and developmentally appropriate for middle level students, and if so, by what process it is best taught.

Middle School Curriculum, Instruction, and Assessment, pages 139–155
Copyright © 2002 by Information Age Publishing
All rights of reproduction in any form reserved.

The Basic School, while helping students become literate and well informed, also has a duty, along with parents and religious institutions, to help children develop the capacity to live responsibly and judge wisely in matters of life and conduct.

Ernest Boyer (1995, p. 156)

It appears that America is in great need of character education today. Columbine, teen pregnancies, Monica, the Matthew Shepherd and James Byrd killings, Timothy McVeigh, and now 9–11, John Walker Lindh, and ENRON emphasize the need for attention to the moral fiber in America. During the 15-year period from the *Turning Points* report (Carnegie Council on Adolescent Development, 1989) to *Turning Points 2000* (Jackson & Davis, 2000), middle school educators have held "the vision of a 15-year-old who has been well served during the middle grades," who is a "good citizen" and a "caring and ethical person" (Davis, 2001, p. 219). A consistent message from middle school educators has been a call to focus curriculum on the developmental needs of adolescents. Character education, however, has experienced a vacillating history in America. As Murphy (1998) suggests, social crises among teenagers such as homicides, suicides, vandalism, and teenage pregnancies have been a catalyst for character education movements. Unfortunately, inconsistent definitions, poorly articulated objectives, and fears over whose values get taught have been impediments to these movements. In light of these impediments, educators must rethink and redefine character education.

Character education curricula, whether purchased or developed by school districts, focus on such ideals as *care, empathy, responsibility,* and *respect* for self and others. *Caritas*, "related to the words charity, caring, and cherish, is a Latin word meaning regard, affection, esteem, and love, and also has the connotation of preciousness" (Noddings & Shore, 1998, p. 222). *Empathy,* for conservative character educator Thomas Lickona (1991) and moral philosopher Mark Johnson (1963), is a more precise term. Lickona equates *respect* with "showing regard for the worth of someone or something. Respect takes three major forms: respect for oneself, respect for other people, and respect for all forms of life and the environment that sustains them" (p. 43). *Responsibility,* he says, is an extension of respect. "If we respect other people, we value them. If we value them, we feel a measure of responsibility for their welfare" (p. 43). Together, respect and responsibility are equal to what Lickona calls empathy.

The purpose of this chapter is to consider whether character education is effective and developmentally appropriate for middle level students, and if so, by what process it is best taught. To accomplish our purpose we first explore two moral philosophies in which empathy is preeminent. Next, we briefly review the history of character education, the instructional processes used, and supportive research. Then, to substantiate the importance of helping young adolescents develop empathy, we examine their cognitive and neurological processes. Following this we consider best practices for infusing character education into the whole curriculum and conclude with recommendations and concomitant benefits.

EMPATHY IN TWO MORAL PHILOSOPHIES

Many moral philosophers of late have been turning to neuroscience, developmental psychology, and evolutionary biology to understand the nature and limits of moral reasoning and to see how people actually reason. Whereas visual perception and language processing have been the complex processes of choice through which neuroscientists studied the brain and mind, many cognitive scientists are looking now to moral reasoning as a complex form of human cognition that challenges their theoretical models. Two such philosophers are James Garbarino and Mark Johnson.

Garbarino: Moral Circles

Empathy for someone places the recipient within one's moral circle, which Garbarino (1999) describes as the line of demarcation separating those things in life for which we accept a moral obligation from those things for which we perceive little or no moral obligation. Inside our moral circle might be our immediate and extended families, our dog, and our best friends. Outside our moral circle might be the one uncle who has been abusive to us, the neighbor's dog that typically growls and threatens us, a thief caught stealing from us, and everyone else. The authors suspect that there are concentric circles with degrees of empathy, though Garbarino considers empathy as an "all or nothing" state in the same way Noddings (1992) describes her construct of care.

The notion of moral circles is also consistent with Noddings's notion of a caring person who she characterizes as having both *engrossment* and *motivational displacement,* where engrossment refers to "an open, nonselective receptivity to the cared-for" (1992, p. 15) and motivational displacement is "the sense that our motive energy is flowing toward others and their projects" (p. 16).

Johnson: Moral Imagination

Moral imagination (Johnson, 1963) is the imaginative structure of our moral concepts and the reasoning we do with them. That is, our ability to envision a variety of plausible resolutions in turn helps us develop moral judgments with which we deliberate and decide what to do in morally complex situations or dilemmas. Moral imagination has four moral elements: prototypes, metaphors, narratives, and moral perceptions.

Prototypes

Humans organize cognitively stored knowledge around prototypical instances of experience rather than around lexical definitions or sensory icons of memory. These prototypes carry with them the meaning, point, and force of the contexts from which they came, implying that they carry with them the affective dimensions that evoke emotions, moods, empathy, and other affective states. "In this way, our basic moral concepts are never pure abstractions, but are always permeated with passion and emotion that move us to action" (Johnson, 1993, p. 199). To properly understand prototypes, May, Friedman, and Clark (1996) suggest:

> We should carefully distinguish exemplars, stereotypes, and prototypes. Exemplars are the concrete instances we encounter during training or learning. Stereotypes are the socially constructed images of 'typical' exemplars of a concept or category (e.g., the stereotypic nurse). Prototypes (as used in most cognitive scientific literature) are the internally represented results of a process that extracts statistical central tendency information from the specific set of exemplars to which an individual system has been exposed. Statistical central tendency information is information concerning which features are most common to the exemplars of some class. (pp. 5–6)

Johnson (1993) says, "We learn about justice, not as an abstract concept, but by prototypical situations of experienced fair and unfair distribution" (p. 191). Prototypes also grow and change over time. Our prototype of a bully easily changes from the playground toughie to overbearing boss to Al Qaeda terrorists. Prototypes, then, are one of the four elements of our process of moral judgment. Another is metaphor.

Metaphors

"A conceptual metaphor is a mapping of a conceptual structure from a source domain, which is typically some aspect of our concrete bodily experience, onto a more abstract or less highly articulated target domain" (Johnson & Gilmore, 1996, p. 51). A metaphor, then, is an abstraction of a sensory experience, and moral metaphors derive from experiences encased in moral consequence. Like prototypes, metaphors are conceptual rather than logical propositions or linguistic statements. Johnson (1993) explains that as abstractions, metaphors are less direct, but more universally applicable than direct encoding of experience, so metaphors may hide as much as they reveal, and what is hidden may be as important as what is revealed (1993, p. 195). Because concepts are "metaphorically defined...we are hardly ever engaged in applying literal, univocal concepts [to moral situations]" (p. 193).

According to Johnson (1996), if Elena does a favor for Hector, then Hector owes her a return favor. If Hector always pays back his debts, then Elena develops a metaphor "Your credit is good," which becomes "wealth and well-being." When Elena does volunteer hospice work, she says, "It enriches my life." Her work engenders her metaphoric response, "wealth and well-being." This sort of response is also available to Elena in times of moral uncertainty, making this metaphor a powerful component of her moral imagination. Knowing our own moral metaphors assists in self-understanding, that is, knowing these moral values have been examined and accepted as our own, rather than merely having unquestioningly accepted someone else's moral value.

Narratives

The third element of moral imagination is narrative or knowing the elements of fiction including setting, character, and plot. Thinking of ourselves as a character in a narrative, called life experience, helps us realize we have a beginning, middle, and end, that we have supporting characters, and that our experiences are contextualized in a physical, social, and emotional setting. Narrative plot, with its crisis–decision pattern of the rising action, provides imaginative and vicarious experience with resolving crises, the will and experience to seek out patterns of events, and the habit of questioning causes. We live in a world of narrative; we are told of the ENRON and O.J. stories, we tell friends the "story" of our lives, and our minds tend to "fill in" the spaces with narrative content when we do not have all the answers.

Martha Nussbaum has argued eloquently for the central role of literature in our moral development: "A tragedy does not display the dilemmas of its characters as pre-articulated; it shows them searching for the morally salient; and it forces us, as interpreters, to be similarly active" (2001, p. 12). Johnson (1993) suggests that fiction is a place to explore the implications of people's character and choices. We watch a particular character in a particular setting and under particular circumstances choose to live her life. He contends that fiction gives us the power to develop our moral sensitivity, develop empathy for others, and make subtle distinctions about the nature and salient moral issues within well-crafted situations.

Moral Perception

Our ability to recognize morally salient aspects of issues as we encounter them is called our moral perception and comes in frames of reference. The way we frame a particular situation is crucial in defining the other elements of moral imagination that we bring to it. Johnson (1993) uses the example of members of a state police force breaking into a home and confiscating some documents that the residents wrote in secret. Suppose this is the mid-1950s at the height of the McCarthy era, and we frame this as an invasion of privacy. Suppose this is just September 14, 2001, and we frame this as confiscation of evidence, perhaps of a terrorist cell operating clandestinely within our national borders. Now we have to decide how to act, and the two frames of reference we have suggested for Johnson's event would bring forth different prototypes, metaphors, and narratives with which to make a decision. While our frames might have seemed clear-cut, we must recognize that communist cells did operate clandestinely in the United States in the 1950s. We must also recognize that racial and/or ethnic profiling has been a serious issue during the latter months of 2001. As we consider the confiscation event, the political and social tenor of the day, heightened moral perception makes us sensitive to situations that we might be callous to otherwise, the communists' cells or the ethnic profiling.

Developing moral imagination seems to require that when we get into a potentially moral situation, we recognize it for what it is as separate from all other possibilities. Then we must bring to bear our moral prototypes and moral metaphors learned in the narrative fabric throughout our lives.

HOW HAVE WE TAUGHT CHARACTER EDUCATION?

Prior to the 20th century, teachers of virtuous and righteous character modeled morality and character. These traits were more valued than good or even sufficient content knowledge (J. H. Johnson, personal communication, February 1999). "In the early public schools and continuing into the twentieth century nothing, including the 3Rs, competed in significance with character training" (Goodman & Lesnick, 2001, p. 126). Later, good character included not only morality but citizenship as well. The story of George Washington chopping down the cherry tree, for example, blends the two. Washington was our first president, and he would not tell a lie. America's first textbook series, McGuffey's Readers (Thompson & McGuffey, 1879), published from 1836 to 1921, infused biblical verses, moral affirmations, and morally didactic stories beginning in *The First Eclectic Reader* and continuing with similar content through *The Sixth Eclectic Reader*, which contained Patrick Henry's speech before the Virginia Commonwealth and the Speech of Paul [the apostle] on Mars Hill.

The "Roaring Twenties," with its immigration, urbanization, and industrialization, accelerated character education with elaborate codes of conduct and extracurricular activities designed "to provide opportunities for practicing the virtues enunciated in the codes" (Leming, 1997, p. 12).

Interestingly, the 1920s and 1930s saw Dewey's (1916) Progressivism and his call for democracy in education (1916). Character education and democratic education have been overlapping entities ever since and have become a reframing and gradual redefining of morality and citizenship.

Seventy years ago, Dewey (1933) acknowledged that while schools may not have a moral education program, they foster moral education through a hidden curriculum. In today's schools, the approach is more direct. As described by Chazan, there has been a "remarkable explosion in reflection, experiment, and programming related to moral education" (1985, p. ix). Character education expert Lickona (1991), presents 10 reasons why schools should commit to developing good character in their students. One of his reasons is that moral questions are among the great questions facing individuals. This is particularly relevant to young adolescents as they embark on their search for a unique identity.

Murphy (1998) studied character education programs in more than 100 Blue Ribbon schools identified by the U.S. Department of Education Blue Ribbon Award Program. She makes it clear that not all schools define character education in the same way. Her research identified six ways in which character education is promoted in Blue Ribbon schools. These include assemblies, community service, curriculum, discipline plans, school awards, and staff models. DeRoche and Williams (2001) report three types of character education programs, including those connected with content-area lessons, those containing supplemental activity programs, and those linked to community-based programs. Review of the literature finds support for all three. Lickona (1991) recommends teaching character education through the curriculum by using the ethically rich content found in academic subjects. Supplemental activity programs that strengthen character are included in Leming's (1997) review of programs. Based on his survey of 50 principals who reported a formal community service program, O'Keefe (1997) describes the variety of character development opportunities available when schools have community connections.

Affective and Cognitive Models

Character education approaches may focus on affective development, cognitive development, or integration of both domains. The Quest Skills for Adolescents program views character education as a learning process dealing with affective responses (Murphy, 1998). This commercially prepared curriculum in self-esteem and decision making helps adolescents gain self-confidence, good judgment, and social skills needed to cope with the challenges of today's world. When educators use Kohlberg's (1969) dilemmas to develop moral reasoning, character education is being approached as a cognitive process. Kohlberg viewed moral development as a sequence of qualitative changes in the way an individual thinks. Gilligan (1982) criticized Kohlberg's theory on the basis that it was limited to a justice perspective. She described a care perspective, one that reflects relationships and concern for others.

Some character development models are add-on programs. Project Essential, one of 10 character education programs reviewed by Leming (1997), provides curriculum that helps students earn their own sense of self-worth. The premise is that adolescent problems can be addressed successfully through the enhancement of self-esteem. The reviewer reports that a 4-year evaluation of the Project Essential curriculum found that teachers reported statistically significant positive changes in student's self-control, respect of others, and acceptance of responsibility. The Character Education Curriculum (Leming, 1997) may be taught as a stand-alone subject. The objective of the program is to teach 12 universal values to students. Evaluation data on the curriculum suggests that the program leads to a reduction in student problems. The questionnaires that were completed by students, teachers, and principals indicated satisfaction with the program.

The research findings for effectiveness of the above models and other programs have typically been based on observations and self-reports. Consequently, a threat to validity exists among much of the research. Research on the effectiveness of character education models that are designed specifically for young adolescents is scarce. To date, research has more often been focused on elementary-grades programs such as the Acquiring Ethical Guidelines for Individual Development (AEGIS), the Child Development Project, and Lions-Quest models.

Interaction and Infusion Models

An alternative to add-on programs is character education that integrates affective learning and cognitive instruction in content areas. Today's world finds a strong demand for both content learning, as mandated by state learning and assessment standards, and affective learning in response to gangs, violence, and community issues. Educators may respond to both demands by integrating affective character education curriculum and cognitive instruction in content areas.

Several character education models provide for integration of character development and content curriculum. Character education may be presented through an approach such as the Heartwood Institute's curriculum that integrates affective and cognitive processes. Reporting on progress at a Pennsylvania middle school, Murphy (1998) explains that Heartwood is a multicultural curriculum that allows teachers to integrate character education into literature, social studies, art, and music. The Community for Caring program (Leming, 1997) was developed as a middle school model. Teachers are encouraged to use the many opportunities present in existing school curricula to focus student attention on the program's five values. For the program to be effective, teachers must adapt their content teaching to include elements of character education. This level of integration would be considered an infusion of character education into the curricula. Infusion of character education is a more pervasive approach than integration. Infusion suggests that character education prevails throughout the whole school in comparison to integration, which focuses more on connecting a content lesson or unit, such as in social studies or literature, with character education.

The research findings for the above models are encouraging. In the research Leming (1997) reported for the Community for Caring program, students' grade point average increased, students gained knowledge of consequences of risky behaviors, and fewer disciplinary problems occurred. Murphy (1998) also describes the Heartwood program as one of the best character development programs that she has found. Using a quasi-experimental design, evaluators found that students who participated in the Heartwood program demonstrated higher levels of ethical understanding and demonstrated improved conduct.

While the research findings on integrating character education into curriculum are limited, a number of educators endorse these approaches. Lickona recommends using the "academic curriculum as moral educator" (1991, pp. 162–163) approach. He warns that teachers are wasting a great opportunity if they fail to use that curriculum as a vehicle for character education. More recently, Johnson (1997) describes the "countless" opportunities for teachers to use the morally rich content of academic subjects including literature, history, science, and art as vehicles to teach moral lessons. In describing teaching strategies at Blue Ribbon schools, Murphy (1998) explains that character education may be integrated with cooperative learning activities, thematic units, whole language instruction, and portfolio assessment. According to Weber (1998), preservice preparation programs for teachers should guide them in how to use subject content as an opportunity for character education.

Infusing character education into many aspects of school life is an extension of the integration approach. Describing this holistic view, DeRoche and Williams (2001) list seven guiding principles from the Character Education Manifesto (http://www.bu.edu/education/caec) that major players in the character education movement created. The infusion approach is revealed in one of those principles: "Character education is an integral part of school life, in which the school becomes a community of virtue fostering modeling, teaching, expecting, celebrating, and practicing responsibility, hard work, honesty, and kindness" (DeRoche & Williams, p. 3). Similar endorsement for the infusion approach may be found in the 11 principles of the Character Education Partnership (http://character.org), wherein character education is seen as a holistic movement that includes recruitment of parents and the community as partners. This approach is consistent with several *Turning Points 2000* recommendations, including involving parents and communities in supporting healthy development and creating a safe and healthy school environment (Jackson & Davis, 2000, p. 24).

CHARACTER EDUCATION IS IMPORTANT FOR YOUNG ADOLESCENTS

The physical, social, emotional development of young adolescents occurs at a rate faster than at any other time in their lives, second only to infancy, in sheer velocity (Carnegie Council on Adolescent Development, 1989). Although infants grow faster, they are not "conscious witnesses of their development as are young adolescents" (National Middle School Association, 1995, p. 6). Fischer and Rose (1998) explain that physical changes in the brain and cognitive changes in thinking and learning occur in repeating patterns, suggesting common growth cycles in behavior and in the brain. A metaphor for this "cycle" of development is the growth of a cube or solid figure. First the dots combine to form a line, then the lines combine to form a square, and finally the squares combine to form the cube (p. 57). Furthermore, these growth cycles occur with a great capacity for plasticity and resilience, plastic in the sense of capable of building tissue and of being formed, and resilient in the sense of capable of being influenced and of recovering quickly from change, resuming its shape and form after being stretched or compressed. In the first cycle, infants develop capacities for representation, and in the fourth cycle young adolescents develop a capacity for abstraction. Fischer and Rose explain:

> Optimal levels for represential capacities develop during childhood, between 2 and 12 years. Eventually a child understands his or her first abstractions (such as literary and mathematical concepts; personality and motivational characteristics; concepts of *society, law, and philosophy*). Optimal abstraction capacities appear between 10 and 25 years of age and produce the capacity to *build principles* relating multiple abstractions (such as evolution by natural selection, *reflective judgment, the Golden Rule.* (p. 58, emphasis added)

If Fischer and Rose (1998) are accurate in identifying these two overlapping periods of optimal growth, from first abstractions to beginning the capacity for building principles and reflective judgment, then this 2–year overlap coincides with the beginning of the middle level years, typically considered to be 10 to 15 years old (Lipitz, 1984; National Middle School Association, 1995, p. 5). The implication is hard to miss, that the transition from childhood to middle level is the optimal time for character education, for their developmental abstract thinking, and for their initial building of principles and reflective judgments. We first examine how neuropsychology confirms the interaction of cognitive and affective processing and how developmental psychology confirms that young adolescents exhibit a new and different way of thinking.

Brain Research: Cognitive and Affective Processing

After the Decade of the Brain, the 1990s, researchers have reinterpreted MacLean's (1978) triune brain theory, which argued that the brain included three distinct parts with separate functions. The brain stem or reptilian brain is responsible for automatic actions that are necessary for survival, for example, the respiratory and circulatory systems. The midbrain or limbic system is responsible for emotional processes. The neomammalian brain or neocortex is responsible for rational or cognitive processes. The interactions of these three parts of the brain are now considered more important than thinking of each as a separate functioning part of the brain.

Today cognitive scientists like Michael Gazzaniga (1985) suggest that the human brain is divided into modules, each module being a semi-autonomous network of neurons working together for a single function. Groups of modules work together to process more complex functions. Dawson and Fischer (1994) argue that cognition is enhanced by emotional responses and that emotions are modulated by rational thinking. Today, neuroscientists generally agree that the midbrain and cortex work in tandem to process and respond to information. Stephan Heckers (2001) demonstrates this as he describes the neuroprocessing of new information as it occurs in three stages: *reception, representation,* and *response.*

Reception begins when one or more sense organs gather information from the environment. Each individual aspect of the perceived source of information is noted independently. When the retina receives light from an object in the environment, some specialized retinal receptors receive shape, for example, while others receive color, shade, movement, or line. The retinal receptors send their information along the occipital nerves to a specialized module or network of neurons in the thalamus in the midbrain. If a noise is heard, then the same process begins for tone, rhythm, pitch, and other auditory information, each received by auditory receptors in the inner ear and sent along the auditory nerve to thalamic modules specialized for auditory processing.

Once information reaches the thalamus, the reception process is concluded, and the representation processes begin. There are two representational processings in the thalamus, that is, information comes in for one level of integration, it leaves, and then it returns for a more complex integration. The first processing integrates visual aspects such as shape, color, shade, and movement into a whole visual display or pitch, tone, and rhythm into an auditory display. The second processing integrates the visual display with auditory and/or other sensory displays. Between these two levels of processing, however, important emotional and cognitive interpretations are applied to the sensory displays.

For simplicity we will follow only the visual display interpretations. After the first associative processing, the visual display is sent through emotional centers like the amygdala and hippocampus to various aspects of the neocortex to determine what it might be and the context or environment in which it was originally perceived. After the second thalamic processing, the display is sent to the prefrontal neocortex for a second assessment: "Is this new information?" "Is it interesting?" "Is it worth keeping?" "How do I want or need to respond?" So the prefrontal neocortex, where so much synaptic growth occurs in young adolescents, and which is the site of high level thinking and the modulation of emotional responses (Dawson & Fischer, 1994), is directly involved in information processing. Furthermore, this young adolescent synaptic growth coincides with movement from Piaget's concrete to formal operations. It also coincides with Erikson's psychosocial stage of seeking identity, seeking answers to "Who am I?" and "What do I value?"

What is now known about neurological processing of sensory information strongly supports the notion that cognition is intricately bound with emotion, the affective domain. The thalamus and other parts of the limbic system interact with numerous parts of the neocortex to construct and to interpret new knowledge. Making assessments about what is new, interesting, or worthy requires both cognitive and affective processing, and both cognitive and affective processing occur in both the cortex and the limbic systems.

Young Adolescent Changes in Thinking

Piaget (1954) postulated that knowledge is constructed when our actions are transformed into thought through reflective abstraction. These newly constructed thoughts can be used to interpret new sensory data and in either familiar or new contexts. Piaget believed that individuals are capable of constructing knowledge of the world around them without formal instruction. While Piaget's first three stages of development are universal, the fourth, formal operations, is not necessarily universal (Aries, 2001; Kagan, 1971; Piaget, 1972). Aries, for example, states that "normal adolescents develop the *potential* for formal operational thought, but whether they actually attain it depends on their environment and whether there is demand for the use of these formal structures" (p. 98). Furthermore, Vygotsky (1978) argued that such construction is taught, though informally, through social interactions with adults and peers. As children develop into young adolescents they change their social surroundings to include adults outside the home and peers, sometimes slightly older peers. The social context in which young adolescents place themselves significantly affects what they learn, and they, in turn, affect their environment (Bronfenbrenner, 1979; Rogoff, 1990). We therefore contend that adolescents' potential for abstraction is better actualized when the social, learning, and conversational environments support, lead, and listen, respectively, to adolescents as they experiment with their early attempts at abstraction.

Kagan (1971) suggests that because puberty brings with it new sexual thoughts, young adolescents of necessity develop a new cognitive competence enabling them to rethink their existing beliefs and to search for inconsistencies between their old beliefs and the ones they hold now. Elkind (1984) claims that older beliefs learned in childhood are not genuinely or personally owned but were handed to them by caregivers and other adults. With the advent of puberty and dramatic social changes, young adolescents begin "thinking in a new key" (p. 23). They give a critical eye to everything adults do, looking for inconsistencies between what adults do and say, and between what adults do and what they themselves do. As they encounter new ideas and values, they have two options. The first and easiest is to simply copy ideas and values from others, taking them as their own, which Elkind calls *substitution*. The other option is to discriminate and separate the differences between themselves and others, and to use higher-order thinking or *integration* to change their views and beliefs. Substitution appears to resemble Piaget's (1954) notion of assimilation, while differentiation and integration resemble accommodation. Elkind claims that youngsters who build their belief systems by substitution develop a patchwork of inconsistencies that continually cause confusion during times of decision and stress. Those who build their belief systems by discrimination and integration develop a whole and well-integrated self, capable of handling difficult decisions and stress with maturity.

If young adolescents are learning to use the synaptic growth in their prefrontal cortex for new ways of thinking and for modulating their emotions, then there appears to be physical and psychological substantiation for the "last best chance" scenario made urgent by *Turning Points*. The argument in that report stated, "Young adolescents face significant turning points. For many youth 10 to 15 years old, early adolescence offers opportunities to choose a path toward a productive and fulfilling life. For many others, it represents their *last best chance* to avoid a diminished future" (Carnegie Council on Adolescent Development, 1989, p. 6, emphasis added). Middle school, then, is an important time for youngsters to have strong character education infused throughout their curriculum to promote integrated self-identities. The alternative approaches of tacking character education onto an already crowded curriculum or integrating it into a unit or two increases the chance of promoting patchwork self-identities.

INFUSING CHARACTER EDUCATION

To summarize, there is support from neuroscientists and from developmental psychologists for integrating cognitive and affective learning, and for recognizing and providing the social opportunities for young adolescents to practice their ability to "think in a new key" about their serious existential questions such as "Who am I?" "What is this world?" "How do I fit?" and "What do I value?" Middle level educators are well advised to infuse character education throughout the entire curriculum. Surely ample opportunities abound for examining prototypes, metaphors, and the narratives in every subject. Two examples are provided.

The first comes from Rosenblatt's (1968) notion of transaction with text. Though she confined her thoughts to engaging literature, they can be applied to any narrative as well. Rosenblatt identified two approaches a reader takes with a text, a response to the form of the artistic piece and a response to the art of the piece. The 1930s and 1940s literary movement known as New Criticism was encouraging readers to focus on content and form unemotionally. Rosenblatt urged teachers to help an "adolescent...encounter literature for which he possesses the intellectual, emotional, and experiential equipment" (p. 25). She asserted that the words of the text bring to the reader's consciousness concepts, sensuous experiences, and images that will determine what the work communicates to him or her. "For the adolescent reader, the experience of the work is further specialized by the fact that he has probably not yet arrived at a consistent view of life or achieved a fully integrated personality" (p. 31).

The second example was specifically designed for informational text that is read for its content rather than its artistry. Teachers often attempt to motivate students to learn by telling them of the value of the information or by threatening them, however benignly, with a test. Mandeville (1992) found it difficult at best to interest students in things they knew little about and so developed two related strategies to encourage students to assign their own affective responses after they learned the material. Value and Interest Elaboration through Writing (VIEW) begins with the teacher developing a concept map of what students know about the topic to be considered or, if students are unlikely to know much about the topic, to develop a concept map as an advanced organizer. Students then read the text and report new information from the text that extends or corrects their prior knowledge. The teacher adds this new information to the concept map in a different color. Students talk about and then write responses to two cognitive questions and three affective questions: "What did I learn that is new?" "How does this new information fit with, or integrate into, my previous knowledge?" "What is most important to my newly integrated understanding?" "What is most interesting?" and "How can I use this newly integrated understanding?"

Mandeville (1994) used the same three affective questions to extend Olge's (1986) KWLA strategy. Both the VIEW and KWLA strategies were shown to improve poor readers comprehension of informational text (Mandeville & van Allen, 1993).

RECOMMENDATIONS

As a result of this study, five recommendations surface for the middle-level educator:

1. Increase emphasis on character education. Recent events have elevated the challenge that young adolescents face in understanding and making judgments on moral issues.
2. Reach a working definition of character education based on thoughtful synthesis of the many concepts and strategies advocated by experts in the field.
3. Recognize the timeliness of teaching character education at the middle level. Consider the recent conclusions of brain researchers that adolescence is a time of development of the brain, a cycle during which young adolescents develop the capacity for abstractions.
4. Carefully evaluate approaches to character education. Recognize the distinct alternatives of add-on program models, curriculum integration models, and the infusion models. Evaluate these, keeping in mind the support for infusion models voiced by many character education experts.
5. Implement character education in a manner that engages both affective and cognitive processes. Brain research presents a strong case that cognition is intricately bound with emotion, the affective domain.

REFERENCES

Aries, E. (Ed.). (2001). *Adolescent behavior: Readings & interpretations.* Columbus, OH: McGraw-Hill/Dushkin.

Boyer, E. L. (1995). *The basic school: A community for learning.* Princeton, NJ: The Carnegie Foundation for the Advancement of Teaching.

Bronfenbrenner, U. (1979). *The ecology of human development.* Cambridge, MA: Harvard University Press.

Carnegie Council on Adolescent Development. (1989). *Turning points: Preparing American youth for the 21st century.* The Report of the Task Force on Education of Young Adolescents. New York: Carnegie Corporation of New York.

Chazan, B. (1985). *Contemporary approaches to moral education.* New York: Teachers College Press.

Davis, G. A. (2001). Point to point: Turning Points to Turning Points 2000. In V.A. Anfara, Jr. (Ed.), *The handbook of research in middle level education* (pp. 215–239). Greenwich, CT: Information Age Publishing.

Dawson, G., & Fischer, K. W. (1994). *Human behavior and the developing brain.* New York: Guilford.

DeRoche, G. F., & Williams, M. M. (2001). *Character education, A quick guide for school administrators.* Lanham, MD: Scarecrow Press.

Dewey, J. (1916). *Democracy and education: An introduction to the philosophy of education.* New York: Free Press.

Dewey, J. (1933). *How we think.* Boston: D. C. Heath.

Elkind, D. (1984). *All grown up & no place to go: Teenagers in crisis.* Reading. MA: Addison-Wesley.

Fischer, K. W., & Rose, S. F. (1998). Growth cycles of brain and mind. *Educational Leadership, 56*(3), 56–60.

Garbarino, J. (1999). *Lost boys: Why our sons turn violent and how we can save them.* New York: Free Press.

Gazzaniga, M. S. (1985). *The social brain: Discovering the networks of the mind.* New York: Basic Books.

Gilligan, C. (1982). *In a different voice.* Cambridge, MA: Harvard University Press.

Goodman, J. F., & Lesnick, H. (2001). *The moral stake in education: Contested premises and practices.* New York: Longman.

Heckers, S. (2001, January). *Brain anatomy for beginners.* Paper presented at the meeting of Learning and the Brain, Cambridge, MA.

Jackson, A. W., & Davis, G. A. (2000). *Turning points 2000: Educating adolescents in the 21st century.* New York: Teachers College Press.

Johnson, M. (1993). *Moral imagination: Implications of cognitive science for ethics.* Chicago: University of Chicago Press.

Johnson, M. (1996). How moral psychology changes moral theory. In L. May, M. Friedman & A. Clark (Eds.), *Minds and morals: Essays on cognitive science and ethics* (pp. 45–68). Cambridge, MA: MIT Press.

Johnson, M. H., & Gilmore, R. O. (1996). Developmental cognitive neuroscience: A biological perspective on cognitive change. In R. Gelman & T. Au (Eds.), *Handbook of perception and cognition: Perceptual and cognitive development* (pp. 333–70). Orlando, FL: Academic Press.

Kagan, J. (1971). A conception of early adolescence. *Daedalus, 100* (4), 997–1012.

Kohlberg, L. (1969). Stage and sequence: The cognitive-developmental approach to socialization theory and research. In D. A. Goslin (Ed.), *Handbook of socialization theory and research* (pp. 347–380). Chicago: Rand McNally.

Leming, J. S. (1997). Whither goes character education? Objectives, pedagogy, and research in education programs. *Journal of Education, 179*(2), 11–34.

Lickona, T. (1991). *Educating for character: How our schools can teach respect and responsibility.* New York: Bantam Books.

Lickona, T. (1997). The teacher's role in character education. *Journal of Education, 179* (2), 63–90.

Lipitz, J. (1984). *Successful schools for young adolescents.* New Brunswick, ME: Transaction Books.

MacLean, P. (1978). A mind of three minds: Educating the triune brain. In A. Mirsky (Ed.), *77th National Society for the Study of Education yearbook: Education and the brain* (pp 31–39). Chicago: University of Chicago Press.

Mandeville, T. F. (1992). The VIEW procedure: Integrating cognitive and affective learning. *Reading Education in Texas, 8,* 15–21.

Mandeville, T. F. (1994). KWLA: Linking the affective and cognitive domains when learning new information. *The Reading Teacher, 47*(8), 679–680.

Mandeville, T. F., & van Allen, L. (1993). Middle school poor readers need more than good literature and skills drills. *Journal of the Texas Middle School Association, 2*(2), 24–29.

May, L., Friedman, M., & Clark, A. (Eds.). (1996). *Minds and morals: Essays on cognitive science and ethics.* Cambridge, MA: MIT Press.

Murphy, M. M. (1998). *Character education in America's blue ribbon schools.* Lancaster, PA: Technomic.

National Middle School Association. (1995). *This we believe: Developmentally responsive middle level schools.* Columbus, OH: Author.

Noddings, N. (1992). *The challenge to care in schools: An alternative approach to education.* New York: Teachers College Press.

Noddings, N., & Shore, P. J. (1998). *Awakening the inner eye: Intuition in education.* Troy, NY: Educator's International Press.

Nussbaum, M. C. (2001). *Fragility of goodness: Luck and ethics in Greek tragedy and philosophy.* Cambridge, UK: Cambridge University Press.

O'Keefe, S. J. (1997). Children and community service: Character in action. *Journal of Education, 179*(2), 47–62.

Ogle, D. (1986). A teaching model that develops active reading of expository text. *The Reading Teacher, 39,* 564–570.

Piaget, J. (1954). *The construction of reality in the child.* New York: Basic Books.

Rogoff, B. (1990). *Apprenticeship in thinking: Cognitive development in social context.* New York: Oxford University Press.

Rosenblatt, L. (1968). *Literature as exploration.* New York: Noble.

Thompson, J. E., & McGuffey, W. H. (Eds.). (1879). *McGuffey's eclectic readers.* Eclectic Educational Series. New York: American Book Company.

Vygotsky, L. S. (1978). *Mind in society: The development of higher psychological processes.* Cambridge, MA: Harvard University Press.

Weber, C. (1998). Pre-service preparation for teaching character and citizenship: An integrated approach. *Action in Teacher Education, 20*(4), 85–94.

CHAPTER 9

RECULTURING MIDDLE SCHOOLS TO USE CROSS-CURRICULAR PORTFOLIOS TO SUPPORT INTEGRATED LEARNING

Sue Thompson
University of Missouri, Kansas City

ABSTRACT

Authentic assessment that reflects a curricular delivery model that is integrative, challenging, exploratory, and promotes learning is necessary if there is to be a connection between curriculum, instruction, and assessment (National Middle School Association, 1995). The purpose of this multisite, qualitative case study was to inquire into the supporting conditions necessary to reculture schools in order to institutionalize curriculum integration and cross-curricular portfolios in five middle schools in a midwestern suburban school district. Data were collected that reflected the many dimensions of curriculum integration and authentic assessment and included the researcher's extensive field notes; samples of integrative thematic units and cross-curricular portfolios; inter-

---

Middle School Curriculum, Instruction, and Assessment, pages 157–179
Copyright © 2002 by Information Age Publishing
All rights of reproduction in any form reserved.

views; observations; and surveys, both written and oral, with teachers, students, and building level administrators. Data analysis resulted in findings that supported the initial belief that the district, the individual school, the interdisciplinary team, and the teacher had to be recultured to create learning environments for young adolescents that resulted in meaningful learning experiences, reflecting their needs, questions, and interests. Findings include the conditions that are necessary to reculture middle schools for integrated curriculum and cross-curricular portfolios.

INTRODUCTION

This suburban district in a large midwestern city was unified in 1965 and since that time has grown between 5 and 20% per year. From 1965 until 1992 the district had the same superintendent. As the district grew, the superintendent began to decentralize the district through the implementation of site-based management. By the mid-1990s, the district held 16,500 students and five middle schools. The average household income for the district is $95,888, and the average home value is $234,069. Seventy-two percent of the adults in the district are college educated, and 50% of the households have children. The district has been described as upscale and the population as well-educated, informed, and very supportive of education.

The average teacher's experience is 12.5 years, and 66 percent of the faculty hold master's degrees. Twelve of the district's schools have received the U.S. Department of Education award for outstanding educational programs, including four of the middle schools. The district has a reputation of hiring competent, skilled teachers and administrators who are willing to try new practices if they result in higher student performance. The district's students score higher than 90% of other students nationally on standardized achievement tests. Ninety percent of the district's graduates attend colleges and universities.

From 1976 through 1988, hundreds of middle school students were served by the middle school program in the district. The middle school program was based on the junior high model where the superintendent had been a former junior high school principal. The departmentalized day consisted of seven periods with some students being grouped by ability. Teachers taught within departments, for example, social studies, language arts, science, and math, across grade levels. Individual teachers knew neither what students their fellow teachers were teaching nor what academic content they were teaching.

The superintendent believed that it was timely and appropriate to review their middle school programs and practices and established a District Middle School Study Committee in 1986. The committee was composed of the junior high school principals, some junior high school teachers, some district office personnel, and several school board members. This committee suggested proposed changes in the middle school program that would be implemented during the 1987–88 school year. The proposed changes were designed to refocus on the needs of young adolescents. The five areas of improvement included implementing interdisciplinary teams, exploratory courses, an advisory program, a more inclusionary student activity/athletics program, and staff development that would support the changes being proposed for the middle schools in the district. The superintendent and Middle School Study Committee also recommended that the district hire a director of middle level education in the summer of 1987. Between 1987 and 1996 the district added two middle schools, for a total of five. These were very similar in demographics and the culture of each school was more alike than different. While some teachers resisted the move to middle schools because they saw the junior high schools as having been successful, other teachers and the middle school administrators were ready for change and embraced the opportunity to change the organizational structure of the middle level schools and create more developmentally responsive schools for young adolescents.

"For the past 25 to 30 years much effort has been expended in changing programs and practices in middle level schools to better meet the needs of young adolescent learners" (Thompson & Gregg, 1997, p. 27). This is the story of one district's quest for meaningful learning for its young adolescents that would focus on their questions, issues, and concerns about their world and the world around them. The district's implementation of cross-curricular portfolios supported democratic beliefs about learning. These new beliefs are ones that provide opportunities for students to be engaged in meaningful activities that allow them to speak up, form questions, advocate their positions on issues, and listen to other students do the same (Kubox, 2000). If democratic classrooms are to be the cornerstone of middle level reform, then integrated learning experiences and student self-reflection must become a part of the school culture.

Fundamental for many proponents of curriculum reform is the belief that to create more meaningful learning, students must be at the center of the learning experience. Consequently, democracy and equality should be the underlying mission of educational institutions (Beane, 1993, 1997). Creating learning communities in schools where teachers have an opportunity to expand their mental models about teaching and learning and develop skills to talk about and create collective mental models should be a part of the school culture in order to move from classrooms that are teacher-directed to classrooms that are student-centered.

REVIEW OF THE LITERATURE

Change in the Context of School Culture

Educational change must be studied in the context of school culture. In defining culture, Owens (1998) pointed out that multiple cultures exist within an organizational culture and subunits, that is, schools in a school district have cultures of their own that possess distinctive attributes. He goes on to state:

> The culture of a given school is likely to reflect certain of the principle characteristics of the school district's organizational culture and, yet, be different in some ways. Moreover, the cultures of the various schools are likely to differ. Further, it is more than likely that the central office will exhibit an organizational culture of its own that is distinctive from that of any of the schools. It is the subunits—such as schools and departments—that regularly bring together people who share some constellation of interests, purposes, and values; they are the settings in which people seek social affiliation in face-to-face groups; they facilitate the sharing and cooperative effort required to get the work done. (pp. 171–172)

Reculturing is defined as changes that occur as a result of educators reflecting upon, evaluating, and expanding their own mental models regarding the education of young people (Senge, 1990). Mental models are the images, assumptions, and stories that one carries in one's mind of oneself, other people, institutions, and every aspect of the world. They shape how one acts and are often untested and unexamined (Senge, 1990). Through the expansion of individual mental models about teaching and learning, collective mental models or visions might be developed that result in more meaningful learning experiences for students. If collective mental models are going to be developed that change the culture of a middle school, teachers must change the way they communicate with one another.

Often, camps develop in a school where the staff is clearly divided on the adoption of a particular program or practice or, more seriously, the direction or vision for the school. Discussions dissolve into exploring ways that people are different rather than ways that people are alike and often end up in debates where each person or group tries to beat the other down through logic. Decisions on new programs or practices are decided by a vote of the faculty, which results in winners and losers. John Meyer and Brian Rowan, in their classic 1977 article, argued that schools are loosely coupled organizations, and the "losers" who do not believe in the new innovation will often shut their classroom doors and teach in a way that is more consistent with their beliefs.

The challenge for middle school educators who wish to truly move into integrated curriculum work and authentic assessment is finding the time to participate in dialogue and metalogue with fellow staff members and reflect upon their own beliefs about teaching and learning. Metalogue is where people think and act as one, creating shared visions and common goals. This new way of communicating will lead to building new shared assumptions—based on brain research, young adolescent development theories, and best middle school practices that become a part of the new culture of the school. Then, and only then, will individuals, schools, and school districts truly become recultured.

Individual teachers and interdisciplinary teams across the United States have stories to share as they have moved away from the traditional curriculum models into integrated curriculum and authentic assessment. However, very few school districts have attempted to expand the mental models of all teachers to move all of their middle schools into integrated curriculum and authentic assessment and significantly change the way all teachers do their work.

Integrated Curriculum

Curriculum as defined by this district for the purposes of this study is that curriculum is the sum total of what is taught, which includes methods of instruction; tools of assessment; materials; activities in which students engage in schools, classrooms, and the community; and the values that are communicated and shared. Curriculum must be centered on student learning, and assessment must be reflective of the curriculum that is being taught and the way the curriculum is delivered.

From a historical perspective, attempts to integrate the curriculum have been cited in studies going back to the 1800s (Vars, 1991). Curriculum integration has been touted as the answer to creating more meaningful learning experiences for young adolescents as schools move beyond the organizational structure changes brought about by the middle school movement (Beane, 1997; Lounsbury & Vars, 1978; Pate, Homestead, & McGinnis, 1997; Stevenson & Carr, 1993). While interdisciplinary teaming is considered a key characteristic of a developmentally appropriate middle school, it has only been in the last decade that middle level educators have, as stated by Swaim in Lounsbury (1992), turned their attention to finding ways "to restructure our pigeon-holed, content-separated curriculum to a more interdisciplinary/integrated one" (p. v).

Two of the most important additions to the National Middle School Association's revised *This We Believe* (1995) are the inclusion of the concept that curriculum is integrative and assessment and evaluation should promote learning. The NMSA states that in developmentally responsive middle schools, curriculum embraces every planning aspect of a school's education program. The NMSA's position paper stresses that middle level curriculum should focus on issues significant to both students and adults. Supporting this view is a large amount of research that supports the integrated approach (Jackson & Davis, 2000). Fifty years of research and more than 80 studies reveal that students in interdisciplinary programs do as well, and often better, on standardized tests when compared with those in the usual separate-subject programs (Vars, 1993).

In summary, curriculum integration is an approach to curriculum development that presents a holistic view of knowledge to learners extending beyond a combination of disciplines. This holistic view includes across-the-domain skills such as thinking, reasoning, and problem solving. With a focus on learning goals based on skills, knowledge, and dispositions determined by middle level educators, integrated studies can teach those skills and knowledge in brain-compatible ways, crossing the boundaries of disciplines and skills to focus on real-world issues. A fundamental shift from textbook-driven instruction to integrated curriculum and authentic assessment is both an opportunity and a challenge.

Authentic Assessment

In this study, authentic assessment reflects students' knowledge, skills, and dispositions determined by the district and promotes student growth through reflection, personal goal setting, and collaborative efforts between students, teachers, and parents. In addressing the area of assessment and evaluation, *This We Believe* (National Middle School Association, 1995) states that "Continuous, authentic, and appropriate assessment and evaluation are essential components of the learning process at any age level, providing information that students, teachers, and family members need to plan further learning" (p. 26). *This We Believe* emphasizes the importance of using assessment to actively promote learning and encourage student participation in all phases of assessment. Vars (2001) states, "Hence it is important to invite students to work with their teachers to make critical decisions at all stages of the learning enterprise, especially goal-setting, establishing evaluation criteria, demonstrating learning, self-evaluation, peer evaluation, and reporting" (p. 79).

Middle school educators should be concerned about what their students know, what their students are interested in, the ways their students learn, and what they learn. Portfolios provide a vehicle for students to collect samples of their actual work over time in order to reflect on their growth and identify areas in which they want to improve. According to Herman,

Aschbacher, and Winters (1992), "A longitudinal approach to assessment puts the results of any one assessment into perspective. At the same time, multiple measures of the same outcomes provide alternative views of performance that combine to create a more complete picture of student achievement" (p. 120).

Students grow in their ability to self evaluate and to value themselves as learners. As stated by Smith and Myers (2001), "Students need time to reflect on their work, to make connections between and among tasks, and to note improvements along the way. Such personal integration of knowledge is the key to good assessment" (p. 11). Portfolios also provide opportunities for students, parents, and teachers to share in the evaluation process. They provide evidence of student growth and a format for students to use in sharing their work with parents and teachers.

Change and Its Role in Reculturing

If integrated curriculum and authentic assessment, that is, cross-curricular portfolios, most clearly meet the needs of the young adolescent learner, the question of why more teachers on interdisciplinary teams are not engaging their students in integrated learning and authentic assessment experiences must continue to be explored. The answer may well be that while the philosophical component of middle school transformation is based on second-order changes that, according to Cuban (1988), seek to alter the fundamental ways in which organizations are put together, including new goals, structures, and roles (e.g., collaborative work cultures), more second-order changes—changes that affect the attitudes, beliefs, and feelings of the teachers, students, and parents—need to occur.

The challenge of schools is to institutionalize more second-order changes—changes that affect the culture and structure of the schools, restructuring roles and reorganizing responsibilities, including those of students and parents (Fullan, 1999). Culture, as defined by Schein (1985), is "the deeper level of basic assumptions and beliefs that are shaped by members of an organization, that operate unconsciously, and that define in a basic 'taken-for-granted' fashion an organization's view of itself and its environment" (p. 6).

Consequently, because these second-order changes have not occurred in most middle schools, established traditional curriculum and pedagogy have been much more difficult to change than the implementation of middle school program components, such as interdisciplinary teaming. Many middle schools that organize their teachers in interdisciplinary teams still develop and organize the curriculum by separate subjects.

In a review of the literature on the effects of teaming and collaborative arrangements, Arhar, Johnston, and Markle (1989) concluded that, "while it is clear that team arrangements reduce teacher isolation, increase satisfaction, and improve individual teachers' sense of efficacy, a single organizational arrangement does not assure that collaboration will occur on such important matters as instructional improvement or curricular integration" (p. 25).

RESEARCH DESIGN

Problem and Purpose Overview

As pointed out by Owens (1998):

The study of organizational culture presents nettlesome problems to the traditional researcher primarily because important elements of culture are subtle, unseen, and so familiar to persons inside the organization as to be considered self-evident and unworthy of discussion. Collecting, sorting, and summarizing data such as the significant historical events in the organization and their implications for present-day behavior, the impact of organizational heroes on contemporary thinking, and the influence of traditions and organizational myths, is a task that does not lend itself to the tidiness of a printed questionnaire and statistical analysis of the responses to it. As the work of Ouchi, Peters and Waterman, Kanter, and Deal and Kennedy demonstrated, it is necessary to get inside the organization: to talk at length with people; to find out what they think is important to talk about; to hear the laughter they use; and to discover the symbols that reveal their assumptions, their beliefs, and the values to which they subscribe. For that reason, students of organizational culture tend to use field research methods as contrasted with the more traditional statistical studies that have long been the stock-in-trade of educational researchers. (pp. 176–177)

This inquiry provided a detailed description of what occurred as a result of the middle school director and building administrators' decision to move ahead with the curriculum and assessment questions and the identification of supporting conditions necessary to have curriculum integration and cross-curricular portfolios become an institutionalized component of a team's culture, a school's culture, and a school district's culture. The issue addressed was reculturing schools in order to institutionalize new educational practices. The new educational practices, for example, integrated curriculum and cross-curricular portfolios, are about giving voice to the learner and moving the young adolescent to the center of the learning experience. By examining the role of the interdisciplinary team, the school culture and the culture of the district in the acceptance or rejection of curriculum integration and cross-curricular portfolios by teachers, principals, parents, and district office personnel, this study should provide valuable information to persons interested in the institutionalization of new practices and innovations, for example, integrated curriculum and cross-curricular portfolios.

Research Methods

A qualitative research design was selected for this study because of the belief that the views of the traditionally unempowered, for example, teachers and students, and as ones directly involved in this change effort, have valuable and necessary information; perhaps as much, if not more, than those in authoritarian positions. Qualitative research methods are reflective of a more democratic philosophy (Bogdan & Biklen, 1992) and allowed the researcher to study issues in depth and have a better knowledge of the subjects and the learning environments teachers create for their students.

Research Questions

This study examined the work of 120 interdisciplinary team teachers in five middle schools in this district and how cultural beliefs of the school district and their individual school impact their feelings, attitudes, and beliefs about integrated curriculum and cross-curricular portfolios. This inquiry focused on identifying conditions necessary to support teachers in expanding their mental models about teaching and learning in order to deliver curriculum in an integrative fashion and assess students' learning through cross-curricular portfolios.

The primary research questions answered were:

1. How do teachers' belief systems change regarding how young adolescents learn, and what kind of curriculum and assessment is most likely to engage the minds and spirits of young adolescent learners in worthwhile studies in order to reculture schools and classrooms?
2. How and why do curriculum integration and cross-curricular portfolios become institutionalized into a school culture?

The supporting questions addressed were:

1. What is "integrated curriculum?" What does this kind of curriculum mean for teachers? What does this kind of curriculum mean for young adolescents?
2. What is "authentic assessment?" What does this kind of assessment mean for teachers? What does this kind of assessment mean for young adolescents?
3. How do teachers get started in this kind of work?

Methodology Rationale

In studying the reculturing of school organizations to incorporate integrated curriculum and cross-curricular portfolios, the methodology had to reflect the nature of the challenge that the researcher had chosen to undertake in this study. The conceptual framework for this study was the concept of culture and how to change culture to reflect more democratic practices, that is, integrated curriculum and cross-curricular portfolios, using second-order change to challenge the beliefs, assumptions, and practices of people within the organization.

Case study research requires the use of multiple sources in order to validate data, studying both census and phenomenological data, and deriving themes from the data rather than from a preordained hypothesis (Denzin & Lincoln, 1994; Merriam, 1988; Yin, 1994). Each of these principles was adhered to in this study. Multiple data sources in the study included interviews and informal conversations with school staffs and students, observations, and school documents. Major themes were derived from these sources, creating triangulation. Documented findings were examined in the context of the participant observer's reaction and interpretation.

Participant Selection

Participants in this study included all 120 interdisciplinary team teachers and 10 building-level administrators, one principal, and one assistant principal, from each of the district's five middle schools. During the course of this study, two new middle schools were built and the staffs at all of the five middle schools were composed of approximately 50% veteran teachers in the district who were a part of the initial transition from junior high schools to middle schools, and 50% of the teachers new to the district. Three of the middle school principals had been junior high school principals in the district and two of the principals had been middle school principals in other districts before coming to this district. Two of the middle schools had been original junior high schools in the district and the other three middle schools were built after the transition from junior high schools to middle schools.

Data Collection

Interviews and informal conversations with both individuals and groups, observations, and a review of formal and informal documents were the data collection techniques used in this study. Formal and informal documents included explanations and agendas of professional development experiences; memos to staff; articles shared with staff related to the innovations; agendas and minutes of meetings with staff concerning integrated curriculum and cross-curricular portfolios; district reports, including formal evaluation of middle school practices; and the participant observer's detailed journal and appointment calendars. This study made extensive use of archival data. Data were collected over a 5-year period. Through the use of a variety of sources, the triangulation of data enhanced the design of this research study.

Interviews

Interviewing is a basic mode of inquiry and at the heart of the interviewing research is an interest in other individuals' stories because they are of worth (Seidman, 1991). Interviews and less formal conversations with both individual teachers, teams of teachers, and larger groups of teachers were critically important in making sense out of a multitude of experiences. Asking teachers to tell their stories about their work with integrated curriculum and cross-curricular portfolios provided a more "unstructured" approach to interviewing than asking a series of questions and was one technique used by the researcher. Teachers and building administrators are cultural informants, the people who offer clarification and insights regarding the cultural scene.

Data Management and Analysis Method

In looking at data management in relation to the conceptual framework of reculturing middle schools, a systems perspective was used to identify themes and reoccurring patterns. The components of systems thinking, in relationship to reculturing that directly impact curriculum and assessment, that were used in coding and analyzing the data for this study were (a) curriculum delivery models and instructional strategies, (b) assessment and accountability, (c) building and district leadership, (d) school and district culture, (e) structure and organization, and (f) professional development.

Analyzing the data to determine philosophical, psychological, and organizational assumptions at work in the culture facilitates an understanding of how and why certain events happened as they did. The challenge for middle level educators has been to move from restructuring to reculturing.

The Researcher

The researcher, the director of middle level education in the district, chose to use a participant–observer approach in an attempt to understand the cultural settings in the five middle schools and to inquire about and investigate cultural changes in these settings. The researcher has strong biases concerning this level of education and those biases have been acknowledged in this study.

ANALYSIS OF DATA

Building Capacity to Develop and Implement Cross-Curricular Portfolios

In order to expand mental models and beliefs about authentic assessment, using dialogue and metalogue, all interdisciplinary team teachers from the five middle schools were invited to attend an all-day session where they would begin to learn about cross-curricular portfolios so that they could construct their own meaning and understanding about this method of assessment. Every middle school team teacher attended one of three sessions about portfolio assessment. The large group broke into 12 small groups and participated in a round-robin reading activity related to portfolio assessment. From the readings they identified big ideas and essential learnings, generated implications or questions from the articles, and shared this information with the whole group.

Teachers worked in groups by school and discussed the benefits of cross-curricular portfolios for the following groups: students, teachers, parents, school, and district. Then the group regrouped by grade level across the district and identified the skills, knowledge, and dispositions they wanted students to have when they exited their grade level. In looking at benefits for students, some of the answers were: can see relationship between subjects; ownership of learning; see progress or improvement; enhanced self-esteem; learn organizational skills; become more self-reflective; learn to set goals; use higher-level thinking skills; and learn how to apply skills and knowledge in real-world situations. They also said that portfolios promote risk-taking; allow students to focus on their improvement rather than be compared to other students; and honor diversity among learners.

The benefits of portfolios for teachers were as numerous as the benefits for students. They were cited as better understanding of students as learners, reaches all levels of learners; pinpoints significant learning; more interaction between students and teachers; compels team members to work together across disciplines; encourages student growth; improves instruction; promotes self-reflection and accountability; and helps teachers better understand their students as learners.

Understanding the reality of needing to prove the validity of the middle school program to parents, teachers felt parents would benefit from portfolios in the following ways: show student's development; show the process and the final product; improve communication between parent, student, and teacher; promote opportunities to connect with the learning process; be more aware of criteria; have a tangible record of child's growth; recognize different learning styles and intelligences; promote better involvement with student's education; treated students as individuals; and awareness of what goes on in school.

Teachers were asked, by grade levels, to determine the essential skills, knowledge, and dispositions they wanted their students to have acquired by the end of the year. Each group organized their thoughts in any way that made sense to them. The teachers needed to be free to explore, reflect, and share without constraints. Freeing up teachers to be the professionals that they are allows them to truly reflect on their beliefs about middle school, young adolescents, and learning. The question was whether they would look at their work as separate-subject specialists only or view their work in an integrated way.

The work reflected, collectively, the beliefs and mental models middle school teachers in this district had about learning and the acquisition of skills, knowledge, and dispositions. Four common strands and definitions were identified:

Communication: A piece of student work that demonstrates effective written and oral student expression.

Problem Solving/Critical Thinking: A piece of student work that demonstrates Problem-solving and critical-thinking skills that could originate in any discipline. The skills could possibly include identifying and solving problems, applying perspective, using manipulatives, making connections to real life, understanding one's own learning style, and gathering, processing, and producing data.

Personal and Social Awareness: A piece of student work that demonstrates evidence of application to the life skills of appreciation of others, common sense, cooperation, effort, flexibility, goal setting, integrity, patience, respect, sense of humor, leadership opportunity experiences, caring, community service, curiosity, empathy, friendship, initiative, moral courage, perseverance, responsibility, and organization/time management.

Academic Development/Integrated Studies: A piece of student work that would reflect the outcomes for the disciplines represented in middle school and that would show the connections between the disciplines. Students would show their ability to use skills and knowledge across the disciplines to complete projects, exhibitions, and other assignments.

The strands reflected the teachers' knowledge and understanding of current cognitive research and the needs and characteristics of the young adolescent learner. The strands also indicated that the teachers valued the integrated curriculum delivery model. At the end of the day, teachers were asked to reflect on their experience. They completed the following open-ended statements: "I feel...," "I liked...," and "I wish...,." Teachers said they felt real good about the future of the assessment process; exhausted, but felt they had worked hard and came up with great ideas; tired; comfortable with the idea of portfolios; this was a good, productive day...even if it was on a Saturday; some ownership as they moved into this work; and that portfolios are the way of the future. Other comments included: "I'm frightened because of class sizes increasing and an ever-increasing job load." "I'm not sure how to proceed." "This was a very informative workshop. It helped me clarify my beliefs about cross-curricular portfolios." Another teacher stated, "With the help of teachers district-wide, we will hopefully get portfolios off the ground in middle schools."

Teachers also said that they felt the district was moving in the right direction and hoped the district would continue this work at a slow place; this day gave them a little more insight into portfolio assessment and more connection to other middle school teachers in the district; relieved, portfolios aren't as scary as they thought they were; overwhelmed with what this type of assessment could mean for teachers. Others said they would be teaching much differently with this idea; it will be difficult to mandate a portfolio approach and the district should take small steps to encourage "buy in" of teachers.

Out of 131 responses to the "I feel" statement, 95 responses were positive, 29 were neutral, and 7 were negative. Teachers indicated that they liked the way they worked in groups to formulate ideas and found that many of the teachers were thinking along the same lines; working in groups and brainstorming; working with peers and getting ideas across the grade levels; sharing of ideas; the way the district was introducing teachers to the concept of portfolios; being exposed to different articles/studies of other school districts and their experiences with portfolios; the reading groups; that it was beautifully organized; and the way they worked in groups, that is, the round-robin reading exercise, because it was like an exploration.

Teachers also said they liked the "hands-on" approach. They liked working collaboratively, not being lectured at; the reading activity because they were able to gain a lot of knowledge in a short time; knowing other teachers were as unsure as they were about beginning this project; learning more about portfolios and having everyone be involved in this project; the way the day was split into different groups; learning in a safe environment and having the chance to share and participate in a large group investigation. Other comments reflected their appreciation for being valued for the knowledge they had about learning and assessment. Many participants said they appreciated the time to interact with and learn from one another. At the conclusion of the meetings, the overwhelming positive responses reflected the importance of group work that results in meaningful dialogue around substantive issues like learning and how little time teachers have to share new knowledge and ideas, construct meaning around new ideas, and begin to formulate new beliefs and mental models about learning.

One of the most interesting discussions among members of the District Cross-Curricular committee was how much guidance this committee should provide for teams. Some teachers wanted to have many rules and regulations and have a standard form for all the portfolios across the five middle schools. Others said it was much more important that each interdisciplinary team struggle with what the portfolio should look like and develop a system for themselves and their students. Eventually, after much dialogue, the committee agreed that they would provide a framework based on the four identified strands and suggested ideas for student reflection, but each team would have the autonomy to develop portfolios in ways that made sense to them and the needs of their students. Again, a more democratic process was chosen as the district moved forward with cross-curricular portfolios.

The district did implement cross-curricular portfolios in every middle school and every interdisciplinary team. Through the interview process, classroom observations, and examination of a random sampling of portfolios, the researcher determined that the cross-curricular portfolios did impact the way teachers taught as teachers continued to struggle to move into more integrated ways of delivering the curriculum. Some teams did a much better job than others, but all teams were moving ahead. Students expressed enthusiasm about being able to select the work that would go into their portfolio. The following goals on student ownership of the portfolios were shared with both students and parents: power, fun, choices, connection to life, strategies to learn, learn more about themselves as learners, self-awareness, pride, improved self-concept as a learner, uniqueness, understanding one's weaknesses and strengths, partnerships with parents and teachers, and goal setting.

Necessary Conditions

Changing schools to fit the needs of young adolescents is an old issue. A curriculum that reflects the questions and interests of young adolescents has been the most difficult goal to achieve through middle level reform initiatives. This study showed that integrated curriculum was occurring at all five middle schools where previously there had been fragmented curriculum with skills and content being taught through a separate-subject approach and assessment that was disjointed and not necessarily tied into larger goals and truly reflective of what students were learning.

When attempting to change something as complex as institutional practices related to student learning, changing the culture of the organization must be the real agenda, not implementing single innovations (Fullan, 1991). In this district, curriculum integration and cross-curricular portfolios were not viewed as isolated innovations or just another middle school component or program to be accomplished through an occasional correlated or multidisciplinary unit. Based on interviews, classroom observations, and examination of curricular portfolios, curriculum integration and cross-curricular portfolios became a part of the middle schools' organizational culture. When these practices became a part of the beliefs, values, and purposes of the middle school teachers, it was evident that the schools were becoming recultured because peoples' beliefs, assumptions, and mental models about teaching and learning had changed to reflect more democratic practices in the classroom, that is, integrated curriculm and cross-curricular portfolios.

FINDINGS

In examining the patterns that have emerged from the research, interviews, history, and artifacts, this study has identified the following conditions to be necessary to sustain integrated curriculum and cross-curricular portfolios in middle schools.

Condition #1: Schools as Learning Organizations

Teachers and administrators began to think of their school as a learning organization and themselves as learners. Teachers began to support one another in building the knowledge and skills necessary to more effectively facilitate learning. Teachers were more autonomous and able to make decisions about their students and learning experiences and had a more active role in decision making.

One of the most powerful ways that organizations can support teachers' and administrators' cognitive growth is to encourage and provide ways for them to engage in reflective thinking, dialogue, and, eventually, metalogue. In moving from junior high schools to middle schools, the district provided teachers and administrators opportunities to learn new information, have new experiences, study new research, and talk to one another about proposed changes in structure, philosophy, and practice. Leaders had to fight the desire to dictate changes through mandates and policies and understand the power of creating a different kind of discourse in schools.

Study groups were established at both the district and building level. At the district level, many committees and task forces provided participants an opportunity to learn about the newest research in specific areas and share ideas about the implementation of new programs and practices. Committee members were given the responsibility to make important philosophical decisions about curriculum, instruction, and assessment. Committees were formed to meet district goals, but they also addressed the needs of individual faculty members.

Again, a different kind of dialogue was created where relationships and the importance of the school being a learning community began to be valued by teachers and administrators alike. This definitely helped the reculturing of the district's middle schools. The dynamics observed in the district suggested that people learned and grew from interacting with one another as they became engaged in relationships.

Condition #2: Proactive Leadership at the Building and District Levels

The superintendent must appoint someone to be responsible for the overall implementation of organizational changes and give that person authority equal to the responsibilities. It definitely helped this district to implement the middle school program with fidelity by having one person oversee all aspects and components of the middle school program. This person kept the middle school program in the district from becoming fragmented and divided into components, rather than a holistic, systemic reform that encompassed all areas, including curriculum, instruction, and assessment.

Leadership was not just the responsibility of formal leaders but the responsibility of teacher leaders. Talented and committed teachers began to believe there might be a better way to educate young adolescents than previous practices. Reculturing occurred because teachers believed in integrated curriculum and cross-curricular portfolios and worked hard to turn espoused theories into actual practice.

Reculturing also occurred because principals and assistant principals believed that democratic practices create high-performing middle schools. Building-level administrators do not necessarily have to be able to do this kind of work or even show people how to do it, but they must believe in and understand this work. They must, at the very least, become "cheerleaders" for curriculum integration and cross-curricular portfolios, provide support and encouragement to their staff, and be able to explain this kind of work to parents and community members. Leaders in the district were perceived by most teachers as being very supportive of middle school philosophy, integrated curriculum, and cross-curricular portfolios.

Condition #3: Professional Development that is Ongoing and Job-Embedded

While a school or district might make decisions about the organizational structure and components that should be present in a middle school, there is no one way to "do" integrated curriculum work. Integrated curriculum and authentic assessment is holistic, complicated, developmental, interactive, and inherently imprecise. This belief guided the district as multiple experiences over time were provided for teachers so that professional development was not a "one shot" experience and teachers had time to reflect, plan, implement, assess their successes and failures, and discover their "own way" to provide meaningful learning experiences for their students.

Building-level administrators in this study were provided with the same opportunities to change or expand their mental models about schooling for young adolescents as were teachers. Fullan (1991) states:

> One should feel especially sorry for those in authority positions (middle management in district offices, principals, intermediate government personnel in provincial and state regional offices) who are responsible for leading or seeing to implementation that they do not want or do not understand—either because it has not been sufficiently developed (and is literally not understandable) or because they themselves have not been involved in deciding on the change or have not received adequate orientation or training. (p. 104)

Condition #4: Time for Collaboration

In order to learn, share, reflect, plan, implement, and evaluate, teachers must have time to collaborate. This study confirmed that time was a necessary condition to begin and sustain integrated curriculum work and cross-curricular portfolios. It was found that daily planning time often did not allow enough time for teachers to address the implementation of new teaching practices.

Time to share and dialogue together often created dissonance within individual teachers and with others. It was this challenge to our own ways of thinking in the district that opened the door to mental models that were shared, and these shared mental models moved teams and schools into shared visions of what schooling and learning should look like for all young adolescents in the district.

Condition #5: Understanding New Research in the Cognitive Sciences

Practitioners must be given opportunities to learn and experience first-hand a different way to learn based on the brain research. Experts in brain-based learning are concerned that traditional instruction is inconsistent with how the brain learns, and that the typical classroom is actually brain-incompatible (Brooks & Brooks, 1993; Caine & Caine, 1994). The brain requires a great deal of input to detect patterns. Therefore, educators' attempts to simplify things for students are misguided. This study assumed that fragmenting content was one of the biggest mistakes schools can make. The brain is looking for meaningful connections; teachers actually cut those off when they reduce learning to memorization of facts that have no personal meaning for the learner. Based on this assumption, it was believed and found to be true that understanding brain research was necessary for teachers to know and understand in order to expand their beliefs and mental models about learning.

Condition #6: Congruent and Coherent Curriculum, Instruction, and Assessment

Teachers talked about ways to decrease the fragmentation that young adolescents often experience in schools. Integrated curriculum and cross-curricular portfolios were a part of the discussion in the curriculum development process. As the schools continued to reflect learning organizations where everyone was learning and students were continually involved in self-improvement, changes in the classroom environment began to take place. Students were engaged in much more active and experiential activities. More students were involved in choosing content and approaches to learning. Students were doing surveys, conducting research, studying community and world issues that were relevant to them, tutoring and teaching one another, making presentations, conducting interviews, and having field experiences. Textbooks were used as references and a wealth of other kinds of materials were used as resources.

Assessment, through authentic performance-based projects and cross-curricular portfolios, reflected the knowledge, skills, and dispositions that had been identified as important for young adolescents to know and be able to demonstrate. Understanding important issues, theories, and models became more important than textbook knowledge. Students didn't just prove they could problem-solve, they actually had to demonstrate an understanding of identified content. More often than not, the lines between instruction and assessment were blurred. Learning was both an active and a reflective process where the teacher and student both assessed the student learning that was occurring. It was complex and it was messy, but it was changing the face of student learning in the district.

Unresolved Issue: The Role of Politics in the System

A school district is a very complex organization. While decentralization was a goal of the previous superintendent, the new superintendent began to dismantle site-based management and return to a more bureaucratic and hierarchical organizational structure. According to Perrow (1986), "Bureaucracies are set up to deal with stable, routine tasks; that is the basis of organizational efficiency" (p. 4). Change, on the other hand, is not simplistic and certainly the transition from junior high schools to middle schools and the implementation of integrated curriculum and cross-curricular portfolios were not stable, routine tasks. Change can be very messy and generate more questions than answers. It is ongoing and definitely not a fully predictable process. The changes in the district related to integrated curriculum and cross-curricular portfolios took over 5 years and changes are still occurring in the district as new teachers and administrators join the school district.

Believing that principals and teachers are capable, caring, competent people who individually and collectively should have the right and the responsibility to make important decisions about learning seemed to be inconsistent with a return to a more centralized organization that valued standardization rather than deregulation. With a new superintendent, management in the district became "top-down," taking away much deci-sion making at the building level.

A change in the superintendent, while not directly impacting the orga-nizational structure of the middle schools, impeded the work that was being done in the areas of integrated curriculum and authentic assess-ment. The new organizational hierarchy protected and preserved the parts of the organization that were resistant to empowering people. With new leadership, more emphasis was placed on standardized test scores and less emphasis was placed on authentic assessment through the use of cross-cur-ricular portfolios.

This study showed that districts that are truly interested in reculturing need to examine the barriers that already exist in their organizational sys-tem that might have to be overcome if educators are truly going to change the way student learning looks in their middle schools. Systems will have to be willing to examine their collective beliefs about student learning, the role of the district office in relationship to schools, and whether, in fact, people are going to be trusted enough to be empowered to change schools so that they look different. There has to be a determination if the organiza-tion is willing to change and/or eliminate those impediments. The system, led by the superintendent and board of education, would have to deter-mine if there would be safety for individuals who challenge the norms and beliefs of the existing culture.

There must be people in the organization who are willing to accept the challenge of changing schools into places where benefiting every student is the focus of all decisions. Superintendents must be willing to work with board and community members in expanding mental models of schooling and learning. People have to begin the process of starting to know them-selves. They have to think deeply about what it means to learn, what it means to teach, why certain values are more important than others, and what it means for students to be actively engaged in meaningful learning. The system has to embrace the concept of being a learning organization. The five middle schools in this study were recultured because many teach-ers expanded their mental model about middle schools and learning. Suc-cess of this acceptance of the middle school philosophy was evident through the teachers' acceptance of interdisciplinary teaming, integrated curriculum, and cross-curricular portfolios. In order for these practices to become institutionalized and to withstand the politics of large bureaucratic systems, administrators and teachers must change their beliefs. Only through reculturing will behaviors change that reflect what research and best practice tell us must become part of the culture of a high-performing middle school that is academically challenging, developmentally appropri-ate, and socially equitable.

REFERENCES

Arhar, J., Johnston, J., & Markle, G. (1989). The effects of teaming and other collaborative arrangements. *Middle School Journal, 19*(4), 22–25.

Beane, J. (1993). *Curriculum integration: From rhetoric to reality* (2nd ed.). Columbus, OH: National Middle School Association.

Beane, J. (1997). *Curriculum integration: Designing the core of democratic education.* New York: Teachers College Press.

Bogdan, R., & Biklen, S. (1992). *Qualitative research for education: An introduction to theory and methods.* Boston: Allyn & Bacon.

Brooks, J. G., & Brooks, M.G. (1993). *In search of understanding: The case for constructivist classrooms.* Alexandria, VA: Association for Supervision and Curriculum Development.

Caine, R. N., & Caine, G. (1994). *Making connections: Teaching and the human brain.* Menlo Park, CA: Addison-Wesley.

Cuban, L. (1988). A fundamental puzzle of school reform. *Phi Delta Kappan, 70*(5), 341–344.

Denzin, N., & Lincoln, Y. (Eds.). (1994). *Handbook of qualitative research.* Thousand Oaks, CA: Sage.

Fullan, M. (1991). *The new meaning of educational change.* New York: Teachers College Press.

Fullan, M. (1999). *Change forces, the sequel.* Philadelphia: Falmer Press.

Herman, J., Aschbacher, P., & Winters, L. (1992). *A practical guide to alternative assessment.* Alexandria, VA: Association for Supervision and Curriculum Development.

Jackson, A. W., & Davis, G.A. (2000). *Turning points 2000: Educating adolescents in the 21st century.* New York: Teachers College Press.

Kubox, P. (2000). Fostering democracy in middle schools: Insights from democractic institute in Hungary. *Social Studies, 91*(6), 265–272.

Lounsbury, J., & Vars, G. (1978). *A curriculum for the middle school years.* New York: Harper & Row.

Lounsbury, J. (Ed.). (1992). *Connecting the curriculum through interdisciplinary instruction.* Columbus, OH: National Middle School Association.

Merriam, S. (1988). *Case study research in education: A qualitative approach.* San Francisco: Jossey-Bass.

Meyer, J. W., & Rowan, B. (1977). Institutionalized organizations: Formal structure as myth and ceremony. *American Journal of Sociology, 83,* 340–363.

National Middle School Association. (1995). *This we believe: Developmentally responsive middle level schools.* Columbus, OH: Author.

Owens, R. (1998). *Organizational behavior in education* (6th ed.) Needham Heights, MA: Allyn & Bacon.

Pate, E., Homestead, E., & McGinnis, K. (1997). *Making integrated curriculum work: Teachers, students, and the quest of coherent curriculum.* New York: Teachers College Press.

Perrow, C. (1986). *Complex organizations: A critical essay.* New York: Random House.

Schein, E. (1985). *Organizational culture and leadership: A dynamic view.* San Francisco: Jossey-Bass.

Seidman, I. E. (1991). *Interviewing as qualitative research.* New York: Teachers College Press.

Senge, P. M. (1990). *The fifth discipline: The art and practice of the learning organization.* New York: Doubleday.

Smith, C., & Myers, C. (2001). Students take center stage in classroom assessment. *Middle Ground, 5*(2), 10–16.

Stevenson, C., & Carr, J. (1993). *Integrated studies in the middle grades Dancing though walls.* New York: Teachers College Press.

Thompson, S., & Gregg, L. (1997). Reculturing middle schools for meaningful change. *Middle School Journal, 29*(5), 27–31.

Yin, R. (1994). *Case study design: Design and methods* (2nd ed., Applied Social Research Methods Series, Vol. 5). Thousand Oaks, CA: Sage.

Vars, G. (1993). *Interdisciplinary teaching: Why and how.* Columbus, OH: National Middle School Association.

Vars, G. (2001). Assessment and evaluation that promote learning. In T. Erb (Ed.), *This we believe...And now we must act* (pp. 78–89). Westerville, OH: National Middle School Association.

CHAPTER 10

ENABLING "ALGEBRA FOR ALL" WITH A FACILITATED INSTRUCTIONAL PROGRAM

A Case Study of a Talent Development Middle School

Robert Balfanz and Douglas Mac Iver
Johns Hopkins University
Debbie Ryan
School District of Philadelphia

ABSTRACT

This case study analyzes the first-year results of implementing an "Algebra for All" mathematics program in a high-poverty, urban middle school. First, we review the constellation of forces behind the push to increase the mathematical complexity of the middle-grades mathematics curriculum. Second, we briefly discuss the obstacles that stand in the way of teaching more students algebra, particularly in high-poverty urban schools. Third, we describe the Talent Development Middle School Mathematics Program and the

Middle School Curriculum, Instruction, and Assessment, pages 181–212
Copyright © 2002 by Information Age Publishing
All rights of reproduction in any form reserved.

school featured in this study, Cooke Middle School in Philadelphia. Fourth, we describe the extent to which mathematics teachers implemented the program and participated in professional development. Then, we compare the achievement gains and math teaching practices observed at Cooke Middle School with those at a demographically matched, district-selected comparison school. The teaching practices and systematic and substantial achievement gains observed lead us to suggest that "Algebra for All" is an achievable goal.

In the United States today, there is broad-based agreement at the federal level, in the business community, in the mathematics education field, and among civil rights leaders and social change organizations that all students should receive challenging and increasingly complex mathematics instruction in the middle grades. There is also growing consensus that this sequence should culminate with either an algebra course or the integrated study of algebra, geometry, and data in the eighth grade (College Board, 1994; Edwards, 1990; National Council of Teachers of Mathematics, 2000; National Council of Teachers of Mathematics and Mathematical Sciences Education Board, 1998; National Research Council, 1998; Silver, 1997, 1998; Steen, 1997; U.S. Department of Education, 1997).

Why has providing all middle school students "an ambitious, focused mathematics program" that includes the foundations of algebra and geometry become such a national priority (National Council of Teachers of Mathematics, 2000, p. 211)? Because of pressing economic and equity concerns (Moses, 2001; Schoenfeld, 2002), "...mastering mathematics has become more important than ever. Students with a strong grasp of mathematics have an advantage in academics and in the job market. The 8th grade is a critical point in mathematics education. Achievement at that stage clears the way for students to take rigorous high school and science courses—keys to college entrance and success in the labor force" (U.S. Department of Education, 1997, p. 5).

The equity argument behind "Algebra for All" stems from research that shows that algebra is a "gateway" course to advanced mathematics and science in high school, college attendance, and consequently access to well paying, technology-based jobs (Moses, 2001; Pelavin & Kane, 1990). For example, this research shows that low-income students who take algebra I and geometry are almost three times as likely to attend college as those who do not (U.S. Department of Education, 1997, p. 6). The National Council of Mathematics Teachers, in its publication *Algebra for Everyone* (Edwards, 1990), explicitly argues that low-achieving and underserved students "must be given the necessary algebraic background, beginning at the elementary school level, so that they can either engage in the formal course or be able to compete in the marketplace, where general algebraic concepts and skills are necessary" (p. v).

The economic argument behind "Algebra for All" has two roots. The first is the perception that both individual and national economic well-being will require a higher percentage of workers in the future who can understand and apply algebra and geometry in their work. The "Mathematics Equals Opportunity" White Paper (U.S. Department of Education, 1997), for instance, argues that,

- "In the job market, workers who have strong mathematics and science backgrounds are even more likely to be employed and generally earn more than workers with lower achievement, even if they have not gone to college" (p. 13).
- "Mathematics ability will be even more important for well paying jobs in the future" (p. 14).
- "Shortages in workers skilled in mathematics and science could affect U.S. performance in global markets" (p. 14).

The second root of the economic argument behind the "Algebra for All" movement in the eighth grade comes from the findings of the Third International Mathematics and Science Study (TIMSS). This study indicates that the middle school mathematics curriculum is a weak link in the U.S. education system. Mathematics achievement in the United States is above average in the fourth grade, falls to below average in the eighth grade, and plummets even further by the twelfth grade. The TIMSS study further reveals that the "middle school curriculum in the U.S. is less challenging than in other countries" and that "although algebra and geometry are integral elements of the middle school curriculum in other countries, only a small fraction of U.S. middle schools offer their students these topics" (U.S. Department of Education, 1997, p. 7). In the minds of some, these findings raise the specter that unless major reforms in middle-grades mathematics education are undertaken, the U.S. will lose the 21st century "brain race."

In sum, a confluence of studies and events has convinced a wide range of policymakers, educators, business leaders, and social change activists that the ability to understand and apply algebra is good for everyone. It is viewed as a pathway to full participation in society by and for groups that historically have been marginalized, a foundation of advanced mathematical study, and a contributor to U.S. economic health and growth. These same studies have also convinced the supporters of "Algebra for All" that the middle grades are where the battle will be won or lost.

MOVING FROM RHETORIC TO REALITY: THE CHALLENGE OF HIGH-POVERTY, URBAN MIDDLE SCHOOLS

The proposition that all students should study a heavy concentration of algebra in eighth grade challenges the U.S. education system. Few middle schools are currently organized to provide the student and teacher supports necessary for this to occur (Silver, 1998). According to the National Assessment of Educational Progress (NAEP) mathematics assessment given in 1996, only 25% of the nation's eighth graders reported taking an algebra course, up from 20% in 1992. It also found that algebra participation rates in the eighth grade are skewed by income. Just 15% of eighth graders who were eligible for the national school lunch program reported being enrolled in an algebra course, compared to 29% of eighth graders who were not (U.S. Department of Education, 1997, p. 17).

Extreme poverty in the United States, moreover (defined as census tracts where at least 40% of the residents are poor), has a geographic basis and is concentrated in urban areas. A study of urban schooling by *Education Week* (1998, p. 2) reports that "Half the children who live in extremely impoverished neighborhoods are in 75 cities" and "In eight states ... more than 70% of the children in concentrated poverty are found in a single city."

The challenges confronting middle schools nationwide as they attempt to provide "Algebra for All" will be particularly vexing in high-poverty, urban middle schools. Analysis of large international and national data sets, survey data, and qualitative research suggest that there are at least three major impediments to achieving "Algebra for All." Each of these, in turn, is exacerbated in the urban middle schools that serve high-poverty populations.

Weak and Unstructured Curriculums

The first impediment is the nature of the mathematics curriculum studied by the typical middle-grades student. Researchers (e.g., Schmidt, 1998) from the Third International Mathematics and Science Study refer to the repetitive, unfocused, and unchallenging curriculum found in many middle schools as a "mile wide and an inch deep." Key findings from this study (U.S. Department of Education, 1998) included:

- Approximately 50% of the class time for U.S. eighth-grade students is spent studying arithmetic, whereas only 7% of class time for Japanese eighth-grade students is focused on arithmetic;
- The typical U.S. eighth-grade mathematics textbook covers 35 topics, while the typical Japanese eighth-grade textbook covers only seven;

- The content of the U.S. eighth-grade mathematics classrooms is at a seventh-grade level in comparison to other countries;
- U.S. eighth-grade mathematics classes require students to engage in less high-level mathematical thought than classes in Germany and Japan.
- In the judgment of independent experts, none of the U.S. lessons evaluated in the TIMSS videotape study was considered to contain a high quality sequence of mathematical ideas, compared to 30% of Japanese lessons, and 23% of German lessons.

The effect of flat, unfocused, and uncoordinated curriculums are compounded in urban middle schools that serve large populations of students with poor prior preparations (Balfanz, 1997, 2000). It is not uncommon for the average student to arrive at a high-poverty, urban middle school two years behind grade level. A common and understandable response of their middle-grade teachers is offer below-grade level instruction in an attempt to close real and perceived gaps in "basic" knowledge. While this remediation strategy may make sense within the confines of an individual classroom, at the school level the cumulative result is disastrous. Less and less new and grade-level content is taught each year (Smith, Smith, & Bryk, 1998). As a result, students leave middle school not only further behind grade level than when they began but woefully unprepared for high school mathematics.

Out-of-Field Teaching

A second major impediment to achieving "Algebra for All" in general and in urban middle schools that serve high-poverty populations in particular is the lack of qualified and trained mathematics teachers. Out-of-field teaching in mathematics is substantial. It is particularly high in urban middle schools. A recent study shows that 43% of all students in Grades 7 and 8 are taught mathematics by a teacher without a major or minor in the field compared, to 19% of 9th through 12th graders. Similarly, in low-poverty schools, 27% of all secondary students (Grades 7–12) are taught mathematics by an out-of-field teacher, but this percentage climbs to 43% in high-poverty secondary schools (Ingersoll, 1999). Within urban districts the amount of out-of-field teaching is strongly correlated with a school's poverty rate. In schools with fewer than 25% of students eligible for subsidized lunches, 28% of students are taught mathematics by out-of-field teachers. This rises to 45% of students in schools with poverty rates higher than 50% (*Education Week*, 1998). Students in high-poverty middle schools not only have a greater chance of being taught by an out-of-field teacher but also have considerably greater odds of being instructed by a provision-ally certified teacher or long-term substitute. Sixty percent of the 1,000 new teachers hired in Baltimore in 1997, for example, were not fully certified. A study of urban school districts conducted by *Education Week* (1998) reports that 44% of secondary schools in urban school districts had at least one teaching vacancy in mathematics. The final teacher quality variable, which is particularly troublesome in urban middle schools, is the high rate of teacher mobility. In urban middle schools, teachers transfer between schools, depart the school district (and the field), and change the grade and subject they teach within a school in large numbers. There are many reasons for this. Urban middle-grades teachers are often the most dissatis-fied. Middle-grade teachers with elementary certifications can freely move between subjects and often try year after year to get a transfer to elemen-tary schools. Middle-grade teachers with secondary certifications are await-ing openings in high schools and the good ones are actively recruited. All of this mobility, in turn, allows the veteran teachers who stay to pick their assignment, few choosing mathematics. The combined result of out-of-field teaching, the lack of fully certified teachers, and teacher mobility in high-poverty, urban middle schools is that many students pass through these schools without ever being taught by a fully trained, highly skilled, and experienced mathematics teacher.

Lack of Teacher Support

A third major impediment to achieving "Algebra for All" in the middle grades that is exacerbated in high-poverty, urban schools is the significant imbalance between the demands placed on teachers and the support they are provided. Teaching a more demanding mathematics curriculum to all middle-grades students is a challenge and change of historical propor-tions (Chambers, 1994). The organizational structures, teacher support networks, and professional development infrastructure needed are not yet in place.

Both the TIMSS study and a recent analysis of OECD countries reveal that U.S. middle-grade teachers have high workloads. They spend consid-erably more time teaching each week than their counterparts in Japan and in many European countries, leaving them with much less time for collabo-rative work with other teachers, professional development, and reflective thought. According to the 1998 Teacher Survey on Professional Develop-ment and Training, conducted by the National Center for Education Statis-tics (Lewis et al., 1999), 64% of middle school teachers report that they are provided with common planning periods with other teachers on their interdisciplinary teams at least once a week. However, only 36% report they have regularly scheduled collaboration with other teachers on a weekly basis. This means that at a minimum nearly two-thirds of middle school teachers are not provided with the formal opportunity to work with their subject-area colleagues on an ongoing basis. In urban middle schools, which serve high populations, moreover, the limited amount of nonteaching time is increasingly being used to provide mentoring and social support services to students and/or in support of school-wide reform efforts. Thus, teachers are being asked to implement new and more demanding mathematics curriculums but few are being provided the time necessary to learn new skills, collaborate with their peers, or reflect upon their practice.

At the same time that teachers are being asked to change the content of their instruction and their pedagogy, their classrooms are becoming more diverse. The 1998 Teacher Survey on Professional Development and Training found, for example, that 54% of teachers taught limited English proficient or culturally diverse students and 71% taught students with disabilities (Lewis et al., 1999). While increasing diversity in the classroom is a positive trend that reflects greater access to schooling by previously underserved groups, it places new and expanded demands on teachers. In the 1998 survey, only 20% of teachers reported that they are well prepared to teach limited English proficient or culturally diverse students and only 21% reported being well prepared to teach students with disabilities.

"When teachers learn, students learn" (Killion, 1999, p. vii). But few middle-grades teachers are currently receiving the amount of sustained professional development, mentoring, and networking that is needed to bring about the significant change in teaching practice that will be required to achieve "Algebra for All." According to the 1998 Teacher Survey, fewer than 10% of middle school teachers received more than 32 hours of professional development during the preceding year, which focused on learning new teaching methods, the integration of technology, classroom management, student performance assessment, or the addressing the need of students with limited English proficiency, from different cultural backgrounds, or with disabilities. A fifth to more than half of the teachers reported receiving no training during the prior year in each of these areas. Moreover, 80% of the teachers reported that they had never been part of a formal mentoring relationship and only 26% reported that they networked with teachers outside their school on a monthly or more frequent basis (Lewis et al., 1999). In short, middle school teachers report that they have few opportunities to learn.

THE TALENT DEVELOPMENT MIDDLE SCHOOL
MATHEMATICS PROGRAM

The Talent Development Middle School Mathematics Program (TDMSMP) has been specifically designed to address the barriers that exist to achieving "Algebra for All," particularly in urban middle schools that serve high-poverty populations. It is part of a larger whole school reform model—the Talent Development Middle School has been developed over the last eight years by researchers and practitioners working at the Center for Research on the Education of Students Placed at Risk (CRESPAR) in collaboration with the School District of Philadelphia and the Philadelphia Education Fund (Mac Iver, Balfanz, Plank, & Ruby, 2000). The goal of this model is to provide urban, low-income students with the learning opportunities and supports they need to achieve at world-class levels and to provide teachers with the training, materials, and support they need to teach standards-based lessons in every classroom, every day.

TDMSMP is designed to provide students and teachers with multiple and reinforcing layers of support. First, all students and teachers use standards- and research-based instructional materials, which are coherent, consistent, and increasingly complex across the grade levels. The TDMSMP curriculum is built around instructional materials developed by the University of Chicago School Mathematics Program (UCSMP). Fifth and sixth graders use the UCSMP Everyday Mathematics series, seventh graders the UCSMP Transition Mathematics text, and eighth graders the UCSMP Algebra text. The UCSMP materials were chosen to form the foundation of the Talent Development Middle School mathematics curriculum for two reasons. First, they are research-based and have a track record of raising the mathematics achievement of students from a wide range of backgrounds (Schoenfeld, 2002; U.S. Department of Education's Mathematics and Science Expert Panel, 1999). Second, they are particularly well suited to achieving "Algebra for All" in the eighth grade. Central algebraic concepts and procedures are introduced in an informal and hands-on manner in the fifth-grade materials and then revisited each year in increasingly complex and symbolic manners. Thus by the time students begin more formal study of algebra in the eighth grade, they have been prepared to succeed. The UCSMP Algebra text, in turn, also contains significant amounts of work with geometry and data, leaving students prepared for either a geometry course in high school or the more integrated study of algebra, geometry, and data. The Talent Development Middle School Mathematics Program works with a school and its teachers to customize, localize, and supplement UCSMP materials to make sure that they are aligned with local standards and assessments and build upon and support ongoing district, school, and classroom efforts to increase student achievement.

The second layer of support that TDMSMP provides is focused and sustained professional development. Teachers are offered at least 36 hours of curriculum and grade-specific professional development per year for a minimum of two years. This consists of two to three days of summer training followed by three-hour monthly sessions throughout the year. The professional development has three main foci: previewing and modeling upcoming lessons, content knowledge, and effective instructional strategies and classroom management techniques. This is all done in a very focused and hands-on manner. Sixth-grade teachers, for example, during the course of the year, will work their way through the UCSMP Everyday Mathematics instructional materials. Each monthly professional development session will demonstrate to the teachers the key lessons and activities in the unit they are about to teach, present the content knowledge central to the unit, and highlight instructional strategies and classroom management techniques that are particularly useful with the material they will teach in the coming month. Another component of professional development is that time is reserved at each session for teachers to share their success, questions, and frustrations with each other. Finally, a central goal of the TDMSMP is to have ongoing staff development delivered by local teachers who are experienced users of the program as soon as possible. In short, the TDMSMP creates an infrastructure of professional development in which sustained and focused teacher learning can occur around a common and clearly defined task and body of materials.

The third layer of support provided by the TDMSMP is intensive in-classroom implementation support. Teachers in Talent Development Middle Schools are provided nonevaluative, in-classroom implementation support by highly respected and trained peers who work as curriculum coaches. Typically these are school district teachers who are placed on special assignment to the Talent Development program. They work alongside teachers in their classrooms to help them successfully implement the TDMSMP and provide a range of assistance that includes modeling and co-teaching lessons, peer coaching and troubleshooting, modifying lessons and approaches, and making sure that teachers have the materials. The amount of assistance teachers receive is partly determined by their need. Curriculum coaches spend the first few weeks touching base with all the teachers they are supporting to make sure that they are up and running. Then, the curriculum coaches establish a series of rotations in which they work more intensively with a smaller number of teachers. The goal is to provide every teacher at least two rotations per year with each rotation involving weekly interaction for approximately three weeks, with some teachers receiving more support and others who are doing well less support. In addition, the curriculum coach establishes the equivalent of office hours, a set day of the week when he or she is available in a school to answer all teachers' questions.

The curriculum coach has two other important roles. He or she is the transmitter of good ideas from one classroom to another. In other words, the curriculum coach is in a position to observe innovations in one classroom and then bring them to others. Debbie Ryan—one of this chapter's coauthors and a school district of Philadelphia teacher who has helped invent the curriculum coach—calls them "Jiffy ideas" because they spread easily. A final role played by the curriculum coach and the true art of the job is determining when, how, and if to support teachers who are not attending the professional development sessions and/or are not implementing the TDMSMP program. The goal of the TDMSMP program is to have effective instruction occurring in every classroom, every day and not the uniform implementation of a particular approach. Thus, in some cases, the appropriate response to teachers with distinctive teaching styles and approaches who are implementing the TDMSMP program or achieving its objectives in an individualistic but effective manner is to make sure they have the materials they need and then leave them alone. In other cases, however, low implementations of the program may be a symptom of a teacher who needs intensive help with content knowledge, effective instructional practices, or classroom management strategies. It is the job of the curriculum coach to sort this out and come up with an effective strategy to help make sure that good instruction is happening in every classroom, every day.

The fourth layer of support is that students who need extra help are provided with at least 10 weeks of additional mathematics instruction. The TDMS uses an elective replacement approach to extra help and enrichment. In lieu of an elective, students attend a Computer and Team Assisted Mathematics Acceleration (CATAMA) class that combines the skill of a classroom teacher with the individualized pacing of computer software and the support and cognitive elaboration engendered by working in partnerships and teams (Mac Iver, Balfanz, & Plank, 1999). The CATAMA lab not only provides support to students but also enables the students' regular mathematics teachers to cover more grade-level material because they know that students who have had poor prior preparations can build their basic skills and receive extra assistance in CATAMA.

The final layer of support provided by the TDMSMP is that it is nestled among a set of larger whole school reforms that are part of the Talent Development Middle School Model. A key element of this model, which provides additional support to mathematics teachers and their students, is a communal organization of schooling. Talent Development Middle School uses small learning communities, semi-departmentalization, and looping (teachers staying with the same students for two or more years) to create closer bonds between students and teachers. Stronger student–teacher bonds, in turn, lead to fewer discipline problems, higher levels of student engagement, and an increase in both teacher caring and daring (Mac Iver et al., 2000; McGrath, 1998; Wilson & Corbett, 1999).

IMPLEMENTING THE TALENT DEVELOPMENT MIDDLE SCHOOL MATHEMATICS PROGRAM AT COOKE MIDDLE SCHOOL

The TDMSMP was first implemented during the 1997–1998 school year in three schools. This case study focuses on Cooke Middle School, the only implementing school in which we were given permission to collect both fall and spring achievement data at all grade levels during that year. The data at Cooke are compared to those from a demographically similar comparison school selected by the School District of Philadelphia's research office. Cooke Middle School was in its inaugural year of implementing the Talent Development model and was following a rapid implementation plan in which most of the model's components were being implemented simultaneously. This chapter focuses on the first-year implementation and impact of the Talent Development Middle School Mathematics Program at Cooke. Cooke is a fairly typical high-poverty, urban middle school. It represents an example of both a challenging implementation site and a site where the mathematics program is working in concert with the other elements of the Talent Development model.

The Setting

Cooke Middle School is a nonselective neighborhood school located in the central, north Olney section of Philadelphia. It is situated two blocks from a main north–south thoroughfare in a dense residential neighborhood that contains a mix of rundown and well-kept two- and three-story row homes. The school serves a racially mixed, low-income population. Approximately 72% of its students are African American, 17% Asian American, and 9% Latino. Eighty-seven percent of the students who attend Cooke come from low-income families. The school, which celebrated its 75th anniversary in 1997, is housed in a four-story brick building constructed in the 1920s. In addition to the main building, the school has an annex in the back of a church several miles away, which is used to accommodate an overflow of students. During the 1997–1998 school year, the annex housed approximately 175 students. Cooke fell near the center of the distribution of Philadelphia's 42 middle schools on the district's baseline 1996–1997 performance index. The spring prior to the implementation of the TDMSMP, only 9% of Cooke's eighth graders scored at the basic level or above on the Stanford-9 achievement test.

During the 1997–1998 school year, Cooke Middle School had several features that both supported and detracted from a strong implementation of the TDMSMP program. On the plus side, it had a strong and skilled principal who played a major role in bringing the Talent Development model to Cooke and worked hard to both reorganize the school's resources in support of the model and to communicate to the staff that a strong implementation of the model would benefit the school's students. Over 80% of the professional staff voted by secret ballot to become a Talent Development Middle School in the spring of 1997. The principal also took a hands-on approach to instructional matters, organized a "cabinet" of lead teachers in each discipline that met weekly along with the curriculum coach in mathematics and the Johns Hopkins English Language Arts facilitator to discuss and troubleshoot implementation issues, and helped create a "Mathematics Seminar" to provide her seventh and eighth grade teachers with guided practice in implementing instructional practices that support open-ended problem solving in the classroom. In addition, the school had the benefit of two lead mathematics teachers who had received substantial staff development through past and ongoing school district and reform initiatives. These two teachers not only played a key role in supporting the implementation of the TDMSMP at Cooke Middle School but also became key trainers in the summer and monthly staff development provided to the teachers at all three schools implementing the TDMSMP.

On the downside, the school was hit with several "shocks to the system" during the school year. The first was that the main school building was closed for the first two weeks of the school year due to roof repair work, which was not completed on schedule. Second, early in October, after the teachers were just beginning to become comfortable with the demands of implementing multiple new instructional programs, Cooke became one of a small number of district schools ordered to participate in a new school support process designed for schools that the district identifies as underperforming. The public pronouncement that the school was in need of help and the newness of the process led to a fair degree of uncertainty and unease among the faculty. Another complicating factor was that the prior school year had ended stressfully, largely as the result of a flare-up of racial tension between some of the school's African American and Asian students. The biggest obstacle, however, to a strong implementation of the TDMSMP was the large number of long-term subs, provisionally certified, and inexperienced teachers who were teaching at the school. Aware that large numbers of students would be entering Cooke with poor prior preparation (the average fifth grader upon entry to Cooke tested at the third-grade level), the principal concentrated some of her strongest teachers in self-contained 5th-grade classrooms and took steps to reduce class size in the 5th grade. As a consequence, six of the eight 8th-grade sections and two of the eight 7th-grade math sections had to be taught by new, inexperienced, or provisionally certified teachers with little or no preparation in mathematics teaching.

Participation, Support, and Implementation Levels

During the 1997–1998 school year, the TDMSMP was fully implemented in the fifth, seventh, and eighth grades, with both the seventh- and eighth-grade students using the seventh-grade UCSMP Transition book during the first year of implementation. Sixth-grade teachers were invited to attend staff development, participated in after-school training organized by the curriculum coach, had access to teacher's editions of the UCSMP sixth-grade Everyday Mathematics curriculum, and in some cases implemented portions of it as replacement units. However, they did not receive regular in-classroom implementation assistance from the curriculum coach nor implement the full sixth-grade curriculum. During the following school year, the sixth-grade teachers began a full implementation of the program and the eighth-grade teachers taught an "Algebra Topics" course that used the last half of the UCSMP Transition book and the first half of the UCSMP Algebra book as the second stage of a 3-year, phase-in plan that culminated with all students taking a full formal algebra course in the eighth grade during the 1999–2000 school year.

Teachers were provided with three days of initial summer training, and then, with monthly 3-hour sessions on Saturdays throughout the year. In addition, the curriculum coach organized additional after-school professional development sessions and provided teachers with information about and access to additional training opportunities provided by the school district. Overall, teachers had access to over 50 hours of professional development during the year. Attendance records show that 6 of the school's 13 mathematics teachers attended more than 70% of the summer and Saturday trainings, and 8 teachers attended at least half. Four of the remaining five teachers attended between 20% and 40% of the sessions. Only one teacher attended none of the sessions. By the terms of the teachers' contract, all of these sessions were voluntary and teachers were paid the district rate of $20 per hour by their school for the sessions they did attend.

During the 1997–1998 school year, the curriculum coach worked at the school two days per week providing in-classroom implementation support to 13 mathematics teachers. In her judgment, on a scale of 1 (low) to 5 (high), 11 of the 13 teachers achieved an implementation level of 3 or greater. Both survey data and focus groups revealed that the overwhelming majority of teachers found both the professional development and in-classroom implementation support to be helpful and on target (Useem, 1999).

Overall, Cooke Middle School had relatively high levels of teacher participation in professional development, in-classroom implementation support, student extra help, and implementation of the Talent Development Middle School Mathematics program. The only area where the implementation did not meet its initial projections was curriculum coverage and pace. The fifth-grade teachers completed the first four units of the Everyday Mathematics curriculum (Numbers, Operations, Geometry, Rational Numbers), which is approximately half of it, but were two units short of the first-year goal. The seventh- and eighth-grade teachers completed the first four units of the UCSMP Transition Mathematics text and selected sections from the remaining chapters. The curriculum coach estimates that the average seventh- and eighth-grade teacher attained about 70 to 80% of the first-year curriculum coverage goal.

We now turn our attention to two main questions: (1) Did the Talent Development Middle School Mathematics Program lead to the systematic and substantial gains in mathematical learning and thinking that will be needed to achieve "Algebra for All" at Cooke Middle School? and (2) Is there evidence that teachers implemented the kinds of teaching practices that the TIMSS study found are supportive of advanced mathematical performance in the middle grades?

DATA AND METHODS

To address the first of our two main questions, we analyzed the growth in mathematical achievement experienced by students at Cooke Middle School from fall to spring during the first-year implementation of the Talent Development Middle School Mathematics Program and compared it to growth at a demographically similar control school selected by the School District of Philadelphia's research office. The appendix at the end of the chapter summarizes the means and standard deviations obtained by each school on each subtest in both Fall 1997 and Spring 1998.

The ambitious goal of the Talent Development Middle School's Mathematics Program is to develop the mathematical talent of every class and of every student. How closely did we approach this goal? As a first stab at answering this question, we computed students' growth from fall to spring in scale score units on the Total Math Battery of the Stanford 9. Then, we figured what percent of class sections and what percent of students met two different challenging growth targets: a 12-point gain (which is the national average fall-to-spring scale score gain made by a middle school student if you average across fifth-grade, sixth-grade, seventh-grade, and eighth-grade norms) and a 24-point gain (double the national average gain for the middle grades). Table 10.1 summarizes what we found. Only one section out of 34 total sections did not meet the 12-point growth target at Cooke. This 97% goal attainment rate is 20 points higher than the 77% goal attainment rate at School B. Similarly, 74% of the students had at least a 12-point gain at Cooke versus only 60% at School B. Cooke's accomplishments look even more dramatic if one considers the percent of sections and percent of students exhibiting more than a 24-point gain.

Table 10.1. Developing the Mathematical Talent of Every Class, Every Student?: Percent of Class Sections and Percent of Students Meeting Challenging Targets for Growth in Total Mathematics Achievement between Fall and Spring

	% of class sections in which students' average growth was greater than 12 scale score points	% of students whose scale score gain was greater than 12	% of class sections in which students' average growth was greater than 24 scale score points	% of students whose scale score gain was greater than 24
Cooke Middle School	97%	74%	59%	54%
School B	77%	60%	13%	33%

Table 10.2 summarizes Cooke's accomplishments in terms of Normal Curve Equivalents (NCEs). A positive NCE gain means that students are catching up against national norms. Unlike scale scores, it is meaningful to compare NCE gains across subscales, so we've added information concerning each subscale to this table. Again we chose two challenging growth targets: a 4 NCE gain and an 8 NCE gain.

Every class section at Cooke made an NCE gain greater than 4 in Total Math Achievement. This was true of only 77% of the class sections at School B. The difference between the two schools was greater on the Problem Solving subtest than on the Math Procedures subtest.

Although a 4 NCE gain is a substantial gain, an 8 NCE gain is dramatic and is indicative of sections and students learning much more than a years' worth of mathematics between the fall and the spring. Seventy-six percent of the class sections at Cooke had an NCE gain that was larger than 8 in Total Mathematics Achievement. At School B, only 27% of the class sections met this growth target. In their study of Philadelphia middle schools, Wilson and Corbett (1999) found that in high-poverty middle schools like Cooke Middle School, there are many classrooms where little learning takes place. The classroom level results suggest that, at Cooke Middle

Table 10.2.   Catching Up to National Norms?: Percent of Class Sections and Percent of Students Meeting Challenging Targets for NCE Gains Between Fall and Spring

	Cooke Middle School		School B	
Outcome Variable	*% of class sections in which students' average NCE gain was grater than 4*	*% of students whose NCE gain was greater than 4*	*% of class sections in which students' average NCE gain was greater than 4*	*% of students whose NCE gain was greater than 4*
Growth in Math Total Achievement	100%	72%	77%	57%
Growth in Math Problem Solving Achievement	88%	69%	53%	53%
Growth in Math Procedures Achievement	85%	63%	57%	56%
	Cooke Middle School		School B	
Outcome Variable	*% of class sections in which students' average NCE gain was greater than 8*	*% of students whose NCE gain was greater than 8*	*% of class sections in which students' average NCE gain was greater than 8*	*% of students whose NCE gain was greater than 8*
Growth in Math Total Achievement	76%	58%	27%	40%
Growth in Math Problem Solving Achievement	74%	56%	20%	40%
Growth in Math Procedures Achievement	71%	55%	40%	42%

School, this did not occur. Consistently high quality learning opportunities were offered in mathematics schoolwide.

Although Table 10.1 and Table 10.2 are quite illuminating, they are no substitute for statistically modeling the learning advantage that occurred at Cooke. Specifically, we used HLM to ask the question, Using the Stanford 9 Total Mathematics Battery as our measure of learning, how much more mathematics did the typical student (the student who was at the grand mean of our sample on the pretest) learn at Cooke than at School

B? Or, more precisely, After taking account of students' prior achievement in math, how large an advantage was it to be a student in one of the 34 math classes at Cooke Middle School compared to being a student in one of the 30 math classes at School B?

Several complementary HLM analyses address this question. Each HLM model uses a students' math total NCE score in spring of 1998 as the outcome measure.

Model 1: School as a Predictor of Between Classroom Differences in Students' Math Total NCE

Model 1 evaluates school effects on students' end-of-year mathematics total NCE scores on the Stanford 9 after controlling for differences in pretest status (total mathematics NCE scores on the Stanford 9 from the fall) as follows:

- $Y_{ij} = \beta_{0j} + \beta_{1j}(\text{Prior Achievement}_{ij}) + r_{ij}$
- $\beta_{0j} = \gamma_{00} + \gamma_{01}(\text{School}_j) + u_{0j}$
- $\beta_{1j} = \gamma_{10}$

Model 1 has an intercept (which represents the adjusted mean end-of-year mathematics total NCE for Class j), a covariate measuring prior mathematics achievement, and a randomly varying error term at Level 1, the student level. At Level 2, the adjusted classroom mean level of achievement is modeled as a function of an intercept, school (1 = Cooke Middle School; 0 = School B), and a randomly varying error term.

Table 10.3 shows the results for this model. This model gives us an initial estimate of the greater growth in mathematics achievement (greater spring achievement controlling for students' prior achievement in the fall) in Cooke Middle School's classrooms than in the comparison school's classrooms. The coefficient for school (3.27) indicates that math achievement NCE gains were much higher in Cooke Middle School classes than in the classes at the comparison school. One useful way of interpreting the coefficients from Table 10.3 is to note that students whose prior achievement was at the grand mean of the two schools reached an NCE 38.1 (and a percentile rank of 29) if they attended Cooke, but reached only an NCE of 34.8 (and a percentile rank of 24) if they attended School B. The effect size of .52 associated with this effect indicates that this effect is more than one-half the size of the between-classroom standard deviation of the outcome measure.

Table 10.3.   Model 1 for End-of-Year Total Mathematics NCE Scores

	Model for Level-1 Intercept, β_0		
Fixed Effect	*Coefficient*	*SE*	*p-value*
Intercept, γ_{00}	34.78	.70	.000
School, γ_{01}	3.27	.97	.001
	Model for Prior Achievement Slope, β_1		
Fixed Effect	*Coefficient*	*SE*	*p-value*
Intercept, γ_{10}	.72	.02	.000
	Variances of the Random Effects		
Random Effect	*Variance Component*	*df*	χ^2
Classroom mean, u_0	9.07	62	172.50
Level-1 effect, r	105.61		

Model 2: Did the Magnitude of Cooke's Learning Advantage in Mathematics Depend upon the Grade Level of the Class?

There was reason to predict that Cooke's learning advantage in mathematics, during its first year as a Talent Development School, might be strong in fifth grade, where a very traditional program was replaced by the standards-based Everyday Mathematics program and the new program was supported by intensive and sustained professional development and follow-up in classroom support. More moderate gains were anticipated in Grades 7 and 8 (moderate curricular change was accompanied by intensive and sustained professional development and follow-up in classroom support), and moderate in Grade 6 (full-scale introduction of Everyday Mathematics at this grade level did not occur until Cooke's second implementation year). Many sixth-grade students, however, received an extra dose of math instruction for at least one quarter and sixth-grade teachers enthusiastically participated in Talent Development's professional development sessions. They received informal coaching from the Math Curriculum Coach and tried out portions of the Everyday Math program with their students as "replacement units" (partially replacing the existing curriculum).

Model 2 examines how Cooke's learning advantage in mathematics varied across fifth, sixth, seventh, eighth, and special-multigrade classes. (Special education and ESOL classes at both schools serve students from multiple grades.) To do this, Model 2 adds four dummy variables (Sixth, Seventh, Eighth, and Multigrade) to the class-level model to estimate the main effect of

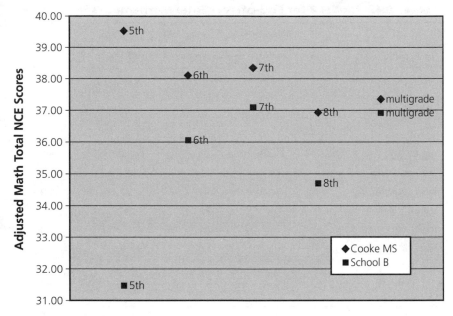

Figure 10.1.   Adjusted math total normal curve equivalent scores as a function of grade and school.

grade of class, and also adds four cross-product terms (School × Sixth, School × Seventh, School × Eighth, and School × Multigrade) to estimate the School by Grade of Class interaction.

Table 10.4 reveals that, as anticipated, the magnitude of the learning advantage at Cooke depends upon grade of class. This significant School × Grade of Class interaction $(\chi^2(1)=8.42, p=.004)$ is depicted in Figure 10.1. As expected, the learning advantage is largest in fifth-grade classes. The adjusted mean NCE at the end of the year in Cooke Middle School's fifth grade was more than 8 NCEs higher than the adjusted mean in School B. For example, a fifth grader who started the year at the overall grand mean (an NCE of 28.2) is predicted to reach an NCE of 39.5 if he attends Cooke but only an NCE of 31.5 if he attends School B. In other words, this fifth grader would reach the 31st national percentile at Cooke but only the 19th national percentile at School B.

Table 10.4.   Model 2 for End-of-Year Total Mathematics NCE Scores

Model for Level-1 Intercept, β_0			
Fixed Effects	*Coefficient*	*SE*	*p-value*
Intercept, γ_{00}	31.46	1.29	.000
School, γ_{01}	8.08	1.82	.000
Sixth, γ_{02}	4.60	1.80	.000
Seventh, γ_{03}	5.64	1.84	.004
Eighth, γ_{04}	3.23	1.93	.099
Multigrade, γ_{05}	5.45	3.45	.120
School × Sixth, γ_{06}	−6.04	2.57	.022
School × Seventh, γ_{07}	−6.82	2.56	.011
School × Eighth, γ_{08}	−5.85	2.61	.029
School × Multigrade, γ_{09}	−7.65	4.83	.119

Model for Prior Achievement Slope, β_1			
Fixed Effects	*Coefficient*	*SE*	*p-value*
Intercept, γ_{10}	.73	.019	.000

Variances of the Random Effects			
Fixed Effects	*Coefficient*	*SE*	χ^2
Classroom mean, u_0	7.14	54	130.18
Level 1 effect, r	105.41		

The learning advantage at Cooke MS was significantly less for classes serving other grade levels, but was still more than 2 NCEs for sixth- and eighth-grade classes and was more than 1.25 NCEs for seventh-grade classes. For example, an eighth grader who started the year at the overall grand mean is predicted to reach an NCE of 36.9 at Cooke MS (the 27th national percentile) versus an NCE of 34.7 at School B (the 23rd national percentile). Only in multigrade classes (special education and ESOL classes) was Cooke's learning advantage too small to be of practical significance.

Did Mathematics Teachers Use State-of-the-Art Teaching Practices More Often at Cooke MS than at School B?

By providing teachers with standards-based curriculum materials and providing multiple levels of professional development and support for teachers, the Talent Development Middle School program seeks to help teachers adopt state-of-the-art teaching practices (practices that are aimed at teaching and learning for understanding and incorporate a variety of nontraditional, active, and cooperative learning techniques). One of the best ways to gauge the frequency of state-of-the-art teaching and of traditional teaching is to ask students to report how often specific practices were used in their mathematics classes during the school year. A student survey concerning mathematics instruction was conducted in spring 1998 in both Cooke MS and in School B. Table 10.5 lists the two subscales (and their component items) that were used to measure the frequency of Traditional Math Teaching and State-of-the-Art Math Teaching in each class. Each class was assigned a score on each item, which represented the mean response of every student in the class. The subscale scores for each class were then computed by averaging across all the items in a subscale.

School and Grade of Class as Predictors of Between-Classroom Differences in Implementing Traditional Math

Traditional Math is measured by a composite that indicates students' responses to three items, which indicate how often their math teacher is implementing a traditional "sage on the stage followed by seatwork" approach to math instruction.

A class-level multiple regression model estimated the main effects of School and Grade Level of Class and the School × Grade Level of Class interaction. This analysis revealed a School × Grade Level of Class interaction ($F(4,56) = 2.43$, $p = .058$). This interaction is depicted in Figure 10.2. As shown in Figure 10.2, fifth-grade classes at Cooke experienced traditional math practices less ($b = -.33$, $p = .016$) than did fifth-grade classes at School B, but multigrade classes at Cooke experienced traditional math practices more ($b = .40$, $p = .06$) than did multigrade classes at School B. The figure also reveals that despite this modest interaction, students at both schools and at all grade levels experienced traditional math practices on "most days" (Grand Mean = 3.04, SD = .28).

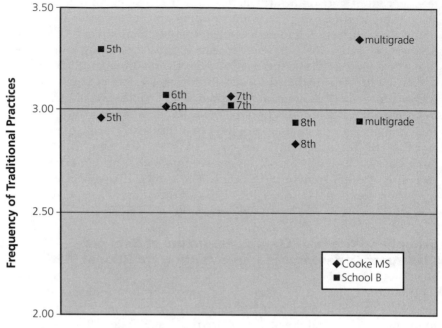

Figure 10.2.   How often do students experience traditional math practices? (2 = "once or twice a week," 3 = "most days," 4 = "every day")

State-of-the-Art Teaching

A class-level multiple regression model estimated the main effects of School and Grade Level of Class and the School × Grade Level of Class interaction. This analysis revealed a main effect of school (F $(1,64)$ = 14.95, p = .000), a main effect of Grade Level of Class (F$(4,60)$ = 6.11, p = .000), and a School × Grade Level of Class interaction (F$(4,56)$ = 6.39, p = .000). The interaction is depicted in Figure 10.3. Cooke students in fifth-, eighth-, and multigrade classes experienced significantly more state-of-the-art teaching than did students in School B, but the frequency of state-of-the-art teaching did not differ significantly between schools for sixth- and seventh-grade classes.

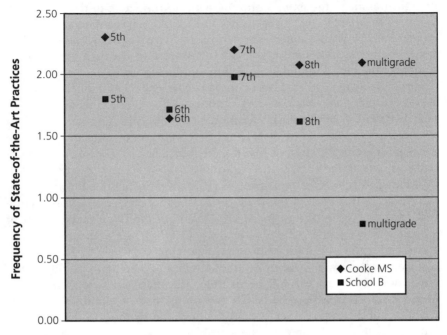

Figure 10.3.   How often do students experience state-of-the-art teaching in math? (0 = "never," 1 = "once or twice a month," 2 = "once or twice a week," 3 = "most days")

DISCUSSION AND CONCLUSION

The multiple analyses of the prior section demonstrate that the achievement gains at Cooke Middle School during its first year of using the Talent Development Middle School Mathematics Program were both systematic and substantial. For a middle school to achieve "Algebra for All," systematic achievement gains need to occur in every classroom, at every grade level, every year. If all students are to receive a common and challenging mathematics course in the eighth grade, it is essential that all students arrive in the eighth grade ready for the challenge. For this to occur, there can be no "cracks in the classroom floor" (Corbett & Wilson, 1997): lost years in which little or no mathematics growth occurs in classrooms that are taught by an unprepared and unsupported teacher. Although such "cracks" are a common experience in urban middle schools, there were no cracks in the mathematics classrooms at Cooke during the 1997–1998 school year. Mathematics learning occurred in every classroom.

The achievement gains at Cooke were ample. For students who attend high-poverty middle schools to succeed in a standards-based algebra course in eighth grade, large gains in mathematical knowledge and understanding need to occur in the earlier grades of middle school. The average student served by Cooke enters the school two years behind grade level in tested mathematics achievement. Such low starting points are typical for students who attend nonselective urban middle schools. This means that to reach a high standard of achievement by the end of middle school, the average low-income, urban middle school student needs to have a substantially higher rate of growth in mathematical understanding per year than the average middle school student in the United States. At Cooke Middle School, for example, students need to demonstrate on about a year and a half's gain in mathematical understanding to close their performance gap by the end of eighth grade. During their first year using the TDMSMP, the data indicate that 74% of the students at Cooke experienced more than a year's worth of growth and that 54% had more than two years' worth of growth. (These gains occurred between October, when the pretest was given, and April, when the posttest was taken.)

Given the intertwined nature of the multiple components of the TDMSMP, it may never be possible to reliably examine the effectiveness of each component. Our working hypothesis is that everything mattered, and, in one classroom or another, every layer of support provided by the TDMSMP proved critical. We know of some teachers who achieved large gains and rarely attended professional development but made substantial use of the in-classroom implementation support that was provided. We know of others who attended staff development regularly but were uncomfortable working with another teacher in their classroom. We also know of cases in which underqualified or unpolished teachers succeeded because they made full use of all the support offered. One case was a provisionally certified teacher who came to teaching as a mid-career change. He had good content knowledge but no experience teaching or working with adolescents. Initially, he had very weak classroom management skills. He came, however, to all the staff developments, followed the curriculum, and worked closely with the curriculum coach. By April, the average student, in all three of his eighth-grade sections, demonstrated considerably more than a year's worth of growth. Another case involved a long-term substitute at one of the other middle schools implementing the TDMSMP. She was covering for a teacher who had been in a car accident and over the course of the first term, an anticipated few weeks' absence stretched into several months. The sub had never taught a middle school mathematics class before. But, with intensive assistance from the curriculum coach—and extra attention provided to her students by the school's elective replacement extra-help mathematics teacher—her two classes, on average, also experienced more than a year's worth of growth.

The problem-solving subscale scores for the seventh and eighth graders at Cooke indicate that the "Mathematics Seminar" invented by the school's principal and organized by the curriculum coach and the school's two lead math teachers also paid off. Numerous teachers commented on how a school-wide instructional program and a cross-school network enabled a professional community to emerge around mathematics instruction; several administrators have stated how a school-wide curriculum prevented students from falling behind when they were moved between sections and teachers.

However, the first year implementation of the TDMSMP at Cooke Middle School was not easy and everything did not go smoothly. Most of the first-year problems reported in the implementation literature occurred at Cooke. Despite an over 80% vote in favor of adopting the Talent Development model, some teachers were at least initially reluctant to implement the TDMSMP. Others clearly felt and reacted to the strain of having to implement multiple new instructional programs (Useem, 1999). There were issues that needed to be worked out with the school's building committee. Despite great efforts, teachers sometimes had to wait longer than promised for critical materials. The school, moreover, could not be easily classified as "ready for reform." The prior year had been difficult, the principal was just starting her second year, and the school's staff was in transition. Yet despite these glitches and difficulties, systematic and large achievement gains occurred. This directly challenges the notion that it takes several years before whole school reform efforts lead to achievement gains. Similarly, large and systematic gains were obtained in Reading, English, and Language Arts as well at Cooke during the first-year implementation of TDMS (Plank & Young, 1999). The gains occurred in our view because the multiple layers of student and teacher support provided in the Talent Development model were strong enough to overcome the implementation difficulties typically encountered in urban middle schools.

This is a source of hope for urban school reform. The 1998 Teacher Survey of Professional Development and Training indicates that the level of support provided to the mathematics teachers during the 1997–98 school year at Cooke Middle School was rare.

It need not be. The central elements of the Talent Development Middle School Mathematics Program—a coherent and increasingly complex standards-based curriculum, sustained and focused curriculum and grade-specific professional development, intensive in-classroom implementation support, coordinated extra help, and a communal organization of school—are broadly reproducible. Nor are they prohibitively expensive. The main costs are 1.5 staffing positions (the elective replacement, extra-help teacher and a half-time curriculum coach), which in some cases can be filled by reassigning existing staff. Other costs include professional development stipends for teachers and trainers and a one-time investment in high-quality research and standards-based instructional materials that support and build "Algebra for All" in the eighth grade. What appears to separate the Talent Development Middle School Mathematics Program from other reform attempts is not a unique curriculum or exotic teaching techniques but the intensity, focus, quality, and multiple layers of learning opportunities and support provided to students and teachers.

A short-term case study can demonstrate what can be accomplished but cannot address issues of generalizability and sustainability. These issues can only be addressed in studies over multiple years in multiple sites. A national field test of TDMSMP is now underway. Thus, in the coming years, we will be able to bring strong evidence to bear on these issues. What the first-year results do reveal, however, is that it is possible to construct an instructional program that directly takes on the major impediments that stand in the way of achieving "Algebra for All"—weak and unfocused curriculums, large amounts of out-of-field teaching, unsupported teachers, and poorly prepared students—and to implement successfully the program in a typical urban middle school to good result.

REFERENCES

Balfanz, R. (1997, March). *Mathematics for all in two urban schools: A view from the trenches.* Presented at the Annual Meeting of the American Educational Research Association, Chicago.

Balfanz, R. (2000). Why do so many urban public school students demonstrate so little academic achievement? In M.G. Sanders (Ed.), *Schooling at risk: Research, polic,y and practice in the education of poor and minority adolescents* (pp. 37–62). Mahwah, NJ: Erlbaum.

Chambers, D. L. (1994). The right algebra for all. *Educational Leadership, 53*(6), 85–86. The College Board. (1994). *Equity 2000: What it takes: Creating a supportive climate for implementation.* New York: Author.

Corbett, H. D., & Wilson, B. L. (1997). *Cracks in the classroom floor: The seventh grade year in five Philadelphia middle schools.* Philadelphia: Philadelphia Education Fund.

Cuevas, G., & Driscoll, M. (Eds.). (1993). *Reaching all students with mathematics.* Reston, VA: National Council of Teachers of Mathematics.

Education Week. (1998). *Concentrated poverty* [Online]. Available: http://www.edwk.org/sreports/qc98/challenges/poverty/p0-n.htm [1999, July 22].

Edwards, E. L., Jr. (Ed). (1990). *Algebra for everyone.* Reston, VA: National Council of Teachers of Mathematics.

Ingersoll, R. M. (1999). The problem of underqualified teachers in American secondary schools. *Educational Researcher, 28*(2), 26–37.

Killion, J. (1999). *What works in the middle: Results-based staff development.* Oxford, OH: National Staff Development Council.

Lewis, L., Parsad, B. Carey, N., Bartfai, N., Farris, E., & Smerdon, B. (1999). *Teacher quality: A report on the preparation and qualifications of public school teachers.* Washington, DC: National Center of Education Statistics.

Mac Iver, D. J., Balfanz, R., & Plank, S. B. (1999). An "elective replacement" approach to providing extra help in math: The Talent Development Middle

Schools' Computer and Team Assisted Mathematics Acceleration (CATAMA) Program. *Research in Middle Level Education Quarterly, 22*(2), 1–23.

Mac Iver, D., Mac Iver, M., Balfanz, R., Plank, S. B., & Ruby, A. (2000). Talent Development Middle Schools: Blueprint and results for a comprehensive whole-school reform model. In M. G.Sanders (Ed.), *Schooling students placed at risk: Research, policy, and practice in the education of poor and minority adolescents* (pp. 261–288). Mahwah, NJ: Erlbaum.

McGrath, A. (1998, April 20). Algebra and sympathy. *US News and World Report.*

Moses, R. P. (2001). *Radical equation: Math literacy and civil rights.* Boston: Beacon Press.

National Council of Teachers of Mathematics. (2000). *Principals and standards for school mathematics.* Reston, VA: Author.

National Council of Teachers of Mathematics and Mathematical Sciences Education Board. (1998). *The nature and role of algebra in the K–14 curriculum.* Washington, DC: National Academy Press.

National Research Council. (1998). *High school mathematics at work.* Washington, DC: National Academy Press.

Pelavin, S., & Kane, M. (1990). *Changing the odds: Factors increasing access to college.* New York: College Entrance Examination Board.

Plank, S., & Young, E. (1999, April). *In the long run: Longitudinal assessments of the Student Team Literature Program.* Paper presented at the Annual Meeting of the American Educational Research Association, Montreal, Canada.

Schoenfeld, A. H. (2002). Making mathematics work for all children: Issues of standards, testing, and equity. *Educational Researcher, 31*(1), 13–25.

Secada, W. G., Fennema, E., & Adajian L. B. (Eds.). (1995). *New direction for equity in mathematics education.* New York: Cambridge University Press.

Silver, E. A. (1997). Algebra for all: Increasing students' access to algebraic ideas, not just algebra courses. *Mathematical Teaching in the Middle School, 2*(4), 204–207.

Silver, E. A. (1998, March). *Improving mathematics in middle schools: Lessons from TIMSS and related research.* Washington, DC: U.S. Department of Education.

Smith, J. B., Smith, B., & Bryk, A. S. (1998, November). *Setting the pace: Opportunities to learn in Chicago's elementary schools.* Chicago: Consortium on Chicago School Research.

Steen. L. A. (Ed). (1997). *Why numbers count.* New York: College Entrance Examination Board.

U.S. Department of Education. (1997, October). *Mathematics equals opportunity.* White Paper prepared for U.S. Secretary of Education Richard W. Riley. Washington, DC: Author.

U.S. Department of Education. (1998). *TIMSS overview and key findings across grade levels.* Washington, DC: Author.

U.S. Department of Education's Mathematics and Science Expert Panel. (1999). *Exemplary and promising mathematics programs.* Washington, DC: U.S. Department of Education.

Useem, E. L. (1999). *Teachers' appraisals of the Talent Development training model.* Paper presented at the Annual Meeting of the American Educational Research Association, Montreal, Canada.

Wilson, B. L., & Corbett, H. D. (1999). *"No excuses": The eighth grade year in Philadelphia middle schools.* Philadelphia: The Philadelphia Education Fund.

APPENDIX

Math Achievement Normal Curve Equivalent (NCE) Scores: Means and (SDs) for Cooke Middle School and School B in Fall 1997 and Spring 1998

	Cooke Middle School			School B		
	Fall	*Spring*	*Difference*	*Fall*	*Spring*	*Difference*
	5th grade (n=142)			*5th grade (n=173)*		
Total Math NCE	19.7 (15.8)	34.2 (17.8)	+14.2	30.2 (17.8)	32.8 (16.9)	+2.6
Math Problem Solving NCE	23.1 (17.4)	36.7 (19.5)	+13.6	33.0 (18.8)	34.3 (17.3)	+1.3
MathProcedures NCE	20.2 (15.9)	33.2 (16.8)	+13.0	30.7 (18.9)	33.3 (18.4)	+2.6
	6th grade (n=170)			*6th grade (n=183)*		
Total MathNCE	25.1 (13.9)	36.4 (15.9)	+11.3	33.2 (17.8)	39.7 (17.8)	+6.5
Math Problem Solving NCE	29.4 (15.3)	39.1 (17.0)	+9.7	34.4 (17.7)	39.2 (18.7)	+4.8
Math Procedure NCE	23.2 (15.0)	34.9 (16.5)	+11.7	34.5 (19.2)	42.4 (18.1)	+7.9
	7th grade (n=172)			*7th grade (n=158)*		
Total Math NCE	23.3 (16.1)	34.1 (15.8)	+10.8	29.3 (38.0)	38.0 (36.5)	+8.7

Math Achievement Normal Curve Equivalent (NCE) Scores:
Means and (SDs) for Cooke Middle School and School B in Fall 1997 and Spring 1998 (Cont.)

	Cooke Middle School			School B		
	Fall	*Spring*	*Difference*	*Fall*	*Spring*	*Difference*
Math Problem Solving NCE	25.1 (18.3)	35.7 (16.4)	+10.6	31.4 (17.3)	38.1 (15.1)	+6.7
Math Procedure NCE	25.5 (16.2)	33.9 (17.6)	+8.4	30.7 (15.1)	39.7 (14.2)	+9.0
	8th grade (n =190)			*8th grade (n=133)*		
Total Math NCE	29.0 (15.0)	37.5 (13.7)	+ 8.5	34.4 (15.3)	40.1 (14.5)	+5.7
Math Problem Solving NCE	31.1 (17.3)	39.1 (14.1)	+8.0	35.9 (16.6)	43.9 (15.8)	+8.0
Math Procedure NCE	29.4 (15.6)	36.0 (14.8)	+ 6.6	35.1 (15.5)	34.8 (15.4)	-0.3

CHAPTER 11

COHORTS IN MIDDLE LEVEL TEACHER PREPARATION

Transformational Possibilities and Complexities

Joanne M. Arhar and Alicia R. Crowe
Kent State University

ABSTRACT

This chapter reviews the literature on cohorts and attempts to further conceptualize the value and role of cohorts as transformative, professional learning communities for prospective teachers, teacher educators, and schools. Drawing on a diverse body of literature that includes cohorts in teacher education, teacher socialization, professional learning communities, group dynamics, and middle-grades reform, a definition of cohorts as transformational agents in middle level schools and middle level teacher education programs is emerging. Cohorts can be viewed as interdisciplinary, student-centered, professional learning communities that function as inquiry groups focused on providing mutual support and the care and nurturance of the spiritual, moral, and intellectual lives of early adolescence. These groups

---

Middle School Curriculum, Instruction, and Assessment, pages 211–231
Copyright © 2002 by Information Age Publishing
All rights of reproduction in any form reserved.

211

work within larger political and social agendas to transform classrooms, schools, and ultimately society to be more just and caring. Awareness of the power relations that come to play between teachers and students attempting to create caring communities is important. Knowledge and application of theories related to group dynamics is essential if cohorts are to reach the potential as described in this review.

WHY COHORTS?

Traditionally, preservice teacher education programs have focused on the development of the individual's knowledge and competencies considered important to teaching rather than the development of a community of learners (Goodlad, 1990; Putnam & Borko, 2000), thus perpetuating the culture of isolation so prevalent among teachers in schools (Lortie, 1975; Rosenholtz, 1989). Meiklejohn and Dewey in the 1920s and 1930s advocated for the concept of student learning communities in higher education as a way of countering increased specialization and fragmentation. Meiklejohn (1932) called for a community of study that would create unity and coherence of curriculum across the disciplines. Dewey (1933) advocated learning that involved student-centered, active learning in shared inquiry. "Learning community models include linked courses, clusters, freshman interest groups, federated learning communities and coordinated studies" (Cox, 2001).

The first policy statement calling for a more communal, cohort-based approach to preparing teachers came in 1986 with the publication of the first Holmes Group Report, *Tomorrow's Teachers.*

> Basically a "non-program" at present [exists in teacher education]; professional courses are not interrelated or coherent. The curriculum [of teacher education] is seldom reviewed for its comprehensiveness, redundancy, or its responsiveness to research and analysis. Advisement is often ineffective, leaving students to wander about, rather than progressing systematically in a cohort through their programs. (p. 50)

Tomorrow's Schools of Education (1995), the third report of the Holmes Group, strengthened the argument for cohorts in teacher education:

> ...we recommend that [teacher education] organize its students into what we call "cohorts." The members of each cohort journeying together along a common path of professional learning and socialization that leads to life-long personal and professional growth and development. No longer should any student in a school of education lack the support of a group of students who form their own small learning community. Each student would be part of a group in which fellow students take an interest in each other's attain-

ments. We expect that the members of a cohort will form a mutually supporting network that endures for many of them throughout their
professional careers. (p. 58)

In *Teachers for our Nation's Schools,* Goodlad (1990) argues:

Programs for the education of educators must be characterized by a socialization process through which candidates transcend their self-oriented student
preoccupations to become more other-oriented in identifying with a culture
of teaching. (p. 288)

He further states that:

Programs for the education of educators must be characterized in all
respects by the conditions for learning that future teachers are to establish in
their own schools and classrooms. (p. 290)

He specifically recommends that teacher educators model what they want
and expect their students to do as teachers.

Tom (1997) agrees with Goodlad's assessment that we have

largely ignored the social dimension of teaching, in which candidates have
relationships with one another and, ultimately, develop collective obligations
to the overall profession…. Rather than being treated as individuals to be
managed bureaucratically, prospective teachers should be grouped into a
cohort that moves through a professional program as a unit. (p. 150)

Tom cites Lortie's (1968) critique of teacher education that it does not create a "shared ordeal." The lack of this shared ordeal, according to Lortie,
contributes to low self-esteem, mistrust between veteran and novice teachers,
and weak collegial bonds. Other problems associated with an individual
(noncohort) approach to teacher education include the time and money
involved in advising, scheduling, budgeting, and tracking the programmatic
progress of students. With cohorts, faculty can team up to do cohort advising, share information with one another, and provide support for prospective teachers who are experiencing difficulties. Finally, Tom argues that
cohorts "provide mutual support for prospective teachers and foster socialization into desirable professional norms and practices" (p. 153).

One of the critiques of teacher education is that it lacks conceptual
coherence around theory, research, and practice. This lack of coherence
and articulation makes educating teachers to form collegial relationships
with other teachers difficult (Arends & Winitzky, 1996). In writing about
professional development schools, Darling-Hammond (1999) argues that
"beginning teachers get a richer, more coherent learning experience when
they are organized in teams to study and practice with these [veteran pro-

fessional development school] teachers and with one another" (p. 232). In these teams, university faculty, school mentors, and prospective teachers can work together around common problems that will help to bridge the gap between theory and practice.

Howey (1996), acknowledging that teacher education programs in general are believed to hold little influence over teacher socialization, believes that coherent teacher education programs would have greater power to exert influence through cohort systems. He also believes in the importance of the critical socialization of the prospective teacher, particularly with respect to developing "dispositions and abilities relative to equity and diversity" (p. 147) so that society can be transformed through teaching.

Arends and Winitzky (1996), also arguing that cohorts may create more coherent teacher education programs, explain how the use of cohorts aligns with research on groups that shows that forces develop within the group that tend to bring the individuals in the group together. In summarizing this research, they explain that "highly cohesive groups are more effective at solving problems and resolving conflicts than groups low in cohesiveness" (p. 546). They warn, however, that merely placing prospective teachers in cohorts will not assure the desired ends of group cohesiveness and articulation.

In summary, cohorts and student learning communities are viewed as a means to (a) facilitate advising and mentoring in a caring, supportive, and nonbureaucratic way; (b) foster shared experiences (Lortie's "shared ordeal") that can help prospective teachers gain self-confidence and professional commitment as they learn to teach; (c) model a collegial approach to teaching in which members share a collective obligation to professional learning; (d) create more coherent teacher education programs; (e) socialize teachers into the profession as individuals and collectively in groups; and (f) involve students in active, student-centered communities of shared inquiry.

In spite of this strong rationale in support of cohorts, the practice has not become prevalent. The Research About Teacher Education (RATE VI) study of 1992 found that less than 35% of the 50 participating institutions reported little or no progress toward student cohort arrangements. Goodlad's (1990) study of 29 teacher education programs also found little evidence of cohort systems.

Why Cohorts in Middle Level Teacher Preparation?

While reports on middle level education do not specify the use of cohorts in the preparation of teachers for the middle grades (see Carnegie Council on Adolescent Development, 1989; McEwin, Dickinson, Erb, &

Scales, 1995; National Middle School Association, 1997; and Jackson & Davis, 2000), it makes sense that teacher education programs model the kind of sustained and supportive teacher–student relationships that interdisciplinary teams are supposed to enable. By modeling the skills, knowledge, and dispositions associated with team membership, teacher education programs may better prepare teachers for the responsibilities as beginning teacher/team members. It also opens up possibilities for beginning teachers to shape the culture of middle level schools that do not use interdisciplinary teaming.

RESEARCH ON STUDENT LEARNING
COMMUNITIES AND COHORTS

Cox (2001) summarizes the research literature on student learning communities in higher education. Students who participate in learning communities develop an educational citizenship (an understanding of mutual interdependence), academic and social support from their peers, increased learning and more engagement in learning, a sense of belonging, and intellectual development (e.g., embrace complexity) (See Cox, 2001, p. 45, for references to this body of literature). An emerging body of literature on cohorts in teacher education is beginning to suggest similar findings.

The teacher education studies that we explored indicate the positive effects of the use of cohorts in socializing teachers toward collaborative, interdependent work and learning to teach (e.g., Beck & Kosnik, 2001; Bullough, Clark, & Wentworth, 2001; Sapon-Shevin & Chandler-Olcott, 2001). However, researchers remind teacher educators that the benefits of cohorts do not arise merely from changing the structure of a program. In general, to help assure positive effects, teacher educators should attend to creating intentional community-building activities; be explicit with students regarding communities, cohorts, and the teacher education process; and model the values and practices they desire to teach (Beck & Kosnik, 2001; Bullough et al., 2001; Radencich et al., 1998; Sapon-Shevin & Chandler-Olcott, 2001). Researchers have also documented some of the problems with the cohort system.

The authors could not locate any studies of middle level cohort studies at this time, but it is hoped that an examination of cohorts elsewhere in teacher education could prove helpful in exploring the possibilities cohorts hold for middle-grades teacher education. We narrowed our search to research preservice undergraduate cohort systems and did not include anecdotal stories about cohorts that are embedded in the literature on teacher education programs. Cohorts are defined variably. However, in the studies that we located, students were grouped together for a significant amount of professional coursework and field experience for more than one semester to provide mutual support and foster a commitment to growth and learning of schoolchildren and knowledge and skill about how to do this in the classroom and school.

Beck and Kosnik (2001) describe research with cohorts in an elementary teacher education program at the Ontario Institute for Studies in Education, University of Toronto (OISE/UT). Their study was conducted with four cohorts of approximately 60 students each. They collected data over a 4-year period, staying with each cohort for a year. In designing and teaching their cohorts, they deliberately focused on the community aspect of the cohort system and their study seeks to understand the effects on their student teachers. Their findings offer promising results reflecting the advantages of using cohorts, with certain conditions in place.

In their study, the researchers found that a teacher education program with a cohort system in place that has a strong focus on community provides an effective program for supporting both the academic and social aspects of learning to teach. Some expected findings included the students' "loyalty, the willingness to pitch in, the caring for one another, the inclusiveness, even the personal and social growth" (p. 945). Beyond these expected findings, they found evidence to suggest that the community emphasis in cohorts can influence the academic and technical learning of members of the program. Some of these influences included "high level of participation in whole class and small group discussions and activities; high quality of the discussion and group work, notably in connection with the action research projects; growth in awareness of the value of collaboration and ability and willingness to seek help and resources from fellow student teachers; willingness to take risks in practicum settings and implement basic changes in approach to teaching; willingness to express their point of view and question each other's and the faculty's opinions, while maintaining positive relationships; [and an] inclination and ability to foster community and collaboration in their own classrooms" (p. 946). Finally, the high demands on faculty of a cohort system can be draining and detrimental to progressing through promotion and tenure decisions.

Sapon-Shevin and Chandler-Olcott (2001) took a more critical approach to cohorts, attempting to problematize the widely accepted notion that cohorts are the optimal way to organize students in a teacher education program. In particular, they were interested in "the extent to which a student cohort with a strong sense of community is the optimal setting for developing the skills of critical reflection" (p. 352). In their study of their own cohort of elementary/special education students at Syracuse University, Sapon-Shevin and Chandler-Olcott found that the positive effects of the use of cohorts, such as cooperation and trust, differed with each cohort and cannot be assumed. The negative aspects include development of cliques, which not only impeded a sense of safety for peers but also lead away from program goals; varying conceptions of community (e.g., some students believed that friendship and lack of conflict were necessary components of a good community that ran counter to faculty beliefs); strong personalities can alter student and faculty attitudes toward cohorts; and ethical dilemmas that arise in faculty decisions to share or not to share information about students with other cohort faculty for fear of coloring their views. They noted that the nature of their curriculum (teaching for social justice) creates dissension and tension in students and that even the dissension has value because it teaches prospective teachers how to handle such topics in their own classrooms.

Upon reviewing their findings, Sapon-Shevin and Chandler-Olcott (2001) provide several suggestions for the development of successful cohorts that parallel what Beck and Kosnik (2001) describe. In particular, they suggest that instructors involved with the cohort should (a) discuss "the rationale, hoped-for benefits, and possible land mines" of participating in a cohort-based system with members of the cohort; (b) incorporate the study of ways of developing and maintaining a community into the curriculum of the program; (c) "implement mechanisms for monitoring and assessing the changes within the student cohort;" and (d) "find ways to exchange information essential to continuity and smooth functioning of the cohort" (p. 362).

Bullough and colleagues (2001) report on a study involving 20 student teachers in a secondary education program who were members of a cohort for 1.5 semesters. The study investigated the attitudes of student teachers regarding the strengths and weaknesses of student cohorts in teacher education. Although the faculty/researchers defined cohorts to mean both working together to care for and nurture the intellectual, moral, and spiritual lives of children and a willingness to invest in one another's development, students reported that the greatest value of cohorts lay in the quality of relationships with peers. They also found that cohorts develop a culture of their own (e.g., gripe session about student teaching that turned quite negative) that may run counter to the goals of the program. It is not surprising that student attitudes about the cohort and the program paralleled the ups and downs of both the high school academic year and the college academic year. Exams, the stress of the job search, and unit plan development, for example, all influenced how members felt about the cohort system. As the pressures of student teaching responsibilities mounted, students chose to neglect their academic assignments in favor of the more immediate pressing needs.

In general, students were pleased with the tight fit of the program with the culture of the school and teachers, leading the authors to conclude that the cohort proved effective in helping students fit in. However, fitting in also meant often rejecting researcher-based knowledge. The support students gave one another was viewed as valuable in dealing with the ups and downs of student teaching (the researchers critique Lortie's language of "shared ordeal," saying that it is more appropriate to war than to teacher education). There was some evidence to suggest that the cohort system seemed able to counter teacher isolation—the tendency to close the classroom door was resisted by students who realized (through their cohort) that working together and supporting one another's professional growth is more beneficial in learning to teach.

As with others, Bullough and his colleagues (2001) emphasize that the positive effects of cohorts on the learning of the students is not automatic. To reach its full potential, the faculty involved with the cohort must deliberately cultivate a culture within the group that respects and desires effective group problem solving. They also feel that greater attention to altering traditional conceptions of teaching (including teacher isolation) as well as teaching students about the developmental issues of student teaching needs to be made explicit so that the program does unwittingly socialize students into the status quo of the culture of the school and teaching.

Radencich and colleagues (1998) focused on the cultures of cohorts in an elementary and an early childhood teacher education program. Within the culture of the cohort system, they wondered about the development of social conscience, which for Radencich and her colleagues meant "behavior guided by a sense of professionalism, a sense of morality and empathy for the needs of others" (p. 110). Their study included a team of 25–40 students from the elementary and the early childhood program. The team spent their junior year, summer session, and first half of their senior year together. From this research, they found that the cohort system turned out to be "either very positive or almost pathological" (p. 112), supporting the findings of Sapon-Shevin and Chandler-Olcott.

Some of the pitfalls they noted were that (a) students, when becoming close and extremely supportive of one another, may become too inward focused and ignore others; (b) within teams, cliques may develop; and (c) an individual or minority members may provoke negative group reactions or place pressure on other members of the group to join in their reaction. The authors suggest team-building activities, communication among all members of the group, and explicit discussion of concepts and practices associated with team building.

These studies seem to point to several issues: when cohorts are going well, students seem to enjoy and value the support that they receive from their peers; some academic and technical benefits relative to teaching exist that arise from cohorts (increased participation, attention to fostering community in their own classrooms, inclusiveness); without careful planning and consideration on the part of faculty to group maintenance and developmental issues of college students, cohorts can simply reinforce the status quo of the isolated culture of teaching or degenerate into "dysfunctional families"; faculty and student conceptions of community may differ; cohorts have a life of their own and one cohort may differ markedly from another. What is clear is that the socialization of teachers into a culture of collaboration is not always easily accomplished and the opposite of what is intended can occur, resulting in a fragmented rather than a coherent program. The emotional and sometimes professional toll taken on faculty also needs to be considered.

THEORIZING ABOUT THE POTENTIAL AND THE PROBLEMS OF COHORTS

Several themes emerge in the above discussion of learning communities and cohorts that merit development. This further examination of the theoretical literature related to both the potential and limitations of cohorts has implications for continued research in this relatively unexplored field and implications for the development and improvement of cohorts in the preparation of teachers for the middle grades. What is important to note is that despite the limitations or problems associated with cohorts, both students and faculty seem to favor them.

The Potential of Cohorts for Transformative Change

The following exploration of the literature on Dewey's views of democratic communities, teacher socialization, professional learning communities for faculty and students, and middle level schools as transformative and collaborative cultures may help to explain the continued interest in and potential for the use of cohorts in teacher education. This potential may or may not have been reached in programs as they now exist.

Teacher Socialization
The teacher socialization literature seeks to understand the process whereby teachers become participants of the teaching profession (Zeichner & Gore, 1990). Zeichner and Gore (1990), in their literature review of teacher socialization, outline three main approaches researchers have taken to understand socialization:

1. Functionalist—researchers study how teachers learn to fit into the role of teacher and the culture of the profession as determined by schools that are essentially bureaucratic.

2. Interpretive—researchers study how prospective teachers attempt to understand (and sometimes shape) the role of teacher and the culture of the profession.

3. Critical—researchers study and critique the broader social, historical, political, and institutional contexts that influence the role teachers play.

They cite research that shows the weak influence of teacher education programs on teacher socialization. The segmentation of the program (including subject area coursework, methods classes and field experiences) and the resultant mixed messages given to prospective teachers by university faculty, mentors, and supervisors are offered as explanations of this lack of influence. On the other hand, criticalists argue that the hidden curriculum of most teacher education programs (which separates theory and practice, fragments curriculum, and views learners as passive recipients of officially sanctioned knowledge) provides powerful lessons to prospective teachers about what is important in teaching. It is this hidden curriculum, they believe, that constitutes a strong influence on teacher socialization. There has been little research on the broader issues of race, social class, and gender and there is general agreement now that socialization is a highly interactive process in which teachers exercise choice in learning to teach.

Cohorts in teacher education are an attempt to socialize beginning teachers into a more collaborative culture and notion of teaching. Collaborative work cultures and professional learning communities have been linked to effective classroom learning, stronger professional confidence, and feelings of self-efficacy among teachers, and teachers' capacity to initiate and respond to change (see Hargreaves, Earl, Moore, & Manning, 2001, p. 165, for references to supporting research).

Dewey's Views of Democracy and Community

How might cohorts be like communities? Dewey's belief that democracy provides the ideal community life is reflected in the ideas of Goodlad, Tom, and others who see cohorts as a place where prospective teachers develop collective obligations to the overall profession. According to Dewey (1916), democracy is a "mode of associated living," a way of living together characterized by "conjoint communicated experience" in which citizens are concerned with developing shared interests that lead them to consider the impact of their actions on others. Arguing against those who fear that interconnection and interdependence are restrictive, Dewey believes that the limitations are "balanced off by the opportunities for genuine growth which they also provide" (Boisvert, 1998, p. 63). Arguing against those who believe that individuality is concerned with self-interest and isolation, Dewey views individuality as the distinctive contribution someone makes to community. Thus difference is viewed as an asset rather than a liability.

Professional Learning Communities for School-Based Teachers and Prospective Teachers

Cochran-Smith and Lytle (1999), in reviewing the literature on professional learning communities in schools and teacher education programs, offer teacher educators a way to think about the potential that cohorts have for inculcating prospective teachers into a more collaborative way of learning to teach. They describe a conception of teacher learning, what they term "knowledge of practice," that occurs in professional learning communities. The assumption behind this view of learning is that "through [systematic] inquiry, teachers across the professional life span—from very new to very experienced—make problematic their own knowledge and practice as well as the knowledge and practice of others" (p. 273). In this view of learning, teachers and the knowledge they construct are connected to larger political and social agendas. Like the work of action researchers who "regard the construction and reconstruction of curriculum as central to the larger project of social change and the creation of a more just and democratic society" (p. 274), these teachers act as "transformative intellectuals" (Giroux, 1998). Classrooms become the site of inquiry and "teacher research...makes visible the ways teachers and students negotiate power, authority, and knowledge" (Lytle & Cochran-Smith, 1992, p. 470). The image of teaching as critical, political, and intellectual means that "teachers learn by challenging their own assumptions; identifying salient issues of practice; posing problems; studying their own students, classrooms, and schools; constructing and reconstructing curriculum; and taking on roles of leadership and activism in efforts to transform classrooms, schools, and societies" (Cochran-Smith & Lytle, 1999, p. 278) that limit students' access to opportunities to learn. In this view of learning, collaborative relationships replace the expert–novice relationship, and the inquiry community is the central context in which teacher learning takes place.

In preservice teacher education programs that create communities for teacher learning to occur,

> work is deliberately structured so that multiple viewpoints are represented, including reading research by school-based as well as university-based researchers and teachers. Time is allotted for groups to work together to hash out issues, write about their experiences, and share the data of their classrooms with one another. The key is that student teachers are socialized into teaching by becoming part of a community of researchers and learners

who see questioning as part of the task of teaching across the life span. (Cochran-Smith & Lytle, 1999, p. 284)

How are such inquiry communities formed and maintained? Cochran-Smith and Lytle's (1999) review indicates there are several dimensions at play:

1. time to work together,

2. a discourse that is characterized by "joint construction of knowledge through conversation and other forms of collaborative analysis and interpretation" (p. 294),

3. group issues related to negotiating agendas, sharing power and decision making, representing the work of the group and dealing with tensions of individual and collective viewpoints and purposes are dealt with, and

4. teachers assume leadership roles in which they critique the assumptions of change efforts rather than carrying out the changes intended by others.

Hargreaves and colleagues' (2001) report on a 5-year study of seventh- and eighth-grade teachers as they work to understand, implement, and cope with a new, mandated curriculum policy in Ontario that includes standards, alternative assessment, and curriculum integration indicate that the kind of support needed for change to occur is similar to Cochran-Smith and Lytle's assessment: time to plan and think through the changes and teacher-directed team approach.

Providing prospective teachers with time for reflection in a team setting would seem an important way to socialize them into a culture that needs proactive, transformative intellectuals. And the literature on school culture indicates that there is much work to do in this regard.

The culture of many schools is highly individualistic, balkanized, or contrived in its collegiality (Hargreaves, 1995) rather than collaborative. Henderson and Hawthorne (2000) summarize Hargreaves's understanding of a collaborative school culture:

True collaboration and collegiality mean choosing to share understandings, perspectives, beliefs, and practices and to engage fully in joint problem solving, creative planning, mutual support, and professional development. Thus, it calls for major changes in the relationships among everyone in a school. Authentic collaboration requires an ethic of caring that extends far beyond conviviality or safe, inconsequential deliberations. It necessarily involves disagreement, rigorous examination of beliefs and ways of working, and a great deal of forgiveness. (p. 161)

Middle level schools offer an alternative to the balkanized, individualistic, and bureaucratic culture that pervades much of education today. And so represent a rationale for using cohorts in middle level teacher education.

Middle Level Schools as Transformative and Collaborative Cultures

Middle level schools built around interdisciplinary teams offer opportunities for deeper learning to occur for both teachers and students (see Backes, Ralston, & Ingwalson, 1999; Felner et al., 1997; Flowers, Mertens, & Mulhall, 1999; and Lee & Smith, 1993, for a discussion of middle school reform and student achievement; see Johnston, Markle, & Arhar, 1988, for a discussion of middle school collaborative cultures and teacher learning) and for students to feel more connected to their teachers (Arhar, 1990). The interdisciplinary team (which bears some similarity to the cohort system in teacher education) also has the potential to actually change the culture of a school from a bureaucracy to what Erb (2001), referring to Skrtic's work (1991), calls adhocracy. Skrtic, applying Toffler's (1970) ideas about the future of organizations to education, defines the difference between bureaucracy and adhocracy as a movement from standardization of skills via training and socialization to the profession, lack of interdependence, and delivery of standard programs toward one of mutual adaptation via teams of workers who solve problems and create novel solutions in a dynamic environment of change.

Hargreaves, Earl, and Ryan (1996), the Carnegie Council on Early Adolescence (1989), NMSA (1995) and Jackson and Davis (2000) among others advocate for the creation of strong, supportive communities (specifically interdisciplinary teams) for early adolescence, arguing that "care, commitment and emotional engagement are largely absent from emerging definitions of professional standards for teaching," which favor subject matter expertise and technical skills (Hargreaves et al., 1996, p. 58). Noddings (1992) argues that not only is care a necessary condition for learning but it also should be a goal of schooling—to promote healthy, competent, moral people. Adler and Moulton's (1998) study of middle school students' perceptions of care, that it constitutes good teaching, supports the thinking of Noddings. Furthermore, a study of 16 schools engaged in middle school reform a la *Turning Points* concludes that care "required open and trusting relationships among colleagues, school leaders, and the larger community" (Ryan & Friedlander, 1998). Yet, according to a study conducted by McEwin, Dickinson, and Jenkins (1996), only half of the middle schools in the country claim to be using interdisciplinary teaming. The contradictions of reform place teacher educators in a difficult position.

One might ask: "Why socialize teachers for schools that do not exist?" If socialization is considered a one-way process of adapting to what is, then it would seem pointless to organize prospective teachers into cohorts. However, if one considers socialization to be an interactive process of what Skrtic (1991) calls "mutual adaptation," then beginning teachers may influence the culture of the school and help to move it to a more collaborative professional learning community. Therefore, socializing preservice teachers in this way is key to developing transformed schools for middle level students.

Faculty Learning Communities in Higher Education

While the literature reviewed thus far is focused on the potential of learning communities and cohorts for prospective teachers and school-based faculty, there is an increasing interest in learning communities for faculty in higher education. Palmer (1998), for example, seeks to redefine teaching as creating a space "in which the community of truth is practiced" (p. 90). Not only do faculty who participate in learning communities (typically a small, cross-disciplinary group of faculty engaged in a year-long program of seminars and other activities about enhancing teaching and learning) develop interest in the scholarship of teaching, but also they become more civic minded and change the institutional culture toward becoming a learning organization (Cox, 2001). Not only is there the potential for the professional learning of middle-grades teacher educators, but also these teacher educators may transform teacher education toward a more collegial, professional learning culture.

While the literature that has been discussed in this section provides ways to think more fully about the potential of cohorts, cohorts also need to be problematized so that their full benefits have the potential to be realized. The following section examines some of the difficulties associated with cohorts.

Problematizing Cohort Arrangements in Middle Level Teacher Education

It would seem "unprogressive" to argue with the virtue of creating a caring supportive community for cohorts of prospective teachers as opposed to a traditional program in which students move almost mechanistically, course by course, toward completion of a license. In actual practice, however, this ideal may manifest itself in uncaring, mechanistic relationships with students that subjectify them and have, ironically, the opposite of the intended humanisitic effect. In her critique of the Report of the Carnegie Commission on Early Adolescence of 1989, Lesko writes:

> The *Turning Points* image of a good middle school emphasizes affectional ties among adults and youth who participate in close, personal communities for learning. Such relationships may seem unequivocally good to White, middle class professionals, but they are institutional creations that use emotional connections to shape behavior and thinking. I believe it is important to acknowl-

edge the particular kinds of interpersonal power orchestrated in such settings rather than to pretend that authority and control are dissipated or absent in schools with "houses," "families," and "good feelings." (1994, p. 145)

Furthermore, is it not possible for teacher education faculty, in the process of collaborating with one another, to provide this nurturing environment for students, to use information gained through this joint sharing to classify, judge, and label students as compliant/noncompliant, good/bad teachers, hardworking/lazy, reflective/nonreflective, collaborative/non-collaborative—in other words, to use what Foucault terms "dividing practices," which turns students into subjects by objectifying them (1983, p. 208). His genealogy of "pastoral power" is a useful one here to help us understand that power issues are at play as educational institutions take on the health and well-being of students in a way similar to Christianity's designation of "pastor," who had a very special form of power:

> It is a form of power whose ultimate aim is to assure individual salvation in the next world...[it] is not merely a form of power which commands; it must also be prepared to sacrifice itself for the life and salvation of the flock...a form of power which does not look after just the whole community, but each individual in particular, during his entire life...[and] cannot be exercised without knowing the inside of people's minds, without exploring their souls, without making them reveal their innermost secrets. It implies a knowledge of the conscience and an ability to direct it. (p. 214)

As it relates to cohorts in teacher education, the knowledge gained through this pastoral power can be used to determine a person's status/continuation in a program and in the profession. According to this view, teacher educators and teacher education programs are far from power-neutral. And as a faculty's time is consumed with the daily management of cohorts, which often includes observation and documentation of progress over time, are they not, to some extent, because of the intensification of their work, sacrificing their scholarly careers toward promotion and tenure for the well-being of their "flock"? Sensitivity to power relations and some of the negative effects of caring relations, both for teachers and students, is an important ethical consideration that has not been explored in the literature on cohorts and professional learning communities.

"Otherness" and Group Pressure as Group Dynamics That Threaten Cohorts as Learning Communities

While cohorts can take on the feeling of a loving family, they can also become dysfunctional. Radencich and colleagues (1998) and Sappon-Shevin and Chandler-Olcott (2001) note the difficulties cohorts present for some faculty, students, and learning. Radencich and colleagues argue that some students and faculty are treated as "others," isolated and in some instances viciously attacked for being different in some way, whether it be a difference of opinion or difference in age or simply being a new member not part of the initial cohort. They cite the anthropology's literature on the "stranger" as a way to understand more fully the issue. Anthropologists (Bohannan, 1981; Shabatay, 1991) write about strangers as "persons who don't count, who can be destroyed, and who must be always on the alert, antennae out, as they struggle to learn the subtleties of the group's verbal and nonverbal communication" (Shabatay, 1991, p. 114). This may help to understand why students gang up on other students who differ from them and why they treat faculty new to a cohort with such scorn.

Group pressure is another potentially difficult issue that emerges in the literature on cohorts. Radencich and colleagues (1998) cite the literature on group dynamics to offer an explanation of how groups function.

> ttenhausen (1991), in a review of over 250 studies on the dynamics of small social groups, stated that "acting in a group lowers self-awareness and heightens group-awareness" and that "the very fact of group membership has a significant impact on how people see themselves...and act in the group" (p. 348). Kohn (1997) points out social psychologists' assertion that it is a fundamental error to attribute "to an individual's personality or character what is actually a function of the social environment." (p. 431)

In studying the group dynamics of a cohort group within an educational administration program and reviewing literature on the ways groups work, Scribner and Donaldson (2001) explain that group dynamics can prove quite important in either impeding or facilitating learning within a group. In their study, they found that the climate of the group, group norms, the roles individuals assumed or were assigned, and the communication and problem solving within the group were important factors in the types of learning that occurred. As with others studying cohorts, Scribner and Donaldson's study shows that placing people in cohort groups does not ensure positive results. In particular, they stress that although group cohesiveness is necessary for groups to achieve the desired learning, it is not the only factor and it is not sufficient for learning to occur.

Drawing on their findings, Scribner and Donaldson (2001) make recommendations concerning the development and use of cohorts similar to what researchers in teacher education have made. They provide three general recommendations. First, members of the cohort need to be prepared for the experience. For example, participants should understand the issues involved with groups such as group dynamics and group development. Second, they recommend that instructors should be aware that the performance of tasks does not equal learning; a group that holds the task as the focus may not be learning what instructors intended. Third, they recommend that formative evaluation of the cohort program occurs. In particular, they suggest that participants and instructors reflect on their experiences with the group.

SUMMARY

Drawing on a diverse body of literature that includes teacher socialization, professional learning communities, group dynamics, and middle-grades reform, a definition of cohorts as transformational agents in middle level schools and middle level teacher education programs is emerging. Cohorts can be viewed as interdisciplinary, student centered, professional learning communities that function as inquiry groups focused on providing mutual support, a collective obligation to the profession, and the care and nurturance of the spiritual, moral, and intellectual lives of early adolescence. These groups work within larger political and social agendas to transform classrooms, schools, and ultimately society to be more just and caring.

Awareness of the power relations that come into play between teachers and students attempting to create caring communities is important. Knowledge and application of theories related to group dynamics is essential if cohorts are to reach this potential. How universities and colleges of education might respond in supportive ways to those faculty engaged in the labor-intensive work of cohorts needs further discussion.

FURTHER RESEARCH

The dearth of research in an area that has such strong recommendations from a wide variety of sources seems to indicate that further research is needed. Because of the transformative potential of teams in middle-grade schools, research related to cohorts in middle level teacher preparation programs may have an impact not only on how teachers are prepared for the middle grades, but also how middle schools (through interdisciplinary teams) are able to live up to their promise.

Beliefs are powerful as they interact with the curriculum of teacher education, but their strength and nature differ across students (Briztman, 1986; Pajares, 1992; Richardson, 1996). Considering this importance, future studies might (a) consider the initial beliefs of prospective teachers about community and teaching and learning in a community as they enter a cohort; (b) track what happens to these beliefs as the prospective teachers move through methods courses, field experiences, and student teaching; and (c) follow the graduates into their first years of teaching and see how those beliefs have evolved. Studies might also examine how these beliefs play out in classroom practice and how teachers from the cohort-based programs think about their role in schools and in the profession.

Studies could focus on how teachers from these programs influence student learning and the profession and how they are influenced by it. Studies could explore questions like: What are the consequences of teacher learning in cohorts (in the type of learning community described by Cochran-Smith & Lytle, 1999), for the learning of early adolescents? For middle school reform? For interdisciplinary teams? For teacher agency within the profession? How do these teachers respond to school-, district-, and state-mandated initiatives in areas such as assessment, promotion, retention, and tracking? Or in mandated professional development?

Case studies of individual programs might shed light on the hidden curriculum of a cohort's experience with diversity, equity, and inclusion. How do the messages of the hidden curriculum match the stated program goals? Are they coherent? What are the difficulties of creating a coherent teacher education program through cohorts? Is coherence the goal or are diverse messages important?

Other questions include how the use of cohorts in teacher education programs help prospective teachers think about the impact of their actions on others. A study might ask: Do prospective teachers become more concerned about the effect of their actions on others? Do they also consider the effect of their actions on their own students' moral, social, intellectual, physical, and spiritual development?

And what of the teacher educators themselves? There is little literature exploring the beliefs of teacher educators (Wideen, Mayer-Smith, & Moon, 1998), including mentors and supervisors. What are their beliefs about community and how do these beliefs play out in their teaching? How do they balance the demands of research and publishing with the demands of a cohort of students? What are their perceptions of their own power? And victimization? How do institutions respond to middle level teacher educators engaged in this labor-intensive work?

And finally, the literature indicates what group processes are necessary for the development and maintenance of healthy, functioning groups. But how do teacher education faculty include the teaching of these processes in an already packed curriculum that is increasingly mandated by licensure exams and state proficiency tests?

While most of the research on cohorts has been interpretive, there is room for exploration within other paradigms, including process–product and critical paradigms. For example, what is the impact of cohort systems on students' construction of knowledge about early adolescents and effective teaching strategies for this age group? What are the gender, social class, and race issues at play in cliques that form within cohorts? How can professional learning communities of faculty working with prospective middle level teachers support the tenure and promotion prospects of middle level teacher educators? Longitudinal, case study, pre–post test designs, and narrative analysis are among a few possible avenues researchers might take to further explore the use of cohorts in preparing middle level teachers. The literature on group dynamics includes methods that would be appropriately applied to the study of cohort groups.

REFERENCES

Adler, N. I., & Moulton, M. R. (1998). Caring relationships: Perspectives from middleschool students. *Research in Middle Level Education, 21*(3), 15–32.

Arends, R., & Winitzky, N. (1996). Program structures and learning to teach. In F. B. Murray (Ed.), *The teacher educator's handbook* (pp. 526–556). San Francisco: Jossey-Bass.

Arhar, J. M. (1990). The effects of interdisciplinary teaming on social bonding of middle level students. *Research in Middle Level Education, 14*(1), 1–10.

Backes, J., Ralston, A., & Ingwalson, G. (1999). Middle level reform: The impact on student achievement. *Research in Middle Level Education Quarterly, 22*(3), 43–57.

Beck, C., & Kosnik, C. (2001). From cohort to community in a preservice teacher education program. *Teaching and Teacher Education, 17,* 925–948.

Bettenhausen, K. L. (1991). Five years of group research: What we have learned and what needs to be addressed. *Journal of Management, 17,* 345–381.

Bohannan, P. (1981). The stranger. *Science, 81,* 18–20.

Boisvert, R. D. (1998). *John Dewey: Rethinking our time.* Albany: State University of New York Press.

Britzman, D. (1986). Cultural myths in the making of a teacher: Biography and social structure in teacher education. *Harvard Educational Review, 56*(4), 442–456.

Bullough, R. V., Clark, D. C., & Wentworth, N. (2001). Student cohorts, school rhythms, and teacher education. *Teacher Education Quarterly, 28*(2), 97–110.

Carnegie Council on Adolescent Development. (1989). *Turning points: Preparing American youth for the 21st century.* New York: Carnegie Corporation of New York.

Cochran-Smith, M., & Lytle, S. L. (1999). Relationships of knowledge and practice: Teacher learning in communities. In A. Iran-Nejad & P. D. Pearson (Eds.), *Review of research in education* (pp. 249–305). Washington, DC: American Educational Research Association.

Cox, M. D. (2001). Faculty learning communities: Change agents for transforming institutions into learning organizations. *To improve the academy: Resources for faculty, instructional, and organizational development, 19,* 69–93.

Darling-Hammond, L. (1999). Education teachers for the next century: Rethinking practice and policy. In G. A.Griffin (Ed.), *The education of teachers (Ninety-eighth Yearbook of the National Society for the Study of Education, Part I)* (pp. 221–256). Chicago: University of Chicago Press.

Dewey, J. (1916). *Democracy in education.* New York: MacMillan.

Dewey, J. (1933). *How we think.* Lexington, MA: Heath.

Erb, T. (2001). Transformative organization for youth and adult learning. *Middle School Journal, 33*(1), 48–55.

Felner, R. D., Jackson, A., Kasak, D., Mulhall, P., Brand, S., & Flowers, N. (1997). The impact of school reform for the middle years: A longitudinal study of a network engaged in *Turning Points*-based comprehensive school transformation. *Phi Delta Kappan, 79,* 528–532, 541–550.

Flowers, N., Mertens, S. B., & Mulhall, P. E. (1999). The impact of teaming. *Middle School Journal, 31*(2), 57–60.

Foucault, M. (1983). The subject and power. In H. L. Dreyfus & D. Rabinow (Eds.), *Michele Foucault: Beyond structuralism and hermeneutics* (pp. 208–226). Chicago: University of Chicago Press.

Giroux, H. (1988). *Teachers as intellectuals.* New York: Bergin & Garvey.

Goodlad, J. (1990). *Teachers for our nation's schools.* San Francisco: Jossey-Bass.

Hargreaves, A. (1995). *Changing teachers, changing times.* New York: Teachers College Press.

Hargreaves, A., Earl, L. A., & Ryan, J. (1996). *Schooling for change: Reinventing education for early adolescents.* Washington, DC: Falmer Press.

Hargreaves, A., Earl, L., Moore, S., & Manning, S. (2001). *Learning to change: Teaching beyond subjects and standards.* San Francisco: Jossey-Bass.

Henderson, J. G., & Hawthorne, R. D. (2000). *Transformative curriculum leadership* (2nd ed.). Columbus, OH: Merrill.

The Holmes Group. (1986). *Tomorrow's teachers: A report of the Holmes Group.* East Lansing, MI: Author.

The Holmes Group. (1995). *Tomorrow's schools of education.* East Lansing, MI: Author.

Howey, K. (1996). Designing coherent and effective teacher education programs. In J. Sikula (Ed.), *Handbook of research on teacher education* (2nd ed, pp. 143–170). New York: MacMillan.

Jackson, A. W., & Davis, G. A. (2000). *Turning points 2000: Educating adolescents in the 21st century.* Columbus, OH: National Middle School Association.

Johnston, J. H., Markle, G. C., & Arhar, J. M. (1988). Cooperation, collaboration, and the professional development of teachers. *Middle School Journal, 19*(3), 28–32.

Kohn, A. (1997). How not to teach values: A critical look at character education. *Phi Delta Kappan, 78,* 429–437.

Lee, V. E., & Smith, J. B. (1993). Effects of school restructuring on the achievement and engagement of middle-grade students. *Sociology of Education, 66,* 164–187.

Lesko, N. (1994). Back to the future: Middle schools and the *Turning Points* report. *Theory into Practice, 33*(3), 143–148.

Lortie, D. C. (1968). Shared ordeal and induction to work. In H. S. Becker, B. Geer, D. Rieseman & R. S. Weiss (Eds.), *Institution and the person* (pp. 252–264). Chicago: Aldine.

Lortie, D. C. (1975). *Schoolteacher: A sociological study.* Chicago: University of Chicago Press.

Lytle, S., & Cochran-Smith, M. (1992). Teacher researcher as a way of knowing. *Harvard Educational Review, 62,* 447–474.

McEwin, C. K., Dickinson, T. S., Erb, T. O., & Scales, P. C. (1995). *A vision of excellence: Organizing principles for middle grades teacher preparation.* Columbus, OH: National Middle School Association.

McEwin, C. K., Dickinson, T. S., & Jenkins, D. A. (1996). *America's middle schools: Practices and progress—a 25-year perspective*. Columbus, OH: National Middle School Association.

Meiklejohn, A. (1932). *The experimental college*. New York: HarperCollins.

National Middle School Association. (1995). *This we believe: Developmentally responsive middle level schools*. Columbus, OH: Author.

National Middle School Association. (1997). *National Middle School Association/National Council for the Accreditation of Teacher Education—Approved curriculum guidelines handbook*. Columbus, OH: Author.

Noddings, N. (1992). *The challenge to care in schools*. New York: Teachers College Press.

Palmer, P. (1998). *The courage to teach: Exploring the inner landscape of a teacher's life*. San Francisco: Jossey-Bass.

Pajares, M. F. (1992). Teachers' beliefs and educational research: Cleaning up a messy construct. *Review of Educational Research, 62*, 307–332.

Putnam, R. T., & Borko, H. (2000). What do new views of knowledge and thinking have to say about research on teacher learning? *Educational Researcher, 29*(1), 4–15.

Radencich, M. C, Thompson, T., Anderson, N. A, Oropallo, K., Fleege, P., Harrison, M., & Hanley, P. (1998). The culture of cohorts: Preservice teacher education teams at a southeastern university in the United States. *Journal of Education for Teaching, 24*(2), 109–127.

RATE VI. (1992). *Teaching teachers: Facts and figures*. Washington, DC: American Association of Colleges for Teacher Education.

Richardson, V. (1996). The role of attitude and beliefs in learning to teach. In J. Sikula, T. Buttery, & E. Guyton (Eds.), *Handbook of research in teacher education* (2nd ed , pp. 102–119). New York: MacMillan.

Rosenholtz, S. J. (1989). *Teachers' workplace: The social organization of schools*. White Plains, NY: Longman.

Ryan, S., & Friedlander, D. (1998). Strengthening relationships to create caring school communities. *Research in Middle Level Education Quarterly, 20*(1), 41–68.

Sapon-Shevin, M., & Chandler-Olcott, K. (2001). Student cohorts: Communities of critique or dysfunctional families. *Journal of Teacher Education, 52*(5), 350–364.

Scribner, J. P., & Donaldson, J. F. (2001). The dynamics of group learning in a cohort: From non-learning to transformative learning. *Educational Administration Quarterly, 37*(5), 605–636.

Shabatay, V. (1991). The stranger's story: Who calls and who answers? In C. Witherell & N. Noddings (Eds.), *Stories lives tell: Narrative and dialogue in education* (pp. 136–152). New York: Teachers College Press.

Skrtic, T. M. (1991). *Behind special education: A critical analysis of professional culture and school organization*. Denver, CO: Love.

Toffler, A. (1970). *Future shock*. New York: Bantam Books.

Tom, A. C. (1997). *Redesigning teacher education*. Albany: State University of New York Press.

Wideen, M., Mayer-Smith, J., & Moon, B. (1998). The critical analysis of the research on learning to teach: Making the case for an ecological perspective on inquiry. *Review of Educational Research, 68*(2), 130–178.

Zeichner, K., & Gore, J. (1990). Teacher socialization. In W. R. Houston (Ed.), *Handbook of research on teacher education* (pp. 329–348). New York: McMillan.

CONCLUSION

Sandra L. Stacki
Hofstra University

In so many publications describing what and how changes have been implemented in middle schools, structural changes such as teacher and student teaming, advisory groups, or block/flexible scheduling have generally succeeded in providing a more personalized environment and stronger community among students, teachers, administrators, and other school personnel. However, what many perceive as the most difficult yet crucial aspects of restructuring—those involving curriculum, instruction, and assessment (CIA)—often become the last components to receive attention. Unfortunately, most middle level schools still require CIA restructuring to implement creative, student-centered practice (Beane, 1993). Thus, recommendations one and two in *Turning Points 2000* (Jackson & Davis, 2000) distinctly emphasize curriculum, assessment, and instruction rather than the earlier *Turning Points'* (Carnegie Corporation of New York, 1989) more general language, which calls for teaching a "core of common knowledge." The newer *Turning Points* version requires "a more complicated vision than that described in the original report of *how* to decide *what* to teach" (Davis, 2001).

Responding to the call to strengthen CIA in middle level schools, the authors in this volume theorize, describe, and explain practices and some specific programs that can help to meet the needs and demands of our current diverse student populations and our dynamic sociocultural, political environment. These discussions give various middle level stakeholders "a more complicated vision" and help us to understand more about how decisions are made about what to teach. The authors highlight influences from the past and of the present, obstacles to CIA, and new directions. They tar-

Middle School Curriculum, Instruction, and Assessment, pages 233–236
Copyright © 2002 by Information Age Publishing
All rights of reproduction in any form reserved.   233

get for us the major dilemmas with which middle level teachers, researchers, teacher educators, and policymakers grapple with in their own realms and often demonstrate the overlapping of these issues and dilemmas into several realms. Many discussions are also couched within a knowledge of the often-conflicting political demands that may pit the standards and accountability movement against the CIA that educators think best meets the needs of the whole child.

As the early chapters emphasize, integration is a recurring theme in this text. CIA itself is an integration represented as a strong, equilateral triangle with each side or component equally important and emphasized in a rigorous approach. As the introductory chapter notes, CIA and its supporting structures must be a "specific kind of scaffold designed to help young adolescents bridge the space between childhood and young adult life" (Gross, Introduction, this volume). This type of scaffolding is thus not only CIA but also recommends a needed balance with affective goals and structures that provide a more holistic approach to middle school. Several chapters also point out that the middle school concept, philosophy, and CIA are clearly infused with influences of progressivism, especially the ideas of Dewey (1902, 1916). Through these discussions, we understand the evolutionary link between the timeless student-centered, developmentally appropriate practices from our progressive past and the still evolving curriculum—a 21st-century curriculum grounded in rigorous, public academic standards (Jackson & Davis, 2000). Beane's (1993) and similar student-centered approaches can trace their roots to progressivism. Authors endorse Beane's focus on integrated curriculum through themes that are student generated and thus developmentally appropriate and relevant in both the personal and social realms.

Also from the progressive period, middle level philosophy can trace its social meliorist tendencies (Kliebard, 1986) that call for a redistribution of cultural, social, and economic capital and power through a revitalized system of education—a focus on education for *all* children. These forms of equity have been central elements of the modern middle level movement as reiterated in national and state documents (National Middle School Association, 1995; New York State Education Department, 2000) and are demonstrated through curriculum interventions that focus on critical pedagogy (Nieto, 1996) and dimensions such as authors in the volume describe: culturally responsive instruction; TESOL, bilingual, and special education; and authentic curriculum including integrated learning and cross-curricular portfolios. As educators, we must understand this progressive past, what its contributions have been, and what we can still learn from its articulated philosophy and practices.

An integration and collaboration beyond the classroom is also acknowledged by many of these authors as they consider the larger political dimensions of how decisions about curriculum changes are made. Thus middle level stakeholders, including parents, need to know more about areas such as brain-level research, developmentally good practices and, what parents and the community can contribute to the total learning goals—both academic and affective. However, they must also be politically savvy about standards, testing, and accountability and the "hidden" messages and meanings involved. CIA decisions may be too politically rendered and not follow what research suggests are best practices. Many otherwise good middle schools and their teacher teams have yet to rise to the challenge or take the risks that are sometimes involved in implementing integrated curriculum or more authentic assessments. Those who have begun and continue these efforts may receive little appreciation.

Yet we must be cautious about faulting them for maintaining the status quo on most CIA when the political pendulum has swung so far to the right that fear and confusion often reign. As administrators and teachers are held accountable for high-stakes test scores, their desire, incentive, and reward for taking risks on student-centered, integrated, and problem-solving CIA is often diminished. When "report cards" of key tests are published in the local newspapers and on websites, a dangerous competitive precedent is set that may rally parents and communities to criticize schools and complain about lower test scores rather than working collaboratively with the schools.

These risks and uncertainties make the call for more rigorous research crucially important—not only for understanding theory and implementing better practices, but also for the needed rigorous and detailed research studies, the "thick description" (Geertz, 1973) that will provide a broader base of support for developmentally appropriate CIA and help politicians to understand and be persuaded by student-centered, authentic CIA within the structures of an exemplary middle school. Research must guide the middle level to strategies and practices. This series and in particular this volume on CIA adds to this knowledge base. Many of these chapters have described concrete practices and programs that have succeeded. This knowledge and these ideas can be analyzed and contextualized to be implemented in other schools and used to improve student-centered and integrated CIA efforts.

Ultimately, although some of these chapters show us contradictions that can be seen as extremes of difference such as the past versus the present, teacher centered versus student centered, or developmental appropriateness versus academic rigor, we must not view these as extremes. These must not remain on a "collision course" as Gross (Introduction, this volume) described in the case of standards, accountability, and testing versus student-centered, authentic curriculum. Middle level stakeholders must view these as interactive dialectics: internal contradictions or tensions working toward a negotiated and productive balance (Kvale, 1996). The point of balance will shift over time as various stakeholders are involved—for instance, as the political parties and agendas change—yet the tension will continue to exist. We must make this a positive tension in which opposing sides on CIA issues continue to communicate and work together for the best results.

As the central stakeholders, teachers will remain at the center of discussions to improve middle level CIA and developmentally appropriate structures. The more empowered teachers are as knowledgeable professionals, the more they will be confident to take the risks needed to change CIA thinking and practices for the benefit of all children. Chapters in this text, most notably the last, which focuses on teachers experiencing professional education as learning communities, begin to address the issue of teacher professional development and what practices in this realm will best prepare teachers to teach at the demanding and challenging middle level. The next volume of *Research in Middle Level Education* will be devoted to the controversial and crucially important areas of preservice and inservice professional development of middle level teachers and administrators.

REFERENCES

Beane, J. (1993). *A middle school curriculum: From rhetoric to reality* (2nd ed.) Columbus, OH: National Middle School Association.

Carnegie Corporation of New York. (1989). *Turning points: Preparing American youth for the 21st century.* New York: Author.

Davis, G. A. (2001). Point to point: Turning Points to Turning Points 2000. In V. A. Anfara, Jr. (Ed.), *The handbook of research in middle level education* (pp. 215–239). Greenwich, CT: Information Age Publishing.

Dewey, J. (1902). *The child and the curriculum.* Chicago: The University of Chicago Press.

Dewey, J. (1916). *Democracy and education.* New York: Free Press.

Geertz, C. (1973). *The interpretation of cultures.* New York: Basic Books.

Jackson, A. W., & Davis, G. A. (2000). *Turning points 2000.* New York: Teachers College Press.

Kliebard, H. M. (1986). *The struggle for the American curriculum 1893–1958.* New York: Routledge.

Kvale, S. (1996). *InterViews.* Thousand Oaks, CA: Sage.

National Middle School Association. (1995). *This we believe: Developmentally responsive middle level schools.* Columbus, OH: Author.

New York State Education Department. (2000). *Essential elements of standards-focused middle level education.* New York: Author.

Nieto, S. (1996). *Affirming diversity.* New York: Allyn & Bacon.

ABOUT THE AUTHORS

Vincent A. Anfara, Jr., is Associate Professor of Educational Administration and Policy Studies at the University of Tennessee, Knoxville. Before entering the professorate he taught for 23 years in both middle and high schools in Louisiana and New Mexico. He is the coeditor (with Kirby, 2000) of *Voices from the Middle: Decrying What Is; Imploring What Could Be* and series editor for *The Handbook of Research in Middle Level Education.* His most recent book is *From the Desk of the Middle School Principal: Leadership Responsive to the Needs of Young Adolescents* (with Brown, 2002). He serves as the President of the Middle Level Education Research Special Interest Group of the American Educational Research Association and is a member of the National Middle School Association's Research Committee.

Joanne Arhar is Associate Professor in the Department of Teaching, Leadership and Curriculum Studies at Kent State University. She is the Coordinator of Middle Childhood Education, preparing teachers for Grades 4–9, and teaches courses in middle childhood education and teacher education. She helped to design the current cohort structure in the program and teaches a cohort of students each year. Her areas of interest are action research, middle school reform, and middle-grades teacher education.

Robert Balfanz is Associate Research Scientist and developer of the Talent Development Middle School Mathematics Program and codeveloper of the Talent Development High School's Mathematics Program. He is also coauthor of the innovative preschool and elementary mathematics curriculums, *Big Math for Little Kids* and *Everyday Mathematics.* He has over a decade of experience in the research, development, design, and implementation of mathematics curriculum. His research interests also include sociology, economics, and cognitive science.

Candy M. Beal is Assistant Professor of Education and the Coordinator of the Middle Grades Language Arts and Social Studies Program at North Carolina State University. She completed her degrees at the College of William and Mary, Duke University, and North Carolina State University. Her research focuses on curriculum development and integration of technology-enhanced environments.

Dave F. Brown is Professor in the Department of Elementary Education at West Chester University in West Chester, Pennsylvania. His contribution to this book is based on information from his book, *Becoming a Successful Urban Teacher* (2002). Dave is the coauthor of *What Every Middle School Teacher Should Know* (with Knowles, 2000).

Micki M. Caskey is Assistant Professor in the Department of Curriculum and Instruction of the Graduate School of Education at Portland State University. She specializes in middle level education, which builds upon her school teaching career. Micki's interests include authentic curriculum, technology integration, instructional strategies, and content enhancements.

Alicia R. Crowe is Assistant Professor in the Department of Teaching, Leadership, and Curriculum Studies at Kent State University. She teaches social studies methods classes and a general methods class in the Middle Childhood Education Program and participates in a cohort of middle childhood education students. Her research interests focus on reflective thinking and learning to teach.

Pru Cuper is a doctoral student at North Carolina State University. Her research focuses on literacy instruction and instructional technology. She was awarded a Kenan Fellowship for her dissertation work on a literacy website, *Literacy Junction*. Prior to graduate school, she taught middle level reading and language arts classes in New Jersey and received the Outstanding Teacher Award from the New Jersey Partners in Education.

Nancy Flowers is Coordinator of Research Programs at the Center for Prevention Research and Development (CPRD) at the University of Illinois in Urbana-Champaign. Nancy has been with CPRD since 1992 and serves as a coprincipal investigator for several projects in CPRD's programmatic area of school reform and innovation. The focus of her work is in the continued refinement and coordination of a large-scale quantitative data collection with middle schools throughout the country, as well as the dissemination of research findings and data to support data-based decision making at the individual school level, the project level, and to inform policy.

Steven J. Gross is Coordinator and Associate Professor of Educational Administration at Temple University, where his research interests focus on initiating and sustaining curriculum, instruction, and assessment leadership in K–16 settings. He is the author of the book, *Staying Centered: Curriculum Leadership in a Turbulent Era* (1998) and has led local, state, and national curriculum reform efforts, including the Vermont Common Core of Learning Project.

Douglas J. Mac Iver is Principal Research Scientist and Director of the Talent Development Middle School Program at Johns Hopkins University. Mac Iver received his PhD from the Developmental Psychology Program at the University of Michigan. His research focuses on middle level education, motivation, and achievement in early adolescence and the social structuring of schools. Mac Iver is coauthor *of Education in the Middle Grades: National Practices and Trends.*

Thomas F. Mandeville is Associate Professor at Southwest Texas State University in San Marcos, Texas, where he serves as Assistant Dean for Assessment and Distance Learning for the College of Education and teaches in the Middle Grades and Secondary Education Programs. He received his PhD from the University of Texas at Austin in Reading Education. He taught middle school and high school reading and English for 15 years before joining a university faculty. He has published widely in the areas of reading and middle school issues. His current research interests include neuroanatomy and physiology among young adolescents. He remains interested in middle grades instruction and in ethical and moral development in young adolescents.

Steven B. Mertens is Senior Research Scientist at the Center for Prevention Research and Development (CPRD) at the University of Illinois, where he has been involved with the research and evaluation of several large-scale middle grades reform projects. Together with his colleagues at CPRD, he has published numerous articles and reports addressing various areas of school reform and improvement. He currently serves as a member of the National Forum to Accelerate Middle-Grades Reform, the National Middle School Association's Research Committee, and as a Council Member for AERA's Research in Middle Level Education SIG.

Peter Mulhall is the Director of the Center for Prevention Research and Development (CPRD) at the University of Illinois. He has a master's degree in Health Studies from Indiana University in Bloomington and a doctorate in Community Health from the University of Illinois at Urbana-Champaign. He has extensive experience in the fields of health, education, and prevention, and he has worked on a number of federal, state and local projects related to the evaluation of programs and interventions that target academic failure, substance abuse, and related problem behaviors.

Billy O'Steen is Assistant Professor of Education at North Carolina State University. He earned degrees from Vanderbilt University and the University of Virginia. His educational experiences include teaching high school English, creating and directing a middle school, teaching in a multicultural education program in Brazil, and teaching English at Lake Tahoe Community College. His teaching and research focus on middle level teacher preparation, experiential education, charter and magnet middle schools, and strategies for at-risk students.

Carol Pope is Professor of Education at North Carolina State University. She completed her doctoral degree at the University of Virginia. In addition to serving in leadership roles within the College of Education at NC State, the North Carolina English Teachers Association, and the National Council of Teachers of English, she has published numerous articles on teacher preparation, middle school language arts, and technology integration.

Rich Radcliffe is Assistant Professor at Southwest Texas State University in San Marcos, Texas, where he teaches in the Middle Grades Program. He received his PhD from the University of Denver. He has directed programs for adolescents including residential summer institutes, regional talent searches, and writing competitions focused on moral judgment issues. Currently he is conducting research on ethical decision making in school administration.

Deborah L. Ryan is a teacher on special assignment from the School District of Philadelphia to the Talent Development Middle School Program. She has a master's degree in administration and educational leadership from St. Joseph's University and over 15 years of experience teaching mathematics to middle school and high school students. She has seven years of experience as a workshop leader, curriculum coach, and teacher trainer.

Graciela Slesaranksy-Poe is Assistant Professor in the Special Education Program at Arcadia University. She received her doctorate in Special Education from Temple University. Her work on disabilities began in Argentina in 1987 and currently focuses on education and community inclusion for all, regardless of people's differences.

Ellen Skilton-Sylvester is Assistant Professor in the Teaching English to Speakers of Other Languages program at Temple University. She received her doctorate in Educational Linguistics from the University of Pennsylvania. Her research interests include immigrant and refugee education policy and practice, biliteracy, and content-based instruction.

Hiller A. Spires is Professor of Education at North Carolina State University. She completed her doctoral degree at the University of South Carolina. Most of her academic career has focused on secondary and postsecondary literacy research and instruction. Currently her research focuses on reading acquisition with Web-based learning environments. BellSouth and the Kenan Institute are funding her latest literacy and technology project, *Literacy Junction*.

Sandra L. Stacki is the Middle Level Coordinator in the Department of Curriculum and Teaching at Hofstra University in New York; she works with preservice undergraduate and graduate students as well as doctoral students. Along with middle level courses, she teaches courses on curriculum change, educational practice, gender issues, qualitative research, and international/comparative education. Her research interests include teacher development and empowerment, women teachers, teaming, partnerships, and qualitative and feminist research in both national and international contexts.

Sue Thompson is Assistant Professor in the Urban Leadership and Policy Studies in Education Division at the University of Missouri at Kansas City. Dr. Thompson has been a middle school teacher, principal and director of middle level education. She serves on the National Forum to Accelerate Middle Grades Reform and is Chair of the national Middle School Association's Urban Issues Task Force. Her research interests include middle school reculturing, leadership, and issues of race/ethnicity, class, and gender as they relate to social equity and democratic schools.

Leonard J. Waks holds doctorates in philosophy and organizational psychology. He has been a professor at Purdue, Stanford, and Penn State, and is now Professor of Educational Leadership and Policy Studies at Temple University. He is the author of *Technology's Schools* (JAI, 1995) and more than 70 scholarly articles and book chapters in philosophy and curriculum theory.

INDEX